Chinese Economic Reform and Development

This book is part of the Peter Lang Political Science, Economics, and Law list.
Every volume is peer reviewed and meets
the highest quality standards for content and production.

PETER LANG
New York • Bern • Berlin
Brussels • Vienna • Oxford • Warsaw

Yining Li

Chinese Economic Reform and Development

Peter Lang Updated New Edition

PETER LANG
New York • Bern • Berlin
Brussels • Vienna • Oxford • Warsaw

Library of Congress Cataloging-in-Publication Data

Names: Li, Yining, author.
Title: Chinese economic reform and development / Yining Li.
Other titles: Economic reform and development in China.
Description: Peter Lang updated new edition. | New York: Peter Lang, 2019.
Includes bibliographical references and index.
Identifiers: LCCN 2018052237 | ISBN 978-1-4331-6056-1 (hardback: alk. paper)
ISBN 978-1-4331-6160-5 (ebook pdf) | ISBN 978-1-4331-6161-2 (epub)
ISBN 978-1-4331-6162-9 (mobi)
Subjects: LCSH: Economic development—China—History—21st century.
China—Economic policy—1976–2000.
China—Economic conditions—1976–2000. | Economics—China.
Classification: LCC HC427.92 .L475148 2019 | DDC 338.951—dc23
LC record available at https://lccn.loc.gov/2018052237
DOI 10.3726/b15012

Bibliographic information published by **Die Deutsche Nationalbibliothek**.
Die Deutsche Nationalbibliothek lists this publication in the "Deutsche Nationalbibliografie"; detailed bibliographic data are available on the Internet at http://dnb.d-nb.de/.

The paper in this book meets the guidelines for permanence and durability of the Committee on Production Guidelines for Book Longevity of the Council of Library Resources.

29 Broadway, 18th floor, New York, NY 10006
www.peterlang.com

Printed in the United States of America

CONTENTS

FOREWORD

The success of China's reform and development in the last thirty-two years has attracted global attention. The major steps which have led to China's success exhibit many Chinese characteristics. Of these the most striking is the ownership reform in the state and other non-private sectors. The theoretical and policy preparations for ownership reform took more than ten years. From being heterodox in the mid-1980s they had become mainstream thinking by the mid-1990s.

Professor Li Yining was arguably the most eminent figure in this process. His most influential public speech on ownership reform entitled, "Basic thoughts on economic restructuring" (Essay No. 3 in this selection), was delivered on April 25, 1986 in Peking University. His famous remark, "Economic restructuring may break down if price reform fails. The success of economic restructuring, however, hinges not on price reform, but on ownership reform, which entails revamping the corporate system," soon appeared in the headlines of a number of leading reformist newspapers and later on became a new proverb in the discourse of Chinese reforms.

In the mid-1980s, "market socialism," which was initially promoted by Oscar Lange and Abba Lerner, was the guiding principle of economic reform in China and Eastern European socialist countries. This principle advocated that the introduction of autonomy to state-owned enterprises (SOEs) would induce SOEs to behave like profit-maximizing firms. Once SOEs became sufficiently autonomous, comprehensive price reforms (i.e., price liberalization) would lead to the final success of the economic reform.[1] In line with this mainstream paradigm, Chinese leaders also endorsed the "big bang" approach and implemented a "one-shot" comprehensive price reform in the late 1980s, which, unfortunately, led to more problems than it solved.

At the other end of the spectrum of the reform debates, criticisms of the theory of market socialism and its reform practices in Eastern Europe since 1968, led by Professor János Kornai, became increasingly influential in the 1980s. Kornai's book *Economics of Shortage* became a bestseller in economics and Kornai himself an iconic figure among young intellectuals in China. His insightful analysis of state ownership and bureaucratic coordination led many young economists to believe that without ultimate private ownership, the expansion of enterprise autonomy and self-management under impersonalized state ownership would not be a medicine that would be effective in curing the soft budget constraint (SBC) syndrome. The SBC syndrome would continue to dull the price responsiveness of enterprises and thereby constrain the effects of price signals. Kornai himself later also concluded that unless state property was sold to private owners at a real market price, an attempt to reduce the percentage of state ownership gradually, i.e., to 95, 90, 85 percent and so on would not be able to make a difference.[2]

In sharp contrast to the above strands of thought, Professor Li had a keen observation of the *de facto* diverse property rights structure existing in SOEs in China. He argued that it was feasible and desirable to adopt the shareholding system in SOEs by quantifying interests among different public owners and then converting such quantified interests into shareholdings. With such a shareholding system in place, an individual public agency would have a measurable stake in the fortunes of a firm from which the agency would draw cash flow and control rights. As a result public agencies could more easily consolidate their material interests and assemble more consistent business strategies when facing market competition. They would find it in their best material interest to increase the value of the firm rather than to extend bureaucratic control over it. Furthermore, mixed ownership for a company as a result of joint investment by public, collective, and private partners and diverse forms of ownership in the economy would stimulate competition and induce further property right reform (also see Essay No. 4 in this selection, first published in 1987).[3]

In the context of China in the mid-1980s, when the official ideology still viewed socialist state ownership as 100 percent ownership by the state on behalf of the whole people, it was analytically valuable, practically significant, and politically brave and skillful to highlight the *de facto* plural property rights structure of existing state ownership and then to link this structure to the feasibility and desirability of ownership reform.

Within academic circles in the West, Granick (1990) appears to have been the first person to analyze this plural structure.[4] Highlighting that Chinese SOEs were in fact agents with multiple principals exercising control over them, he asserted that these multiple principals acquired property rights through past investment in SOEs or traditional associations with individual SOEs. He cited a 1966 slogan "whoever builds and manages the enterprise has the use of its output." This slogan was regarded as epitomizing property rights relationships of the 1970s, i.e., instead of control rights being derived from ownership, *de facto* control rights now define ownership. In other words, this practical property rights arrangement is opposed to the usual textbook teaching in which the right to management is an attribute of ownership.

Rooted in the Chinese reality, the analytical work of Professor Li reveals that the conventional wisdom on state ownership in both the West and East is descriptively narrow. The claim that private investors should own the firm, despite its importance, is not the unique logical prerequisite of free markets and free enterprise. Diverse ownership and governance forms can emerge and evolve that are compatible with the evolutionary development of free market and free enterprise. The Chinese like to create a nickname for someone famous for a particular legacy and, not surprisingly, Professor Li is now known throughout China, as "Li Shareholding."

Another area to which Professor Li has made an important contribution is comparative economic history and the history of economic thought (cf., Essay No. 11 in this selection, published in 1993).[5] Integrating such comparative studies with his deep understanding of economic practices in China, he proposed an innovative argument on disequilibrium theory. As presented in Essays No. 5 (published in 1988) and No. 12 (published in 1993) of this selection,[6] he distinguishes two types of disequilibrium based on whether the majority of firms in the economy are viable profit-makers or not. The first type corresponds to the one dealt with in the existing disequilibrium theory, which features excessive demand or supply due to market friction, stickiness of prices and wages, and demand or supply constraints, rather than non-viability of firms. The second type is characterized not only by an underdeveloped market but also enterprises under various forms of bureaucratic control. He argues that China's economy has belonged to the second category throughout its transition process. To make the transition from the second type of disequilibrium to the first, the top priority is the reform of enterprise system with the aim of producing viable and profit-oriented enterprises.[7] This line of thinking provides a further support to his famous remark "ownership restructuring holds key to the reform."

In addition to constructing this second analytical foundation for his ownership reform theory, Professor Li's work on the Chinese economy in disequilibrium also emphasizes the fundamental importance of achieving and maintaining healthy economic growth and social development in China under the conditions of the second type of disequilibrium. The majority of his essays in this selection discuss various coordination issues across economic reform, growth and development, and the urgency of finding solutions to immediate practical policy dilemmas. The central normative guideline has been that the reform and transition are means to serve economic growth and social development and, furthermore, that economic growth and social development are means to serve the well-being and happiness of ordinary citizens in society.

In dealing with the immediate policy dilemma, Professor Li has incorporated the methodology of "dialectical thought and synthetic analysis" of traditional Chinese medicine, which emphasizes holistic connections among many facets of human anatomy and physiology and examines the effect of the social and natural environment on the interrelations and conditioning of *yin* and *yang*. He pays particular attention to both the "treatment effect" and "side effect" of each policy pill, as well as its short-run and long-run effects. For instance, the first essay of this selection was published in June 1980 when the high urban unemployment rate was at the top of policy agenda. With a thorough and comprehensive analysis of the historical and structural roots of the high unemployment rate, Professor Li suggested that in the short and medium run, the solution would be to actively develop labor-intensive manufacturing industries and labor-intensive export processing to take advantage of China's abundant low-skilled labor force. However, in the long run, China has to develop human capital intensive manufacturing and services industries and actively promote human capital intensive exports so as to convert the persistent population pressure into an emerging comparative advantage. Therefore, it was strategically important to significantly increase investment in education in the 1980s so that China would no longer suffer high unemployment rates in the next two to three decades and become well prepared for the inevitable era of human capital-intensive production and exports. Clearly, this vision is still valid today.

The publication of this *Chinese Economic Reform and Development* enriches the literature in English that examines the past, present and future prospects of China's reforms, transition, and development. Although all the essays in this selection are well-known in China, they provide carefully examined alternative perspectives which scholars and students in the West may not be familiar with. I am honored to write the foreword for this excellent selection and commend it enthusiastically to scholars, policy makers, business professionals, as well as to more general readers, who are interested in the dynamics of China's transition and the growing importance of China in the world.

Sun Laixiang
Academician, the Academy of Social Sciences, UK Professor and Head, Department of Financial & Management Studies, School of Oriental & African Studies, University of London
August 9, 2010

Notes

1. For an excellent critical review on market socialism in general and its manifestation in the 1980s in particular, see Kornai János (1992), *The Socialist System*, Princeton: Princeton University Press. For a leading essay on market socialism for China, see Sun Yefang (1982), "Some theoretical issues in socialist economies," originally published in Chinese in the period 1958–1961, in Fung K. K. (ed.), *Social Needs versus Economic Efficiency in China*, Armonk, NY: M. E. Sharp. For an influential essay which promotes comprehensive price reform in China, see Wu Jinglian and Reynolds Bruce L. (1987), "Choosing a strategy for China's economic reform," *American Economic Review*, Vol. 78, No. 2, pp. 461–466.
2. See Kornai János (1990), *The Road to a Free Economy*, New York and London: W. W. Norton & Company.
3. For more detailed and systematic discussions on multiple property rights and ownership reform by Professor Li, see Li Yining (1986), *Political Economy of Socialism*, Beijing: Commercial Press; Li Yining (1987), *An Exploratory Study of Economic System Reform*, Beijing: People's Daily Press; and Li Yining (1989), *Thoughts on China's Economic Reform*, Beijing: Zhongguo Zhanwang Press. All these three books are in Chinese.
4. David Granick (1990), *Chinese State Enterprises: A Regional Property Rights Analysis*, Chicago: University of Chicago Press.

5. Also see, for example, Li Yining (2003), *The Rise of Capitalism: A Study of Comparative Economic History*, Beijing: Commercial Press; Li Yining (2006), *The Economic History of Rome-Byzantine Empire*, Beijing: Commercial Press. Both books are in Chinese.
6. More detailed and systematic analysis on this topic is presented in Li Yining (1990), *Chinese Economy in Disequilibrium*, Beijing: Beijing Daily Press. This book is in Chinese.
7. An important parallel research on the viability issue of SOEs in China (and other transitional economies) has been conducted by Professor Justin Yifu Lin. Lin employs the analytical perspective of comparative advantage and argues that the firms in heavy industries prioritized by the government in transitional centrally planned economies are not viable in open, competitive markets because their activities are inconsistent with the economy's comparative advantage. This viability problem is another root of the soft budget constraint (SBC) syndrome. If the viability problem is not solved, the SBC syndrome will not be eliminated even though the socialist government is overthrown and all firms are privatized. See, Lin, Justin Y. (2003), "Development strategy, viability and economic convergence," *Economic Development and Cultural Change*, Vol. 53, pp. 277–308; Lin, Justin Y. (2005), "Viability, economic transition and reflection on neoclassical economics," *Kyklos*, Vol. 58, No. 2, pp. 239–264

PREFACE

The 17 essays featured in *Chinese Economic Reform and Development* were chosen from amongst those I wrote and published during the period 1980–1998. They are reflections of my thoughts on certain important issues pertinent to the economic development of China in the intervening years.

For instance, the opening piece, "The Role of Education in Economic Growth," was published in 1980, when the nation was setting about the task of confronting and resolving long-neglected issues shortly after the adoption of the policy of reform and opening up to the world. I was keenly aware of the fact that as a result of the decade-long "cultural revolution" that started in 1966, education had been seriously damaged and its development gravely held back because it was despised by leaders and the masses alike. Consequently, it was imperative to attach the utmost importance to developing education and cultivating talents, and it was against that background that the paper was written. In it I pointed out that if education continued to be scorned in such a manner, China would lose both its present and its future.

"Basic Thoughts on Economic Restructuring" was written in 1986, a little more than seven years after the initiation of economic restructuring in this nation in 1979. By that time, a household contract system had been adopted in rural areas nationwide, which brought about a dramatic increase in farm produce output and an initial improvement in rural living standards. However, in urban areas, the development of state enterprises was hampered, as their management was encumbered by government intervention and their property rights were ill-defined. The promotion of urban economic restructuring thus became the next crucial task. In that paper, I suggested that corporate reform be put before anything else, but that its main thrust should be directed at introducing the joint stock system and transforming state enterprises into firms that were liable for their own profits and losses, enjoyed autonomy in business activity, and were operated by a wide spectrum of investors. I believed that this suggestion, if adopted, would ensure success in economic restructuring and provide institutional guarantees for smooth economic growth in this nation in the years to come.

In "A Tentative Study of Socialist Ownership Structure," published in 1987, I introduced diverse forms of ownership that might work for the Chinese economy in the long term. I predicted that the nation's ownership system would eventually include two economic forms: first, a small number of large corporate groups each funded by several investors; and second, legions of medium-sized and small private and cooperative firms, including self-employed industrial, commercial, and farming households under a contract system, the majority largely invested by individuals and cooperatives. This dual economic system would play a positive role in promoting economic growth and technological progress, in relieving the pressure on employment, and in raising resident income.

"Coordinating Economy and Environment in Less Developed Regions" was published in 1991, the year I, as advisor for the State Council Commission of Environmental Protection, spent considerable time on environmental economics. During my field surveys, I was able to see more and more clearly the intimate relationship between the economic development of impoverished areas and environmental protection. I realized that if we went single-mindedly to help local communities defeat poverty without working to coordinate the economic and environmental concerns, we could end up getting half the result with twice the effort, thus failing to deliver those communities from poverty and lead them onto the road of prosperity. A year later, the Chinese government established the China Council for International Cooperation on Environment and Development, and I was appointed as a Chinese member on the council and director of a working panel of experts in environmental economics. That position enabled me to go on with my research and policy consultancy service in this field.

In 1993, overheated investment triggered high inflation, which riveted the attention of economists in this country and prompted them to search for solutions to the problem. I wrote "Growth and Fluctuations in Economic Disequilibrium" to spell out my opinions on government regulation policy. Specifically, I focused my analysis on two "alert lines" under conditions of disequilibrium. Given the imbalanced development in the Chinese economy, I asserted, it was inevitable for either the unemployment rate or the inflation rate to run higher than zero, and therefore, it was impossible to set the alert line on a zero unemployment or inflation rate. At what level of unemployment or inflation the alert line should be set should be determined in light of the actual situation. Moreover, there should be two alert lines, designated respectively as the first alert line and the second alert line. Accordingly, the operational space for the entire economy should be divided into four segments along the zero unemployment axis or the zero inflation axis, and along the first and second alert lines.

In Segment One, the economy runs below zero unemployment or inflation, which is deemed abnormal. This gives rise to workforce shortfalls or deflation, which calls for macroeconomic regulation and control steps.

In Segment Two, the economy runs above the zero unemployment or inflation axis without breaking through the first alert line, which is deemed normal, and does not necessitate governmental micro-economic regulation and control.

In Segment Three, the economy runs above the first alert line without breaking through the second alert line, which is slightly abnormal and calls for moderate macroeconomic regulation and control.

In Segment Four, the economy runs above the second alert line, which is abnormal to a grave extent and calls for intensified macroeconomic regulation and control, and, when things come to a head, extraordinary control steps.

In 1997, when Southeast Asia was engulfed in a major economic crisis and the Chinese economy was affected to a certain degree, I wrote "Meshing Fiscal Policy with Monetary Policy." Its gist was that whether in dealing with this crisis or in executing the national economic policy, we have to learn how to coordinate financial policy and monetary policy. To tighten or loosen financial and monetary policies at the same time is something that can be done only under extraordinary circumstances. Under normal circumstances, a tight financial policy should complement a relaxed monetary policy, or vice versa. Only thus can good results be achieved in regulating national economic development.

"The Dual Foundations of Efficiency" was published in 1998. It was written at a time when, with marketization making steady headway, the public had sufficiently understood the importance of efficiency but was yet to see the importance of the foundations on which efficiency rests. I pointed out in this paper that efficiency rests on two foundations, that is, the material and technological foundation, and the moral foundation. Equipment, factory buildings, raw materials, and workers' technological attainment are elements in the material and technological foundation of efficiency, while its moral foundation consists of people's faith, confidence and cultural and moral attainments. History has proved that the material and technological foundation can only engender conventional efficiency. The moral foundation, however, can generate super efficiency. This bears out the momentous value of people's faith, confidence and edification in culture and morals. In developing its economy, the nation is faced with the urgent task of bolstering up the moral foundation of efficiency, so that the moral and cultural character of the population can play a still greater role in economic development.

Having given a glimpse at the essays selected in this book, I believe that readers who have read this book will gain some insight into my basic thoughts on Chinese economic development from the 1980s through the 1990s.

In publishing *Chinese Economic Reform and Development*, I have benefited from the unstinting help of Professors Hao Ping, Ling Yuan, Norman Apritchard, Cai Hongbin, and Zhou Li'an. Without their unstinting assistance, it would have been impossible for me to put the book on readers' desks in such a short span of time. My heartfelt gratitude is also due to Director Yu Chunchi and Chief Editor Cai Jianfeng of Foreign Language Teaching and Research Publishing, who made this translation project possible in the first place. Ultimately, I am immensely grateful to Wu Hao, managing editor of humanities and social sciences publishing, and translator-editors Zhong Zhilan, Ren Xiaomei, and Peng Lin, for doing a good job in producing this highly readable English edition of my selected economic essays.

Li Yining
Guanghua School of Management
Peking University, China
January 30, 2010

· 1 ·

THE ROLE OF EDUCATION IN ECONOMIC GROWTH

In my speech "Technology education and capitalist industrialization: a study of the rise of technological power in Western Europe and America,"[1] I dwelled on the relationship between education and economic growth in light of economic history. What I was driving at was that education is a major recourse for nations to groom technological personnel, and that only by putting a premium on education and the cultivation of talents can less developed nations boost their economic growth rates and catch up with and surpass the developed countries. As I put it in that speech, the role of education in economic growth has five aspects:

"First, education provides society with a supply of researchers and designers who can venture into the unknown, innovating in science, renovating and transforming productive technology. Without such contingents, the best a nation can do is to tag along after other nations, but in that way you cannot score major breakthroughs in science and technology.

"Second, education provides society with engineers and technicians who can master and apply advanced means of production. Without such technocrats, even if a nation has acquired sophisticated tools of production, it cannot put them to best use.

"Third, education brings forth production and technology managers well adapted to society's level of industrialization. Without teams of such managers, the production process can be prone to colossal waste in human, material and financial resources, making it impossible to benefit from the superiority of advanced productive technology.

"Fourth, education enhances society's scientific and cultural attainment, and sets the stage for promoting new products and disseminating and upgrading knowledge in science and technology. At the same time, education also lays the groundwork for the future growth of a nation's technological prowess, and guarantees the supply of a constant stream of high-caliber researchers, engineers and managers, and skilled workers.

"Fifth, education enables society to preserve and disseminate its accumulation of scientific knowledge and productive experience free from barriers of time and space and national boundaries. It is through education that such accumulated knowledge and experience are spread from one nation to another and from one generation to another as humanity's shared assets."

I would like to go on with my observation of the relationship between education and economic growth on the basis of the speech I made and published two years ago. However, this paper has a different focus. While in my previous speech I looked into the major role education plays in expanding the economy and raising its growth rate, this paper underlines education's important role in ensuring economic stability and sustained growth, and in providing effective solutions to problems that have occurred or may occur in the process of economic growth. In other words, my previous speech was about economic growth per se, whereas this paper is a study of employment, balance of international payments, income distribution, financial balance and other issues occurring in the process of stabilizing and sustaining economic growth. Furthermore, while my previous speech proceeded from the perspective of the economic history of Western Europe and America, this paper takes China's socialist economy as its focus and background.

This paper is delivered in four chapters dealing respectively with education's relationship with employment, balance of international payments, income distribution, and fiscal balance, so as to illustrate education's role in guaranteeing economic stability and sustained growth.

The "Structural" Nature of the Employment Problem Can Be Solved by Developing and Restructuring Education

Theoretically speaking, any nation can grow its economy either by expanding its workforce or by investing more in machines and equipment and improving workers' technical knowhow and skills. The adoption of labor-saving technology and equipment may help cut down the material production sector's demand for workers in the course of economic growth. Consequently, given a constant population growth rate, economic growth itself cannot ensure full employment. The number of jobs to be created through output increase is determined not only by the rate of production expansion, but also by which approaches are adopted for such expansion. If a country develops its economy not by hiring more workers but by adopting new technology and equipment and improving workers' cultural and technical proficiency, then the ability of its material production sector to absorb the workforce will be limited.

On the other hand, economic growth also entails a process of change in a nation's economic structure. The inexorable law of material production is that some old manufacturing industries decline or are phased out while new ones rise and grow. The ratio between material and non-material production in the national economy is changing as well. It is an irrevocable trend in economic growth for some non-material production industries to grow in strength along with their shares in the national economy. With the national economic structure changing constantly, those working in languishing or failed industries need to find new jobs elsewhere. The rising industries in material production, and particularly the burgeoning industries in non-material production, often run short of workforce. Thus the emergence and growth of new industries in both material and non-material production are major reasons why a nation can increase employment amidst economic growth.

The changing economic structure of a nation implies changes in both industrial and geo-economic structures. In China, underdeveloped regions may achieve a relatively higher economic growth rate, whereas developed regions may slow down, or grow at a relatively lower pace. Regions that either suffer a low growth rate or maintain a high growth rate mainly by spending more on technology and equipment will produce a glut of factory layoffs that will have to seek employment elsewhere, whereas regions with a high growth rate, those with a labor shortage in particular, are likely to accept the job-hunters.

These situations prove clearly that the employment problem confronting a country in the process of economic growth is mainly "structural." That is to say, the success or failure in tackling this problem hinges on whether the workforce structure—the makeup of workers of different trades, industries and locations in a region's total number of workers—is commensurate with local economic growth rates and economic structural changes, and whether the workforce itself can meet the technical needs of local economic growth. When the structure of a workforce does not match the local economic growth rate and the changing local economic structure, and when workers' technical proficiency level falls short of the needs of economic growth, unemployment will unavoidably exist alongside a surplus of unfilled job vacancies.

This paradoxical coexistence of unemployment and superfluous vacancies means that while people are looking frantically for jobs, many jobs are left unfilled. How is it that people lose jobs while the economy keeps growing? The answer is that if economic growth is achieved for the most part by raising labor productivity while the population growth rate remains high, those coming of employment age are likely to fail to land suitable jobs. Even if these people are a non-factor, industries and regions with slow or stagnant growth lay off workers. This is particularly true of developing countries, where agriculture—known for its low labor productivity—often dominates the national economy. In the industrialization process, large numbers of villagers who have just quit farming may find it hard to land jobs. Unemployment—concealed unemployment[2] included—thus becomes unavoidable.

Why, then, are there vacancies that remain unoccupied? This is because, when the workforce structure does not tally with the prevailing economic growth rate and economic structure, the rising industries in both material and non-material production cannot find what they want badly: skilled workers and competent engineers, technicians, researchers, and managers. The same labor shortage can also occur in established industries in material production that maintain growth by relying heavily on new technology and equipment, so much so that even workers on their payrolls cannot measure up to what such new technology and equipment require of them. Seemingly unwanted jobs may also occur in newly developed places where required workers are in short supply. This is an outstanding problem with developing countries, where, for historical reasons, skilled workers that can keep pace with industrialization are scarce.

Generally speaking, the number of the jobless can never match the number of jobs awaiting them in a national economy. The ratio between the two numbers differs with the changes and readjustments in a nation's economic growth rate and economic and workforce structure. However, even if the two numbers match each other, they cannot offset each other, because workers of different proficiency levels and fields of work are not interchangeable under modern production and technological conditions. In the long run, the coexistence of unemployment and unfilled job vacancies in a nation's economic growth is not temporary, but, most probably, perpetual. That is to say, job vacancies may disappear when long-time job-seekers have found their jobs, but will occur again when new layoffs arrive on the scene. Unemployment, concealed unemployment included, is a waste of human resources, while job vacancies left unfilled are a waste of material resources—for them to exist at the same time is not only detrimental to economic growth, but also holds back the adoption and popularization of new technology and economic restructuring. The result is that the economy remains mired in low efficiency. Chronic joblessness can also be a major destabilizing factor for society.

In a nutshell, employment problems in a growing economy are attributable to the failure in reconciling the conflict between unemployment and unfilled job vacancies. Such is the "structural" nature of employment.

The employment problems confronting China are complicated. Some are universal to all economies, some are common to developing nations in economic development, but others are peculiarly China's own. These three categories of employment problems are intertwined. The universal ones stem from the fact that the increasing use of sophisticated machines and technological equipment has whittled down producers' need for workers, unskilled workers in particular. Those common to developing nations arise from the new job needs of large numbers of unskilled laborers that have just quit farming at the time of an agrarian society's transition to industrialization. The employment problems peculiarly of China's own are partly to be blamed on incompetent labor administration, but most of them are attributed to the lopsided economic development resulting from the ten-year chaos of the "cultural revolution" that considerably narrowed down people's job options. These problems were aggravated by the excessive population growth in the late 1950s and the early 1960s. Today, those born in those years are coming of age or will soon become eligible for jobs. If the employment problems for these people cannot be properly handled, both society and the economy will be in jeopardy. The situation is also complicated by a dire shortage of skilled workers and the low labor productivity of those in their jobs. The dilemma facing China today is that while many job-seeking youths are having trouble finding jobs, factories, too, find it hard to fill jobs with qualified workers. A nation's aggregate volume of labor resources are derived by multiplying the total number of workers with their average level of technical competency—the chief indicator of labor quality. In that sense, China's aggregate volume of labor resources is by no means abundant because its workers' average skill proficiency is low despite their sheer numbers.

The solution to our nation's employment problems, in the final analysis, is to create a constant supply of new jobs to keep pace with economic growth. If we cannot create new jobs, the need for labor will shrink with the adoption of new technology, even if population growth is kept at a low level.

How to create new jobs? This involves the diverse economic sectors and forms of public ownership under the socialist system, as well as such factors as economic administration, various types of technical innovation, and the ratios between sectors and economic growth rate. These issues, however, are beyond the scope of this study. The topic at hand is this: Supposing substantial numbers of new jobs are created by readjusting and revamping the ownership structure, the economic system and the ratios between economic sectors, and by riding the nation's robust economic growth, can the nation come to grips with its employment problems? Given the "structural" nature of employment in our country, we can assert categorically that the disparity between the structure of the workforce and that of the national economy will never be eradicated without corresponding development in education and without restructuring the education system. The dilemma between "people hunting for jobs" and "jobs seeking takers," too, will remain for a long time to come. The important role of education in tackling employment problems rests precisely on its ability to deliver the nation from that dilemma.

Developing education and spending more on it can help dovetail the workforce structure with a growing economy's need for workers at different technical levels and in different fields of work. To achieve that end, we have got to adapt our educational structure to the changing economic growth rate and structure, and act on the long-term need of economic growth to readjust the categories of schools and the setup of academic programs, and to variegate the schooling terms. Long years of observation reveal two options in this regard. In the first option, when existing and prospective job-seekers are not outnumbered by anticipated unfilled job vacancies, the main thrust of our effort can be directed at further improving education and raising workforce quality, so that every worker that has been educated or trained can qualify for more demanding jobs, thereby enhancing labor productivity and further promoting the adoption of new technology. In this way, not only can the needs of economic growth be met, but the number of unfilled job vacancies can be curtailed as well. In the other option, when the total number of existing and prospective job-hunters outgrows the anticipated number of unfilled job vacancies, we can lay equal stress on improving and universalizing education, so that more high-caliber professionals can be cultivated for the national economy while legions of job-waiters are tooled with one kind of skill or another to qualify for suitable jobs. To achieve this end, apart from further restructuring the economy to increase job vacancies, attention should also be paid to developing secondary technical and vocational education so as to put more job-seekers through training. The school term for students can be lengthened so as to curtail the number of prospective job hunters and better prepare students culturally and technically for future economic growth needs. In other words, we would rather let our youngsters learn more knowledge and skill than keep them waiting for jobs when they are ill prepared in both skill and knowledge.

As things stand today, it is believed the second option is more workable for China for a long time to come. Thus, in education development and reform, we cannot go single-mindedly after improvement to the neglect of the role of education in tackling the "structural" employment problem.

We should also remember that education reform cannot be accomplished overnight. For one thing, economic growth itself demands that our schools supply large numbers of well-educated and skilled workers who measure up to its needs. Failing this, stable and sustainable economic growth will be out of the question. For another, the economy's ever-changing sectoral, regional and technological structures call for the adaptation of the education system.

A certain level of national economic development is always consistent with a certain structure of education, with the latter changing in sync with the former. This fact should be considered when mapping out long-term national human resource plans. So much for my analysis of the "structural" employment issue. The employment problems facing China today are "structural" in the main, but they do not stop merely at being "structural." "Individual occupation selectivity" is another social employment issue for present-day China. When job openings are available, people can still choose to stay jobless. They do not lack the needed education and skill, but they make this choice out of occupational considerations. The causes of this employment problem are manifold, but education can still play a role in tackling it. This is because the mission of educators is not limited to teaching cultural knowledge and technical expertise. Character building and education in revolutionary values are essential to students in this country.

Investment in Education as a Prerequisite for Developing a Knowledge-Intensive Economy; the Gradual Increase of Knowledge-Intensive Exports as a Strategic Measure to Improve China's Balance of International Payments Amidst Economic Growth

As to the patterns of technological innovation for developing nations in the modernization process, I have voiced my opinions in my article "On the roles of capital-intensive and labor-intensive economies in the modernization process of developing nations" (*World Economy*, issue No. 6, 1979). Because what I wanted to drive at in that article was that developing countries are not going anywhere if they choose to develop a capital-intensive economy more than anything else, I made no mention of the differences between skilled and unskilled labor and of the developmental trends of a labor-intensive economy. In this study, however, to explain why investment in education is a boon to stable and sustained economic growth, I find it necessary to look further into the patterns of technological innovation, or, to be specific, the role a knowledge-intensive economy can play in economic growth.

Theoretically speaking, a nation out to seek economic growth must boost its financial savings and raise funds for investment purposes. If the supply of funds is in shortage at home, something can be done to procure foreign funds under appropriate credit conditions and in light of the situation of the world capital market. The plus side of the use of foreign capital is that it helps overcome immediate foreign exchange and capital shortfalls and brings in advanced technology from other lands. However, in the long run, the commitment to repaying both principal and interest will eventually become a problem for the borrower. If the nation cannot increase its foreign exchange revenue from exports or other sources, balance of payments deficit may become a major hindrance to sustaining its economic growth.

Let us imagine a nation that is before or at the beginning of industrialization that has an abundant workforce, whose wages are low, and whose traditional exports of labor-intensive products have a competitive edge on the world market. Such a nation can use its foreign exchange earnings from exports to meet its domestic demand for technology and commodity imports and improve its balance of international payments. However, when industrialization reaches a certain stage, labor-intensive exports will gradually lose their edge and put the nation at a disadvantage for the following reasons:

First, a growing economy inevitably boosts national income gradually. While per capita national income rises on a yearly basis, worker wages go up as well. As a result, the gap in average wage between the nation and the developed industrial nations is likely to narrow down, thus diminishing the benefits of the "entry ticket" the nation can get from its low wages on to the world market. What merits particular attention here is that industrialization is a common trend for all nations. When industrialization arrives at a certain stage in the said nation, other less developed nations will follow suit and strive to expand exports and absorb advanced foreign technology. These "latecomers" are most probably in the possession of abundant workforce and even lower wages, and their exports of labor-intensive products are more competitive on the world market because they are made by workers with even lower pay. If the said nation goes on to depend on labor-intensive products for exports after it has increased workers' wages on the basis of economic growth and increased national income, it is bound to come across newer and tougher competitors on the world market, a situation that is obviously not in its favor.

Second, a considerable part of the products of a labor-intensive economy are primary ones. Economic growth is likely to boost the demand for primary products in nations pursuing industrialization. For instance, the demand for mineral products or farm and sideline produce tends to swell with the rise of new industries, urban development, development in communications and transport, and improvement in people's material and cultural lives. Yet the effort to sustain massive exports of primary products can be inhibited by economic growth and growing domestic demand for such products. If that happens, the nation's balance of international payments will be adversely affected.

Third, even though the output of labor-intensive products can grow in pace with a nation's economy, such a growth rate is generally low. Moreover, their supply is restrained by natural resources and productive technology. This is because living labor accounts for the lion's share of production costs, whereas materialized labor makes up a smaller portion of it. As a result, the growth of labor productivity is relatively slow. Supposing a nation in economic growth needs to import advanced technology constantly and repay the principal with interest on procured foreign capital, it must expand exports to meet that need. If that nation counts mainly on labor-intensive exports in return for foreign exchange earnings, it may not maintain its balance of international payments by expanding such exports because of their low growth rate and serious supply restraint. If the nation wants to expand its exports and maintain its balance of international payments, it can only have one of the three options. Option One: to export more non-labor-intensive products to pick up the slack in the slow growing supply of labor-intensive products. Option Two: to slash domestic demand for labor-intensive products and curtail its growth rate to guarantee exports. Option Three: to transform production technology for labor-intensive products and increase their labor productivity, so as to increase output and expand supply. Option One calls for changing the nation's traditional dependence on labor-intensive products for export revenue. Option Two is predicated on cutting home demand and restraining domestic growth rate, that is, to expand exports at the expense of domestic demand and economic growth. Option Three will bring down labor intensity in the nation's labor-intensive economy and gradually deprive it of its competitive edge. No matter what option is chosen, it is not only difficult but also against the law of economic growth for a nation to keep counting on labor-intensive products for export revenue when industrialization reaches a certain stage of development.

It should also be noted that even if a nation can still benefit from labor-intensive exports at a certain stage of industrialization (when, for example, its wages are low enough, there are still no tough competitors on the international market scene, domestic demand for primary products has not grown strong enough to affect exports, or its labor-intensive economy is still robust enough to stabilize such exports), it gets a raw deal if it goes on selling labor-intensive products in return for non-labor-intensive imports. This is because the history and system of the world economy have determined that trade between non-labor-intensive and labor-intensive products on the international market is an unequal exchange of value, a situation that is not going to change anytime soon. This being the case, why should nations stick to labor-intensive products as the major source of export revenue after they have gone through a certain stage of industrialization? Why can't they replace labor-intensive products with non-labor-intensive ones that can definitely stand them in good stead in world trade?

As shown previously, observed from whatever perspectives, heavy dependence on labor-intensive exports should definitely be relinquished when industrialization reaches a certain stage even though it is a necessity at the beginning. On no account should the practice of letting labor-intensive products take up the lion's share of exports become a long-term state policy.

This poses a problem: Since it is both difficult and inappropriate for a nation to allow labor-intensive products to go on dominating its exports at a certain stage of industrialization, what is to be done with its balance of payments deficit in the course of economic growth? Supposing that nation's international revenue from non-trade items is fixed, what should it do to increase exports so that it can boost imports and repay the principal and interest of foreign debts?

The way out rests in developing a capital-intensive economy, exporting capital-intensive products, or replacing home-made capital-intensive products with similar imports. Feasible though these options are, they are by no means simple. Some developed industrial nations in the world economy today have turned international trade to their advantage through long years of painstaking maneuvering. This, plus the abundant capital in their hands, is of good service to them in exporting capital-intensive products. It is no mean task to compete with the capital-intensive products from these countries, let alone gain the upper hand in such a competition.

For this reason, developing nations that are latecomers to industrialization should spare no effort to develop and export something else after they arrive at a certain stage of industrialization, and that is the products of a knowledge-intensive economy.

The knowledge-intensive economy, observed from the perspective of labor quality and technological innovation, is actually a way of categorizing innovations, industries and products. As illustrated in the foregoing, the strength of a country's labor resources manifests itself in both the number and quality of laborers. Labor quality is not factored in when categorizing national economies into capital-intensive and labor-intensive types. Rather, economies are differentiated in this regard merely in terms of the ratio between labor and capital goods inputs in production by natural physical units. By contrast, in calculating the labor input by natural physical units, every person (or work hour) represents an equal amount of labor input; in calculating the input of capital goods, only their values are taken into account—the degree of sophistication of technology embodied in the capital goods and the technical proficiency of the workers using such goods are not factored in. However, an analysis in light of labor quality shows, firstly, labor input is naturally divided into skilled and unskilled labor input, and secondly, the input of capital goods is also naturally divided into those that, on one hand, embody technological sophistication and are applied by skilled labor, and on the other, do not embody the sophistication of technology used and are operated by unskilled labor. Thus national economies can also be categorized into skilled-labor-intensive ones and unskilled-labor-intensive ones. In a skilled-labor-intensive economy, labor is skilled, and the input of capital goods embodies mature technology in the hands of skilled labor. By the same token, products can also be classified as either skilled-labor-intensive or unskilled-labor-intensive. Knowledge-intensive products are exactly skilled-labor-intensive products.

If a nation rich in workforce can not only keep upgrading workers' scientific and technical proficiency, imbue them with high labor productivity, and enable them to innovate production technology, but can also employ skilled workers and use capital goods that embody the sophistication of technology in production, then its products will not customarily be labor-intensive but skilled-labor-intensive or knowledge-intensive. Such products are a crystallization of the latest science-and-technology achievements mastered by that nation's labor—workers, technicians, scientists and researchers included—and the advanced technical levels they have attained. They also epitomize the latest progress in production technology and the high labor productivity the nation has achieved. If that nation can export this kind of product in return for unskilled-labor-intensive imports, rather than sell labor-intensive products in exchange for capital-intensive products, it can still be competitive on the world market even though its wages are rising with economic growth, and it can also open up one market after another to promote sales. Furthermore, because the nation has stopped exporting labor-intensive products, it can steer clear of the extant terms of exchange in international trade that are detrimental to labor-intensive products, thereby forestalling economic losses that might be incurred by the system of unequal exchange.

Technological innovation knows no bounds; nor will improvement of labor productivity stop at a certain level. A developing nation striving for modernization enjoys broad prospects in both economic growth and balance of international payments so long as it sets its skilled-labor-intensive economy on a track of ceaseless development.

Thus the important role of educational investment becomes apparent in coordinating economic growth and the balance of international payments. Without steady follow-up investment in education, we can never achieve universal and remarkable development in the workforce's technical and work proficiency, bring forth high-caliber scientists and researchers, and revamp productive technology without letup. For this reason, investment in education is the prerequisite for developing a skilled-labor-intensive or knowledge intensive economy.

To sum up, increasing investment in education is a strategic measure for improving the balance of international payments in the course of economic growth. Ours is a socialist nation. Where is our comparative strength in international trade? It lies in none other than the export of certain labor-intensive products. We have got to make the most of this strength, and develop it unremittingly. However, we should never make it a long-term state policy for foreign trade, to say nothing of the inevitability that this strength of ours will dwindle gradually with national economic growth. From a strategic point of view, we must heighten the skilled-labor intensity of every export commodity and the skilled-labor intensity of every exporting company. Our nation will stay competitive on the world market for a long time to come if our exports of farm products are no longer customarily labor-intensive, but improved strains and quality products that epitomize advanced science and technology and the latest research and development achievements; if our exports of industrial goods are no longer run-of-the-mill products of the labor-intensive processing industry, but quality goods that reflect the distinctively innovated Chinese technology and nascent research results; and if what we sell to the world market are no longer ores, coal, crude oil or other mineral products but a good variety of quality products that are fashioned out of mineral raw materials and that mirror China's new achievements in science and technology. Then the more productive our industrial and agricultural departments are, the more competitive our country will be on the world market. All these things, when done in due course, will put our nation's workforce at an advantage not only quantitatively but also qualitatively. With our "knowledge" crystallized in produce and labor service, we will remain invincible in the world market.

To Increase Wages and Improve Economic Efficiency Is the Nation's Cardinal Mission That Can Be Attained—to a Certain Extent—Through Investing in Education

The topic of this chapter is the relationship between income distribution and economic efficiency. In a capitalist economy, the trade-off between "equality" and efficiency has special connotations. Under capitalist ownership of capital goods, "equality" is based on recognizing the capitalist hired-labor system, whereas efficiency is an outcome of capitalist competition. Fundamentally speaking, there will never be true equality so long as the capitalist hired-labor system remains, but this is irrelevant to the theme of this study. Nevertheless, the relationship between income distribution and economic efficiency is a major issue that merits attention.

To care for people and cultivate them is the purpose of socialist production. To develop production is to improve people's material and cultural well-being, and bring forth workers' talent. However, to develop production, we have got to be particular about efficiency and motivate our workers. Theoretically speaking, the principle of distributing to each according to one's work, if carried out to the letter along with sound social welfare measures, is conducive to the development of production and enhancement of efficiency, as well as a guarantee for workers' pay raise provided development in production is ensured. However, workers' average income in this nation is low, and the influence of egalitarianism on income distribution very much alive. Both facts hamper economic growth, sap people's enthusiasm, and render workers' pay rise all the more difficult. The egalitarian pattern of income distribution that has kept wages at a low level for a long time cannot be eradicated without painstaking efforts.

To illustrate this issue, and to explain the role education can play in readjusting the relationship between income distribution and economic efficiency, it is necessary to begin this study with the income distribution theory.

Generally speaking, in economic growth there may be two income distribution patterns. One is to pay workers entirely according to the quantity and quality of work done. Under the other pattern, the state takes steps to regulate people's income by making allowances for low-income earners and limiting or deducting from the income of those highly paid. Proponents of the first pattern argue that paying people entirely according to the quantity and quality of work done represents a fair and square evaluation of the labor or service provided by every member of society, and that this is the only way to duly reward those who work hard and sanction those who malinger or dillydally, and to motivate people to work to the best of their ability and talent. Supporters of the second pattern hold that to reward people entirely according to the quantity and quality of work done is unfair because such quantity and quality are not entirely determined by whether people work hard or not. They argue that people differ in the ability to earn a living because there are broad differences in talent, intellectual attainment, physical strength, family background and education, and especially because people cannot choose the social and work environment and the capital goods they are supposed to use in production. For example, because some happen to be using highly productive machines while the others are not, someone may have worked hard, but the quantity and quality of work he does compare unfavorably with what is done by someone else who does not exert himself but has better talent and family background and works in a better environment. These factors embody the limits of the practice of rewarding people entirely according to the quantity and quality of work done, and are responsible for the fact that some people work harder than others but make less money while others do not work as hard but earn more. It thus stands to reason for the state to adopt regulating measures to give allowance to low-income people and limit the incomes of highly paid people.

Supporters of either income distribution pattern try to make their cases also by citing income distribution's beneficial effect on economic growth. Supporters of the first pattern believe that paying people entirely according to the quantity and quality of work done can inspire every worker to take the initiative into his hands and improve his expertise and skill, thereby promoting national economic growth. According to them, people's enthusiasm will be dampened, and their work efficiency reduced, if they are not paid according to the quantity and quality of work done, or if their incomes are evened up arbitrarily. Supporters of the second pattern believe that the first pattern tends to widen the income gap between members of society, thereby adversely affecting the mindset of some people, so that low-income people may become so frustrated and disappointed as to hurt the national economy.

The controversy surrounding these two income distribution patterns, however, makes little sense for capitalist economies. A capitalist society cannot possibly pay workers according to the quantity and quality of work done, and its class nature determines that it cannot regulate the income of members of various classes in reasonable ways. The superior socialist system makes fair income distribution possible, as it can maximizes economic growth by dispensing income on a rational footing. The superiority of socialism, however, is yet to be brought to full fruition in China. Egalitarianism in income distribution and low average worker income are established facts in this country for a variety of reasons. Ambiguity in production goals compels people to produce for production's sake year in, year out. The belief that the more egalitarian it is, the better income distribution becomes makes it impossible to distribute income reasonably and motivate workers with it. As a result, the economy grows at a snail's pace, labor productivity remains penuriously low, and workers' disposable incomes cannot be increased, so much so that social stability and unity are affected. The situation has reached a point where something has got to be done about it. But what exactly is to be done? In my opinion, when we discuss how to regulate the relationship between income distribution and economic efficiency, we must proceed from our nation's established income distribution pattern, from the egalitarianism that has been prevalent across the land for years, and from the current average income of workers. History cannot be reversed. It won't do to conjure up an income distribution pattern based on the assumption of "what we would have done if we were living in the pre-liberation year of 1949." Important though it is for us to explore such a pattern, it cannot solve real-world problems because the established wage standards make it easy to raise wages and hard to reduce them, and because the established welfare benchmarks make it easy to raise welfare and hard to reduce it.

Given the status quo in our nation, we are not getting anywhere if we stop paying people according to the quantity and quality of work done and increasing people's average income, and allow egalitarianism to go unchecked. It will not work, either, if our government acts impetuously, turns a blind eye to the real practices of income distribution and the welfare steps that have been taken, and carries to extremes the practice of paying people strictly according to the quantity and quality of work done. Considering the historical circumstances under which the current income distribution practice has come about, I believe the order of the day should be to gradually increase workers' pay in the process of developing production. Egalitarianism and low average worker income are the main causes behind low work efficiency; and low work efficiency is a major hindrance to economic growth. Our mission at hand is to root out egalitarianism and carry out the principle of distributing to each according to his work. That is to say, under the precondition of raising workers' actual income, we must do what we can to pay them in light of the quantity and quality of work done. If we keep doing this, workers' income is bound to grow considerably within a few years. However, a universal rise of average worker's pay may also result in the income of some people rising more quickly than others, thereby widening the income gap. If the growing income gap disgruntles some people, it will not be too late for the government to remedy the situation with regulatory steps, such as increasing the private income tax rate and levying an inheritance tax within the framework of a progressive tax system. In my opinion, we have got to foresee this potential trend and refrain from taking premature countermeasures. The problem will be taken care of sooner or later.

Coordination between income distribution and economic efficiency amidst economic growth involves not only the long-standing distribution pattern and the past and present wage and welfare systems, but also a number of ideological issues. For instance, such important ideological issues as workers' political awareness, social mores and values, and people's understanding of what "equality" and "happiness" really mean can affect, one way or another, people's enthusiasm, initiative and efficiency at work, and the balance between income distribution and economic efficiency. We must be careful about the countermeasures we are going to take against these ideological issues if we are to increase workers' pay without crippling their enthusiasm for work or hurting economic efficiency.

What, then, is the role of education in coordinating the relationship between income distribution and economic efficiency? Can education investment speed up the accomplishment of the abovementioned tasks? There is no doubt that education has a certain ideological impact on those being educated, thereby helping them foster a sound outlook on life, a sense of social responsibility and other values that should not be overlooked. It is also indisputable that this impact is not an issue. What is at issue is the content of such education and the approaches to it. In this study, however, I want to draw attention to the following four pertinent economic issues:

First, as education can improve people's money-making ability by raising their cultural and technical levels, an effective way to help low-income workers make more money is to put them through certain professional education or training. If the principle of distributing to each according to his work is followed in real earnest, a worker schooled in professional knowledge and technical expertise can earn more than those who lack such knowledge and expertise. Thus he is a beneficiary of the education he has received. Regular and spare-time education can both help individuals increase their private income. Therefore, those who have passed a certain level of academic or technical examinations should be issued a diploma or certificate and paid accordingly in the workplace. Developing education can upgrade the quality of the entire nation's workforce and boost the work efficiency of those who have been educated. This is particularly the case in this age of modern science and technology, where a growing economy badly needs quality workers who can never be replaced no matter how many low-quality workers there are. Low-income people will be stuck in the low income brackets, and their work quality will remain low if they do not receive professional training. It is thus clear that developing education helps bridge income disparity, increases efficiency, boosts the economy and increases workers' average income.

Second, the lack of labor mobility is detrimental to the effort to enhance economic efficiency and increase income. However, labor mobility is a complex issue that is beyond this study. What I want to say right now is this:

Supposing the workforce in our nation has become somewhat more mobile through institutional and other reforms and readjustments, this leaves another important problem to be addressed, that is, there are people who, for lack of professional knowledge and skills, are not able to adapt themselves to the changing economic structure and ever-improving technology by changing their jobs. In the course of economic growth, large numbers of villagers quit farming as a result of raised productivity in agriculture, but their poor adaptability to new careers makes it hard for them to be absorbed by other sectors in need of workforce. Thus large numbers of them have stuck in agriculture, where their labor cannot be fully utilized. Social efficiency suffers as a result. What merits particular attention is that, under these circumstances, low efficiency, lack of vocational adaptability, and low income are interrelated, and can also be addressed by relying on education development. Only through education can low-income people change their jobs when and where necessary, and get higher pay; only when their abilities and talents are brought into play in their new jobs can society reduce its loss in efficiency.

Third, low income not only affects its earners but also carries over to their younger generation. This is true everywhere, and socialist China is no exception. A socialist society is theoretically free from hereditary tenures, workplace discrimination and cliquishness, but children from low-income families have few schooling opportunities and even fewer opportunities to go to college. When they start work, they have fewer chances to get new jobs, let alone jobs with high pay. I think we should admit that their problem is caused by economic factors. A comparison of low-income families with high-income families shows that if income disparity has become a reality in the first generation, by the time of the second generation, a few low-income families may quit poverty, but most of them will remain poor or even become poorer. This is because, judging from the Chinese reality, among the generation of people in their forties and fifties, families with poor education generally have more children than others. In these families, few housewives hold jobs, a factor which keeps their per-family income at a low level. Low income leads to low level of education, and low level of education leads to low income, and the vicious cycle goes on and on. It goes without saying that the government may take steps to provide children of low-income families with more educational opportunities. But this way of doing things can backfire, because in an environment where higher education is underdeveloped while the remnant influence of feudalism still lingers, government steps can degenerate into some people's tools for selfish gains. When that happens, there will be serious consequences: The efficiency of the national economy will be eroded, and a drain of precious human resources will occur. To break the vicious cycle suffered by low-income families without affecting economic efficiency and dashing talented people's hope for education, we must develop education. We must expand higher education and vocational education dramatically to increase the rate of school enrolment of low-income families' children and prepare them for high-income jobs in the future. At the same time, we should never do anything that might either erode society's economic efficiency or deprive gifted people of the opportunity to continue their education and bring their talent into full play.

Fourth, with the whole picture of the national economy in mind, low-income people and their families cannot be asked to improve their income level on their own. If our economy today were still under the kind of turmoil and sabotage that we saw during the decade-long "cultural revolution," or if our economic growth was very slow, little could be done to address the low-income levels as a social problem, no matter how hard these people worked to raise their incomes or improve their and their children's future money-making ability. The effective solution to income distribution problems in the course of economic growth comes down to national economic development, GDP growth, consistent technological innovation, and ever-increasing labor productivity. This is precisely where the role of education comes into play in regulating the relationship between income distribution and economic efficiency amidst economic growth. As I have said in the previous chapter, improving labor quality is a major guarantee for economic growth, while any achievements in innovating technology and raising labor productivity can be regarded as the accumulated results of investment in education.

Incidentally, I use the term "high-income" in this study as a reference to a certain group of individuals or families in the context of China's income distribution situation. It is relevant only to what happens in China, where the income levels of both workers and government functionaries are on the low side. This renders any comparison of China with the absolute statistics on average international income meaningless. Instead, it makes a lot more sense to compare the consumer-goods structure (the percentage of food expenses in a family's income in particular) and the hourly wage's purchasing power (the exchange ratio between hourly wage and durable consumption goods in particular). For this reason, while riding economic growth to raise the income level of low-income families, we should also work to improve the income of all workers and government employees, so that every family can see changes in their consumption composition and the exchange ratio between hourly income and durables. Of course this arduous task cannot be accomplished without a whole package of government steps. To develop education and increase funding for it is one such significant step. This is because only with a quality workforce and robustly growing labor productivity is it possible for everyone to make enough money and for production costs to drop enough to bring down the prices of consumer goods, change every family's consumption structure, and raise everyone's hourly income higher enough to afford more consumer goods. These changes are interconnected and mutually promoting. Universal changes in family consumption structure and universal increases in worker wages can yield more jobs and make it easier to solve employment problems.

Despite the Conflict of Rising Educational Funding With Fiscal Balance at the Present Stage of Economic Development, Investing in Education Helps Boost Fiscal Revenue Amidst Economic Growth

Developing education calls for more funding. Where shall the money come from? The mere mention of this question arouses concern about an added burden on state treasury. That is why people are saying the need to develop education and increase the funding for it is in conflict with the effort to maintain fiscal balance.

At the present stage of China's economic development, government funding is crucial to education development. But is government the only source of funding for education? Of course not. To solve employment problems and create more jobs, we cannot count on direct government investment alone and turn a blind eye to nongovernmental fund-raising efforts. By the same token, we cannot set our eyes only on state coffers and relinquish social fund-raising efforts if we are to develop education and put more people through school. In this study, however, let us forget about raising funds for education from nongovernmental channels and suppose that government funding is the only financial resource for education in this country.

In that case, there is no lack of theoretical support for the concern that increasing educational funding will result in fiscal deficits. Supposing the financial revenue is fixed or its growth rate is rather low while the growth rate of educational investment and spending on teachers' salaries are high, then financial deficits become unavoidable. Deficits increase money supply, which in turn causes prices to rise. Furthermore, if fiscal revenue is fixed while expenditure for national defense, administration and other purposes is curtailed to a maximum, increasing educational funding is likely to cut directly into investment in material production. This may reduce the economic returns from material production (or its profit growth rate), and inflate production costs (or bring down the cost reduction rate). In both scenarios, fiscal revenue and balance will be adversely affected, which may eventually trigger price increases.

However, we may see another possibility if we look a bit farther. Increasing educational investment is beneficial to both economic growth and the effort to maintain fiscal balance in the course of economic growth. Other things being equal, the source of increasing net revenues for an enterprise lies in its success in managing labor productivity to outgrow wage costs, expanding commodity production and reducing consumption of raw materials induced by improved labor productivity. As far as the entire national economy is concerned, increasing labor productivity to boost enterprise revenues is a reliable way to raise fiscal revenues and stabilize prices. In this light, the role of boosting educational investment speaks for itself. This is because, as I have said previously, increases in labor productivity can be regarded as an outcome of educational development.

This point of view can be further elaborated in three ways.

Firstly, insofar as its nature is concerned, education investment should be seen as a productive investment. Like investment in material production (such as building a factory or adding machinery and equipment), educational investment can also help increase the GDP. The difference between the two kinds of investment is that while investment in material production embodies itself in increasing the quantity and quality of material products, investment in education is reflected in workers' improved cultural and technical proficiency or in increasing the number of laborers who measure up to certain industrial or job requirements. The results of the former investment are plain for all to see, whereas the outcome of the latter can be easily overlooked, so much so that educational expenditure has for a long time been regarded as non-productive. If the role of education in promoting national economic development is still perceived in that old light, the inevitable conclusion is that adding educational funding can only upset fiscal balance. If, on the contrary, spending on education—an investment in human capital—is deemed conducive to heightening the cultural and technical proficiency of the workforce, thereby raising labor productivity and speeding up economic growth, then it is ultimately beneficial to fiscal balance.

Secondly, spending on education as a productive investment is characterized by a cycle that is longer than the construction cycle of the infrastructure, such as transportation and power supply. Of course there is no lack of cases in which educational spending brings quick economic returns, such as certain short-term training programs for technical workers. Generally speaking, however, it takes time to groom workers to a certain proficiency level in culture and technology, and it takes a much longer time to bring forth professionals of a certain caliber. Such facts give rise to the misunderstanding that education is like "distant water that cannot slake immediate thirst." As a matter of fact, that misunderstanding can be averted if people take a strategic point of view and regard education as a productive investment capable of yielding lasting economic returns, and if they can see the continuous role education can play in economic growth. To put it another way, if you are frustrated to see money being spent on education year in, year out, then you must be patient enough to wait until the number of laborers of a high cultural and technical caliber starts growing with each passing year. Just as education spending has about the same long harvesting cycle as infrastructure investment, so it can bring the same significant benefits to the national economy.

Thirdly, as a productive investment, education benefits society with its salubrious effect on the national economy as a whole. That effect can be easily neglected if we lose sight of the whole picture of society and the national economy, or if our vision is limited to a certain region, industry or firm. Of course, the direct effect of education investment can be felt in an individual region, industry or firm, especially in the case of certain types of local school or a factory's training school for technicians. This, however, is less important. Social gains from educational investment are a lot greater. Such gains are reflected, for one thing, in the fact that, by changing jobs or locations, educated workers will spread to all economic sectors and regions, and for another, in the improved scientific and cultural attainments of the entire population and the emergence of a rich crop of new inventions and innovations. Every invention or innovation is the fruit of long-accumulated investment in education, and, therefore, belongs to the entire society. With these inventions and creations, society is able to raise labor productivity, promote economic growth, improve workers' living standards and work conditions, create more jobs, and increase per capita national income. All these are the benefits society can reap from education. In all, if we shift our point of departure from a single region, industry or firm to take in the panorama of society, our judgment of the actual economic returns of education will not be limited to what a region, industry or firm has spent on education, nor shall our evaluation of the beneficial effect of education investment be restrained by the size of a partial investment. Clearly, even though increasing education spending in the course of economic growth may temporarily expand fiscal expenditure or curtail the income of some localities, from a long term point of view and by taking the overall situation into account, such spending is paramount to raising labor productivity, and effective in sustaining growth in national income and fiscal revenue.

Now that the benefits of developing education to the maintenance of fiscal balance in the long run are established, how should we look at the conflict between short-run increases in education spending and the need for fiscal balance? Let us return to the two hypotheses I have set at the beginning of this chapter.

Hypothesis One: Fiscal appropriation is, at present, the only source of funding for education. As a matter of fact, it is unnecessary to regard fiscal appropriation as the only source of funding for education, because nongovernmental fund-raising efforts hold great potential in this regard. How such potential should be tapped depends on the making and enforcement of government policy. We can save a huge amount of government spending on education as long as our policy allows nongovernment entities or individuals to run schools. Schools can be run effectively by involving nongovernment entities or collectives, and there is no lack of success in this field. I see nothing wrong with individuals running schools. Accomplished doctors, artists, accountants, translators and so on, are doing our nation and our youngsters a service by taking apprentices and teaching them knowledge or skills individually or by teamwork. These individuals are doing a lot of good to both the country and people when they run private vocational, technical or continuous education schools by tuition and cultivate talents for society without asking the government for a single penny. We would rather see young people in school than have them stay idle. As well as schools, an abundance of work-study programs are available for these people. To insist on running schools according to certain "rules" or "stereotypes" can do nothing but hold back development in education and put unwarranted burdens on the state treasury.

Hypothesis Two: Supposing fiscal revenue is fixed and defense and administrative expenditures have been pared down to a minimum, more spending on education can mean less investment in material production and result in fewer economic returns, to the jeopardy of fiscal revenue. Reality, however, has never been that simple. As we all know, investment in material production is just one condition for boosting aggregate production. There is at least another condition, and that is the economic returns from investment. If we can increase economic returns from investment in material production, speed up funds' turnover rate, and maximize the economic returns for every dollar spent, then we will see no reason why such investment cannot be downscaled. The former condition has been overestimated for a long time while the latter condition is overlooked, as if the more the investment is made, the higher the accumulation rate will become, with no consideration given to the economic returns of such investment. Astonishing waste is the inevitable result, and there is no lack of bitter lessons in this regard. Given a fixed fiscal revenue, why can't we do more to raise the turnover rate of funds and improve the efficiency of investment in material production? To speed up the training of technicians and managers is an effective way to enhance the economic returns of investment in material production. As long as we can find ways to raise the economic returns of such investment, it will not hurt the aggregate output, companies' economic returns, or government revenue to develop education with money saved from it under a fixed fiscal revenue.

Conclusion

In this study, I have looked into the positive role education investment can play in tackling problems in employment, international payments, income distribution, and long-term fiscal balance in the course of China's economic growth. We have no alternative but to speed up educational development by spending more money on it, if we are to ensure stable and sustained economic growth, tackle the nation's "structural" employment issue and weaknesses in international trade, and coordinate the relationship between income distribution and economic efficiency. The economic history of other nations indicates that it is easy to achieve temporary economic growth, but difficult to gain stable and sustained economic growth on the basis of coordinated development in all fields of socioeconomic development.

In the West, class antagonism and other fundamental conflicts inherent in capitalism are worsening; and unemployment, inflation, international payment deficits and unequal income distribution are entangled with the need for economic growth in an insoluble mess. Even if these capitalist nations can increase investment in education, the best they can accomplish is to ease the situation temporarily—there is no way they can find real solutions to their problems. Despite that fact, since the 1960s Western economists have been emphasizing the role of education in economic growth and urging their governments to take human capital investment policy and human resource planning as important measures to ensure long-term economic growth.

Socialism is a superior system. Problems of one kind or another do occur in our economy, but these problems are not inherent in the socialist system. On the basis of eliminating private ownership of capital goods under capitalism and carrying out the distribution policy of "from each according to his ability, to each according to his work," it should be a great deal easier for our nation to coordinate diverse social and economic interests in the course of economic growth. Education definitely has a bigger role to play in this regard than under the capitalist system. How is it, then, that education has not played such a role in the past? This question merits careful thinking. In my opinion, apart from long years of interference from ultra-leftist ideology and the sabotage of the Lin Biao Clique and the Gang of Four, it also has a lot to do with our short-sightedness, our failure to consider socialist economic development from the viewpoint of national development strategy, and our lack of understanding of the role of education in long-term economic growth. To those who cannot see the nature and role of education in perspective, education is a "soft" task that can be laid aside or delayed at will. Something is amiss, however, with that line of thinking. Therefore, I wrote this article with the same intention as when I wrote my thesis "Technical education and capitalist industrialization: a study of the rise of technological power in Western Europe and America" two years ago. That is, to send this message to our government policymakers: You have got to put a premium on education! When you mobilize society to raise money and open up schooling opportunities for our workforce, please make sure you will increase fiscal spending on education by a wide margin and thereby accelerate the development of education in our nation.

— *Journal of Peking University* (*Philosophy and Social Sciences*), issue No. 6, 1980

Notes

1. This speech was delivered at Peking University's 1978 "May Fourth" Science Forum, and carried in *Social Sciences Front*, issue No. 4, 1978.
2. Referring to individuals who know that no suitable jobs are available but choose not to register as being employed, even though they would prefer to have a job—*Translator*.

· 2 ·

EFFECTIVE AND RATIONAL INVESTMENT UNDER SOCIALISM

What is effective investment? To put it simply, it is the kind of investment that works promptly in putting together production capacity, boosts the supply of aggregate social product, and stimulates economic growth. What is rational investment? In short, it is the kind of investment that maintains basic price stability, creates many job opportunities, and raises labor force income while spurring economic growth. Whether investment is effective or not is determined by whether it has increased aggregate social product; and the effectiveness of investment is measured by the growth rate of aggregate social product. In contrast, whether investment is rational or not is determined by whether it has met the following goals: (1) boosting the economy; (2) maintaining basic price stability; (3) creating more jobs; and (4) raising labor force income. And the rationality of investment is measured by its actual results in meeting these goals. Effective investment may or may not be rational investment. Under socialism, it is not enough for investment to be merely effective. No effort should be spared to turn effective investment into rational investment, and with the largest possible degree of rationality at that.

Investment—Primary Dynamo Behind Economic Growth

Economic activity is a dynamic process in which one period of production, distribution, exchange and consumption circumscribes the next period. To allow production, distribution, exchange and consumption to take place on a larger scale in the next period, a certain amount of national income from the previous period must be spent in investment. The amount of investment determines the degree of changes in economic scale. Therefore, for a given return on investment, economic growth rate is always predicated on a given rate of investment, i.e., the percentage of national income spent on investment.

Investment always manifests itself as the primary driving force behind economic growth. The term "primary driving force" refers to the initial impetus that can set a stagnant economy on the track of growth. Without this initial impetus, no economy can be delivered from stagnation.

The relationship between supply and demand or between production and consumption may be thrown off balance in economic activity. The same can happen between economic sectors and between economic regions. If this lack of coordination is allowed to deteriorate further, it can bring down the economic growth rate or, worse, lead to zero or negative growth. Investment is indispensable if this situation is to be remedied and sustained economic growth ensured. Here, investment is still the primary driving force in adjusting economic structures, coordinating supply and demand, and maintaining economic relations in equilibrium.

Stagnant development of productive technology, worn-out equipment and outdated technological processes, misuse of equipment and raw materials, or failure to eliminate weak production links in good time in the course of economic activity can erode workforce productivity or inflict financial losses. If these conditions are allowed to continue, they will not only hold back economic growth but also adversely affect government revenue for the obvious reason that financial losses in enterprises invariably diminish government revenue. To reverse shrinking workforce productivity and compensate for enterprise losses, it is necessary to increase investment while adopting necessary management countermeasures. This is precisely where investment can be used as the primary driving force to renovate production technology, raise workforce productivity, and boost corporate profits and government revenue.

The reason why investment becomes the primary driving force on these occasions is that the significance of investment does not lie in the demand for it, but in the chain reactions it causes in economic activity. The demand arising from investment is, after all, limited, but the chain reactions it causes in economic activity can play a much larger role in national economy.

More investment means higher income, and higher income can stimulate investment. If this virtuous cycle can be made to last, a cumulative process will result in which investment brings along more investment, and income brings about still more income. This is how economic growth happens, how technology is upgraded and labor productivity grows, and how growth in corporate profit and government revenue are realized. By the same token, without the initial investment, there will be no subsequent investment; and without the income yielded by the initial investment, a constant flow of income will be out of the question.

This being the case, it is clearly unwise to underestimate or overlook the tremendous role investment can play as the primary dynamo behind economic growth.

My above analysis is, of course, built upon a given condition of management. It is not uncommon that mismanagement results in low labor productivity, sluggish economic growth, and financial losses. For this reason, this situation can be changed to a certain extent simply by improving management, without increasing investment.

My analysis is also based upon the initiative and motivation of the workforce. It is not uncommon that the lack of initiative or motivation, or the failure to motivate the workers and give full scope to their initiative limits workforce productivity to such a low level as to reduce the economic growth rate and incur corporate losses. In that scenario, we can also change the situation not by investing more but by taking proper steps to motivate workers and put the initiative into their hands.

Effective and Ineffective Investment

The effectiveness of investment rests with its ability to fuel economic growth, but not all kinds of investment have such ability. Investment may also be ineffective. Ineffective investment refers to the kind of investment that yields zero or negative growth.

Investment effectiveness or ineffectiveness has dual implications: microeconomic and macroeconomic. In microeconomic terms, investment becomes effective if it can boost the investor's output (that is, increase the investor's net output value). Otherwise, it is ineffective. In macroeconomic terms, investment becomes effective if it causes the national economy to grow (that is, increases national income); failing this, it is ineffective.

Because all investment must go through certain processes from the start of the action to the yield of increases in production and national income, the time factor must be considered, that is, the length of interval from the beginning of investment to the date when output begins to grow and national income begins to rise. That duration varies in length with the situation in different sectors. However, no matter how long it takes, the effectiveness or ineffectiveness of investment hinges on whether the economic growth it has brought about is positive, zero or negative.

If the time factor is not considered, investment is ruled ineffective only if it cannot enhance production capacity or contribute to aggregate social product. Any investment can be ruled effective if it enhances production capacity or increases aggregate social product. Thus the number of ineffective investment should be kept low, because most investment can yield production capacity and add to aggregate social product after a certain period of time, thereby contributing to economic growth one way or another.

However, it is far from enough to judge the effectiveness of investment or the lack of it this way. The time factor must be taken into account, that is, the length of time it takes from the onset of an investment action to the realization of output and national income increases. I have defined effective investment at the beginning of this article as something that is prompt in bringing about production capacity. In other words, no investment can be effective if it is overly time-consuming.

You may wonder why my definition of effective investment should contain the word "prompt." In what light should we understand that word? How can we tell whether investment is effective or ineffective based on our understanding of that word? As we all know, investment refers to the occupation of a certain amount of available capital for a certain period of time, whereas the available capital occupied by investment is part of the newly created value in the national economy that may be put to other uses in material production. Used properly, it can raise aggregate social product and elevate economic growth. Therefore, investment entails a certain degree of "probable" or "potential" increase in aggregate social product and economic growth rate. If this amount of money used as investment is prompt in bringing about production capacity, this "probable" or "potential" increase can be converted into an actual increase in aggregate social product. If this amount of money is left idle, it will never yield actual increase in aggregate social product. If an amount of money that can be invested to yield production capacity promptly is left idle, it obviously means losses in aggregate social product and national economic growth rate.

Supposing this amount of money is used as investment but takes a longer time than usual to enhance production capacity, it does absolutely nothing to boost aggregate social product or economic growth during that extra inactive period of time. Because, in this regard, inactivity is synonymous with losses in both aggregate social product and economic growth. During that extra time this amount of money should be regarded as ineffective investment. Moreover, even after it has yielded production capacity and begun to contribute to aggregate social product, it must make up for the losses it has caused previously to the national economy. Only after that can it qualify as effective investment.

This is why, in assessing investment effectiveness, due consideration should be given to the time needed for investment to put together production capacity.

How, then, should the word "prompt" in the wording "being prompt in yielding production capacity" be understood? Because of the differences in industries and investment projects, it is necessary to use the average time it takes for a specific industry or investment project to build production capacity as the benchmark. Investment that takes less than the average time to achieve the anticipated result can be regarded as being "prompt." The less time it takes to be effective, the "prompter" it becomes. Investment projects that take more than the average time to foster production capacity should be deemed "tardy in bringing about production capacity." The more time it takes in this process, the "tardier" it becomes.

With this benchmark, the effectiveness or ineffectiveness of investment can be defined as follows: (1) Investment that cannot yield production capacity or contribute to aggregate social product is ineffective investment; (2) Investment that takes less than the average time to yield production capacity is effective investment; (3) Investment that takes more than the average time to yield production capacity can be deemed effective only after it has reaped production capacity, contributed to aggregate social product, and made up for the losses it incurred during the extra time it took to yield such a production capacity. Before it has met these goals it should be regarded as ineffective investment.

Rational and Irrational Investment

No study of investment is complete if it focuses only on whether it has furthered economic growth or not. As the primary driving force behind economic growth, the positive role of investment lies not just in boosting aggregate social product and economic growth rate, but also in coordinating economic relations and goals of development. In that sense, investment is actually a balancing force in an economy, and hence investment is deemed rational only if it acts as such a balancing force.

Investment, however, may play an opposite role, that is, to disrupt the balances of economic relations and goals of economic development. Instead of keeping the economy on an even keel, it can throw the economy off balance or aggravate economic disequilibrium. Such is one of the attributes of irrational investment.

If investment is irrational, it may still help increase aggregate social product in the short run when it is effective. But in the long run, what appears briefly as effective investment can disturb economic relations, cause or aggravate economic disequilibrium, and result in a stagnation or downturn in aggregate social product.

Thus it is more important to see whether investment is rational or not than to judge if it is effective or ineffective. The concept of rational and irrational investment belongs in macroeconomic investment theory. When we talk about rationality or irrationality of investment, we do it in the context of macroeconomics.

Whether investment is rational or not depends on what role it plays in (1) economic growth, (2) price stability, (3) job creation, and (4) increase in labor income. Investment is considered irrational if it performs badly in one of these four fields, but it can be regarded as rational if it contributes to one field while the other three fields remain roughly constant. Investment becomes more rational if more such fields have improved while fewer of them remain constant.

Thus the definition of rational investment can be put more specifically:

As far as the role of investment in the aforementioned four fields is concerned, investment is rational if it has improved one of these fields while the others show no sign of decline.

If economic growth has picked up after investment is made, and the other three fields remain intact, that is, they have neither improved nor deteriorated, this is a typical case of effective investment also being rational, or to put it differently, effective investment and rational investment becoming the same thing. The minimum requirement for investment to be at once effective and rational is that it can at least promote economic growth while maintaining the status quo of the other three fields.

To combine effective investment with rational investment under that minimum requirement is just the starting point of arranging investment. We should try to improve all the four fields after investment is made. The more rational investment is, the more effective it becomes and the longer it can stay effective. The reason for this is clear: Without increasing aggregate social product, basic prices stability cannot be maintained, new job positions cannot be created in the national economy, and labor income will decline, and as a result, the national economy as a whole will deteriorate, and sustained economic growth becomes out of the question.

As much as the time factor should be taken into account when investment effectiveness or ineffectiveness is studied, the same should be done when investment rationality or irrationality is observed. This is because only by generating production capacity can investment play its role in coordinating economic relations, but it takes a period of time for that to happen. The length of this period is determined by the characteristics of the economic sector and the investment project in question.

What merits attention in this regard is that investment impacts price stability, the creation of jobs, and labor income in different ways. Before production capacity is generated, because there is only financial input and no output in aggregate social product, the amount of currency in circulation grows, which will have a negative impact on price stability. If, after production capacity is yielded, the growth rate of aggregate social product resulting from the investment is still lower than the growth rate of the amount of currency in circulation, it may still have a negative impact on price stability, a possibility that should not be overlooked. The situation, however, is different with the creation of new jobs. Investment may begin creating jobs immediately after it is made, because the investment action itself can absorb some workers. However, after investment has brought about production capacity, it may either increase employment (including the jobs created by this investment itself and the jobs created by other industries or firms under its impact), or reduce employment (including fewer job opportunities in other industries or firms under the impact of this investment and fewer job opportunities directly caused by the termination of the investment project). With regard to real labor income, apart from the investment-induced changes in price level and employment that are likely to affect labor income, the investment-induced changes in labor productivity are a more important factor that inevitably affects changes in labor income. Before production capacity is realized, few significant changes will happen to labor productivity. Therefore, during the interval from the start of investment to the materialization of production capacity, changes in labor income are mainly related to changes in price level and employment, whereas after production capacity is created, changes in labor productivity will have an increasing impact on labor income.

Thus, to judge if investment is rational or not, not only its impact on price stability, job creation, and real labor income after it has brought about production capacity, but also its impact on these fields during the interval from the outset of the investment to the yield of production capacity should be observed. If the former impact is considered but the latter neglected, it is likely that the investment in question may have already had a negative impact, and a seriously negative impact at that, on the balance of national economy before it reaps production capacity. In that scenario, even if investment has generated new production capacity, its earlier negative impact on national economy may be so grave as to hold back the effectiveness of production capacity or offset its positive impact on balancing the national economy.

Discrepancy Between Effective and Rational Investment

As I have pointed out in the foregoing, the criteria for judging effective investment are different from those for rational investment. The roles of effective investment and rational investment in the economy are different as well. Effective investment is not necessarily rational investment. Even if effective investment is also rational, it is not necessarily the most rational investment. On the other hand, although rational investment must also be effective, it may not be the most effective investment. The discrepancy between effective investment and rational investment is apparent.

For instance, a specific investment project or investment in one certain field may be effective because it can raise aggregate social product, but it may have a negative impact on price stability by taking up so much funding for so long as to affect the amount of currency in circulation before it creates production capacity. After creating production capacity, the investment in question may also diminish the job positions it has created and cause other industries and firms to reduce their job positions. Even if it has created production capacity, the investment can still cause real labor income to dip due to price changes, job market fluctuations and declining labor productivity.

Given these possibilities, and by taking its multiple goals and the balance of national economy into consideration, effective investment is likely to be irrational or have just a small degree of rationality at best.

Observed from the perspective of multiple goals and the balance of national economy, a certain investment is rational because it has improved at least one of the four fields—economic growth, basic price stability, job creation, and labor income—while the other fields have shown no sign of deterioration. However, because rational investment has to attain multiple goals, its capacity to boost aggregate social product may be lower than maximal (for instance, if the investment is not put into a highly sophisticated automated factory), although it can still boost aggregate social product to a certain extent. In this case, it cannot be counted as the most effective investment.

How, then, should we deal with the discrepancy between effective and rational investment? We may study the question from a normative or a positive approach.

A normative approach calls for realigning the goals of investment in the order of importance, urgency and priority of the multiple goals that the investment aims to attain. Then overall consideration should be given to the problems to be solved through this investment and the means of solving these problems, so as to find out to what extent effectiveness and rationality of this investment can be coordinated. According to the aforementioned definition, investment is rational if it has improved at least one of the four fields while the others show no sign of deterioration. The question now is which one of these four fields should be improved first. The answer must be based on a study of the actual situation to see which one of the four goals is most attainable. However, the answer also involves judgment of values, that is, which goal is more important and which goal is less important. To observe investment through normative analysis is to prioritize the four goals from judgment of values in order to make rational investment.

The positive approach follows established norms and rules, or is based on the assumption that all goals are equally important, to find ways to coordinate effective and rational investment. The solution to the discrepancy between effective and rational investment is related not only to the preconditions of a given investment but also to the methods of raising and operating the fund needed for this investment. The next chapter explores, from the viewpoint of positive study, the preconditions of investment and how to raise and operate the fund of investment.

Resource and Marketability for Effective and Rational Investment

The shared attributes of effective and rational investment are that, firstly, both can only take place where there are sufficient and usable economic resources, and secondly, there must be markets for the products of the production capacity they have created. In other words, economic resources and marketability are prerequisites for investment to be at once effective and rational.

Economic resources fall into two categories: material and human. Material resources, that is, means of production, include production equipment, raw materials, fuels and power, means of transportation, and storage facilities. Human resources encompass unskilled and skilled labor force, the latter including technical and management professionals. These resource conditions are indispensable for every investment project.

Now that effectiveness of investment hinges on its speed in putting together production capacity and boosting aggregate social product, it is difficult, or even impossible, to turn investment promptly into production capacity in the absence of means of production and human resources. Even if an investment project has been completed, it still cannot increase aggregate social product if it has no sufficient supply of means of production—such as raw materials, fuels, power, and spare parts for maintenance and repair purposes—and adequate labor force, or if transportation, storage and other factors fail to meet production needs. In this regard, investment—the primary driving force behind economic growth—is based upon the adequacy of useful economic resources. Investment can put together production capacity rapidly where idle productive resources and a variety of idle workers are available. It can also quickly bring about production capacity where productive resources and labor force are unavailable but can be obtained through minor readjustments, or where economic resources are in short supply but there is an adequate foreign exchange reserve to be used to buy those deficient resources from foreign markets. However, in the latter scenario, things tend to be complicated because it involves the balance of foreign trade and of international payments. In the absence of all the abovementioned conditions, investment becomes ineffective because it cannot promptly create production capacity.

Given that the rationality of investment is determined by whether it can meet the four goals of economic growth, basic price stability, job creation, and real labor income, effectiveness—that is, promptness in creating production capacity—becomes the minimum requirement for rational investment.

Because adequate supply of economic resources is a prerequisite for the speedy creation of production capacity, such supply must also be guaranteed for rational investment. Otherwise it cannot meet all four goals at the same time.

The next consideration is the market conditions for investment, that is, the product salability of an investment project. Whether such a product is made for production or consumption purposes, there must be people willing to buy it at a certain price. If production is carried out only for the purpose of meeting certain output quotas and the product cannot be sold out and has to be piled up in warehouses, the investment will not be able to contribute to economic growth. This conclusion is understandable, because investment can be rational only if it contributes to aggregate social product, maintains basic price stability, creates new jobs, and increases real labor income. Those roles can never be realized if nobody wants to buy the product of an investment project. Furthermore, investment may have a negative impact on prices and labor income if its product cannot be sold out. Such investment is irrational.

Is product marketability also a prerequisite for effective investment? Because whether investment is effective or not is determined by whether it can bring about production capacity promptly and boost aggregate social product, people may argue that the effectiveness of investment is irrelevant to product marketability. They believe that investment is effective as long as it can produce a certain amount of products, regardless of product salability. In their eyes, investment becomes ineffective only if it cannot create production capacity or cannot do it fast enough—investment should not be deemed ineffective if it can bring about production capacity speedily even though its products are unwanted on the market. This idea, undoubtedly, is not correct.

This idea is wrong in that it only accepts the literal meaning of production capacity, and severs production capacity from product marketability. It is, therefore, a misunderstanding of production capacity. We know that the production capacity of a factory built with an amount of investment is only nominal if it does not produce and supply products. If the factory's products cannot meet market demand and only belong in warehouses, this factory is a non-factor at best because of its failure to supply society with usable products. We would rather this kind of factory did not do anything, for the fuel, power, raw materials and so on it consumes could have been used for meaningful purposes. Therefore, production capacity created by investment should be real, rather than nominal. It should supply society with marketable products instead of things that cannot be sold out. If the effectiveness of investment and the creation of production capacity are understood in that light, product marketability must be regarded as a precondition for effective investment.

The argument that the effectiveness of investment is unrelated to the marketability of its product exactly mistakes nominal production capacity for real production capacity. The effectiveness of investment rests in real, rather than nominal, production capacity it creates.

Profitability of Effective and Rational Investment

Investment profitability is an important theoretical issue. Even if the product of an investment project can be sold out, what will be the consequences if it can only be sold out at a lower price than its production and interest costs?

First of all, this kind of investment cannot be recouped in that case. Moreover, even after the investment project is completed, further expenses are needed to keep production going; otherwise even the original scale of production cannot be maintained. This kind of investment, even if it can bring about production capacity and its products are marketable, poses more losses than gains, and should never be allowed to happen.

Nevertheless, if we extend our vision from an individual investor to the entire national economy, different opinions may occur on investment profitability.

The national economy is an integrated entity, in which all sectors are organically connected. Some sectors or firms may have the needed economic resources and their products can meet market demand. But, for one reason or another, their products are priced equal to or lower than their production costs and interest expenses, and therefore, they cannot generate a profit. Should investment be made in such a sector or firm? Is profitability an overriding condition for investment? It seems that neither question can be answered with a simple yes or no, because both involve how the macroeconomic effectiveness of investment should be measured.

As illustrated in the previous chapter, effective investment has both macroeconomic and microeconomic implications, while rational investment belongs in the macroeconomic realm. Observed from a macroeconomic point of view, some kinds of investment in certain sectors or firms are unlikely to make a profit, but can contribute to faster growth in other sectors or firms and to the balance of national economy and coordination among investment goals. This kind of investment is still necessary, and can be regarded as both effective and rational.

Defenders of investment that is at once ineffective and irrational in practice may also cite the macroeconomic effectiveness of investment to back up their argument that this kind of investment should not be cancelled. They may accuse those who want to do so of lacking macroeconomic farsightedness. They can always find a "reason" to justify any investment project they like, arguing that it is so important to the national economy that it cannot be ditched even if it is not making money. Indeed, this issue can easily become controversial, and can never be settled if we accept the existence and significance of the macroeconomic results of an investment project without setting benchmarks for its effectiveness and rationality in macroeconomic terms.

This is where econometrics comes in handy. Despite its limitations, the methods of econometrics are still useful for analyzing investment effectiveness and rationality in macroeconomic terms on certain occasions and under certain premises and presumptions.

The resource and market conditions for investment should be considered in the first place. Investment, no matter what kind it is, must be guaranteed with an ample supply of means of production and human resources, both of which are prerequisites for production capacity. The products invested in should also meet market demand, otherwise they can only become part of warehouse stockpiles and their production capacity is nominal at best. Various econometric methods can be employed when we analyze the resource and market conditions for an investment scheme. Generally speaking, the input-output analysis can be employed to determine the situation regarding resource supply and market demand.

The conditions for investment profitability come next. Investment profitability in microeconomic terms can be computed with cost-benefit analysis. Relationships in this regard are relatively simple. By factoring in the given output and price conditions, as well as production costs and interest expenses, we can clarify whether an invested project is making or losing money. Then the deadline for recouping the investment normally a major benchmark for judging the microeconomic effectiveness of an invested project—can be set with reference to the production cycle.

The situation is a lot more complex when it comes to judging if an investment project is making a profit or not from a macroeconomic perspective.

Investment rationality in the field of material production and investment effectiveness in macroeconomic terms cannot be studied without comparing various relations in the national economy and dissecting the input-output relationship between sectors in the national economy. If the product of Sector A is not only supplied directly to consumers but also needed by Sectors B, C and D for their production, while the products of Sectors B, C and D are also both supplied directly to consumers and needed by Sectors E, F, G and H for production purposes, and if that cycle goes on and on, then the results of follow-up investment in Sector A will be reflected not just in that sector's augmented income but also in the augmented incomes of Sectors B, C, D, E, F, G and H. Suppose there is a certain ratio between income and employment, then the results of follow-up investment in Sector A will be reflected not just in its increased number of jobs but also in the changes that have taken place in the number of jobs in the other sectors. Using counterfactual analysis, we can compare the results of the following two approaches: first, to study total income, net income, employment and other variables before Sector A was invested in; second, to study the changes in the variables such as total income, net income, and employment in the other sectors after Sector A was invested in. From this comparison we can get to know the degree of profitability of investment in macroeconomic terms. Suppose that a certain investment project does not make money for itself, but contributes to the growth in total income, net income and employment in other economic sectors, and the benefits to the national economy from the growth in these sectors outweigh the losses caused to the national economy by the investment project's failure in making a profit, then the investment can still be considered as a gain to the national economy. As a matter of fact, there is an investment-recouping period for the project, but such a period is reflected in the national economy. If, on the contrary, a comparison of the two approaches indicates that the investment does make a profit for itself but has inflicted losses in total income, net income and employment on other sectors, or that the investment is losing money while these sectors' increases in gross income, net income and employment are negligible so that the benefits the investment has yielded for the national economy are barely enough to offset the losses it has inflicted on the national economy, such an investment is deemed detrimental to the national economy. If allowed to continue under the excuse of cherishing its macroeconomic results, the said investment becomes irrational, and—in macroeconomic terms—ineffective as well.

Relationship Between Investment Fund Supply, Public Finance and Investment

To make investment both effective and rational, due attention must be paid to the supply of funding. Suppose an investment project has favorable resource and market conditions and its product can be sold briskly enough to guarantee an after-sale profit, but it cannot continue or has to stop midway because of fund shortage, then it cannot put together production capacity in good time, and cannot become effective investment. Furthermore, this kind of investment is irrational because it is a loss to the national economy when the money spent fails to yield production capacity.

If, on the contrary, an investment scheme can yield production capacity promptly but spends too much to achieve the purpose, it may also disrupt public finance or money circulation, thereby exerting an adverse impact on price stability. Thus it can never become rational investment.

What can be done to avoid improper supply of funding and ensure effectiveness and rationality of investment? Let us begin answering this question by studying the relationship between investment and public finance.

Under socialism, fiscal appropriations are an important source of reinvestment. They generally have a direct impact on the volume and scale of investment and its effectiveness. More importantly, the impact of such appropriations also extends to the relationship between the multiple goals of investment and to investment rationality.

When we try to coordinate the relationship between economic growth and basic price stability, we face the urgent task of preventing the demand for monetary funds from running out of control, or, to put it another way, we must prevent the amount of currency in circulation from growing too fast. Inflation is eventually attributed to the failure of the growth in aggregate social product to outpace the growth in the amount of currency in circulation. Inflation can be prevented or erased only by boosting the growth rate of aggregate social product, reducing the growth rate of the amount of currency in circulation, or both.

Fast growth in the amount of currency in circulation is mainly an outcome of fiscal deficit or bank credit expansion. Therefore, when there is a serious fiscal deficit, especially when such a deficit has lingered for several years, fiscal appropriation designed to increase investment funding must be used cautiously. Otherwise the amount of currency in circulation may be further increased.

However, insofar as investment is the primary driving force behind economic growth, the lack of sufficient investment can neither boost aggregate social product nor change the situation where aggregate social product grows slower than the amount of currency in circulation. Tightening up investment alone can neither eliminate fiscal deficit nor effectively keep inflation away from the door. This is because economic sectors are interlinked and only by constantly restructuring these sectors and their products can the proportional relationships in the national economy be coordinated. However, restructuring sectors and products calls for followup investment on most occasions. If investment is tightened up merely to eliminate deficits and forestall inflation, the national economy will fall further out of proportion and coordination. Worse, it can also land some industries or firms that may expand production and make a profit in financial loss, thereby doing a disservice to the effort to turn the fiscal situation around and eradicate inflation.

From the perspective of increasing aggregate social product, technical renovation and equipment upgrading are material conditions for labor productivity increases, but both call for follow-up investment. If investment is tightened up merely to wipe out deficits and forestall inflation, it is very difficult to boost labor productivity and aggregate social product by improving their material conditions. Furthermore, if other conditions remain unchanged but equipment cannot be upgraded for lack of necessary investment, workforce productivity will decline. As a result, the industries and firms that could have been producing and making a profit will lose money, and public finance and the effort to control inflation will be jeopardized as well.

To ascribe the rise of financial deficits or inflation merely to investment growth is to oversimplify a complex matter. Effective and rational investment is actually an important means by which to eliminate deficits and inflation, rather than to aggravate them. It is ineffective or irrational investment—investment that drags on and fails to yield production capacity, investment in unmarketable products, investment that is made in marketable products but incurs heavy losses or distorts economic relations—that should be held responsible for deficits and inflation.

This being the case, what merits the attention of the fiscal department is that they should curtail or cancel all the investment projects that lack resource and market conditions or fail to yield macroeconomic returns. However, investment projects that yield production capacities promptly, produce marketable products, make profit, and are conducive to the growth of total and net income of various sectors in the national economy, should not be curtailed or axed. Effective and rational investment is a dynamo behind a robust and booming national economy, and a robust and booming national economy is the solid foundation of public finance and a guarantee for stable fiscal revenue. The financial department can avoid inappropriate supply of investment funding as long as it takes a scientific attitude toward investment, that is, to invest in what should be invested in and not to invest in what should not be invested in.

Choice of Investment Funding Raising Channels

Fiscal funding is a major financial source for investment, but certainly not the only source for it. Under socialism the money needed for investment purposes comes from at least four avenues: fiscal appropriations, non-governmental fund-raisers, business reserve funds, and bank credits.

Short-, medium- and long-term bank credits can be used as a source of money for all purposes of investment. Their strength lies in that they can urge investors to tighten up financial auditing and pay due attention to the microeconomic results of their investment projects. The bank, by screening investment plans and monitoring the spending, plays a definite role in enhancing the macroeconomic results of investment.

Apart from money raised by way of savings and bond purchases, the funds from non-governmental sources also include the money procured from people of all walks of life to run cooperative firms and boost domestic development.

Business reserve funds refer to the portion of profit that firms are allowed to retain on the principle of autonomy to buy equipment, upgrade technology, expand production, reduce costs, and increase output.

Of the four major sources of funding, fiscal funding is not always the principal one. People can make their choices according to investment needs and financial situation. No matter what source is chosen, however, the aforementioned investment conditions should always be kept in mind. On no account should ineffective and irrational investment be made. Whenever an investment project gets off the ground, no effort should be spared to maximize its effectiveness and rationality.

A point that can be easily forgotten is that non-governmental fundraisers are not only a substitute for government investment but also a method to withdraw money from circulation. The role of such fundraisers in substituting for government investment comes through when investment projects originally to be funded with fiscal appropriation revert to social fund-raising. However, investment is not just a supply of money. Guaranteed material supply is indispensable, too. The money raised from non-governmental channels needs to be spent on means of production. However, means of production needed for investment purposes are basically provided by the government department in charge of supplying them. If the government department does not possess sufficient means of production needed for an investment project, it means that the resource conditions for the project are not ripe. Just as I have said in my analysis of investment conditions, investment without adequate supply of means of production is ineffective and irrational and, therefore, should be abrogated. By the same token, if a nongovernment-funded investment project fails to get off the ground, it will not adversely affect the national economy. If the government department has sufficient means of production for an investment project, it means that the material conditions are ripe and that the project in question can be undertaken. In this case, the government department contributes to the national economy by supplying the needed means of production and withdrawing money from circulation. Otherwise, if non-governmental funding is replaced with fiscal funding, it cannot withdraw money from circulation even though it could also be used for investment purposes.

From another point of view, in the absence of fund-raisers, what is the best use for money held in non-governmental hands? This kind of money may end up in banks as saving deposits, or be spent on consumer goods. If it ends up as saving deposits, banks will have to think about how to put the money to good use. When there is investment demand, supply of money by bank credit plays the same role as non-governmental money-raisers. However, if the money does not become saving deposits but is spent on consumer goods, especially on those in short supply, market supply will be strained. For this reason, if investment conditions are suitable and money can be raised from non-governmental sources, such investment projects are more rational than others.

—*Finance & Trade Economics*, issue Nos. 1 & 3, 1982

· 3 ·

BASIC THOUGHTS ON ECONOMIC RESTRUCTURING

Years have passed since economic restructuring came under way in this nation. What is to be done next? Here I would like to share my thoughts, which come in twenty-eight points, and involve seven issues altogether. Some of these ideas may be controversial, but I see controversy as a good thing. Without discussion and debate, there will be no economic prosperity.

Ownership Reform Holds the Key to Economic Restructuring

1. Economic restructuring may break down if price reform fails. The success of economic restructuring, however, hinges not on price reform, but on ownership reform, which entails revamping the corporate system. This is because price reform serves the main purpose of shaping an environment in favor of the growth of the market economy, but only ownership reform or corporate system reform can address such issues as interests, responsibility, motivation, and incentives.

2. The purpose of ownership reform is to build state firms truly liable for their own gains and losses. Being "truly liable for their own gains and losses" means that, for one thing, firms should bear all the consequences of financial

losses, and for another, gains and losses must be symmetrically treated not only for firms but also for their leaders. The most crucial task of ownership reform is to make state firms really accountable for their successes and failures, and, even more so, to answer the question of what is to be done with firms in the red. Symmetrical treatment of gains and losses means that firms should enjoy their profits while absorbing their losses rather than passing the ball to the state, which is exactly what firms are doing today. Taking responsibility for their own losses will stimulate them to improve management. The reason why some non-state firms can stay dynamic and motivated under pressure is because they can treat gains and losses symmetrically—meaning that they have all the economic gains to themselves while being totally liable to economic losses, bankruptcy included. As things stand in this nation, the best that can be done with a failing state firm is to demote its general manager or shift him to another post. This way of doing things cannot be sustained. Gains and losses must be treated on a balanced footing. Mismanaged firms should go bankrupt, and bankrupt firm should be liquidated. There should be both a bankruptcy law and a social security act, and issues such as reemployment for layoffs should be tackled in real earnest.

3. Collective firms may adopt the shareholding system. State firms may also be transformed into shareholding companies, holding companies, or socialist enterprise consortia.

The shareholding system talked about here is not about selling stock shares to workers or other individuals (although of course, some of the shares can be sold to workers and other individuals), but about distributing interests among public owners according to the number of shares they hold. There can be a variety of public shareholders. After a state firm has its current assets evaluated, its net assets should be counted as state shares because they come from state investment. The investment added by a local government to a state firm becomes locally owned state shares, while the shares in the firm's possession come from its own investment. In addition, investment made by other state enterprises also becomes shares owned by these enterprises. The positions of the stockholders on the board of directors are arranged according to how many shares they hold, but it is the board of directors that decides the policies and principles for a shareholding firm. Only in this way can the difficult problem of detaching government administration from business management be effectively addressed. The board of directors is established through the shareholders' congress. In this case, all shareholders are public owners. In such a structure, even if some shares are sold to individuals, they are unlikely to take up a large portion of the total stock.

The holding company system is another option that works under public ownership. Once a state firm becomes a shareholding company, its shares can be put up for sale. In the West, a holder of less than 51% of the shares of a company can control it and turn it into his branch company. We can do the same. If, under the holding-company system, a powerful state company can turn itself into a socialist enterprise consortium by buying shares to control a number of companies, it can change the behavior of these companies, and shift their focus from short-run business to long-term operations with a broad strategic vision. In that position, the socialist company can adapt its policy decisions to long-term development goals. Whatever it does, an enterprise consortium must take the overall scheme of things into consideration. For instance, it can take the lead in oil development in northwest China. If it has foreseen a boom in the petroleum industry coming to that region in a few years, it may consider investing part of its profits there. To boost development, it may also engage in trans-sectoral or trans-regional business operations in return for an average internal profit. China's western region should not be developed piecemeal by an assortment of small concerns, but should be handled by such giants as socialist consortia.

4. The tactics for ownership reform should differ depending on industry, locality, and business size. Firms may be categorized into industries according to their importance to the national economy and the scarcity degree of the resources they need, before deciding which industries should be shored up first and what kind of firms—public, collective or private—should be developed in the main. Such industries and enterprises should also be considered in the light of local conditions, and categorized according to their sizes. Large state firms in important industries or regions should be preserved, while other companies can be leased or subcontracted out; some of them can be sold to collectives or individuals. In this way, the state can let go of most small firms in order to keep those essential companies that form the backbone of the economy under socialist ownership. These "backbone" firms may be developed into competitive socialist enterprise consortia, or transformed into multinational corporations that will be a force to be reckoned with on the world market. At the end of the day, however, they will remain state owned.

How about medium-sized and small firms? This depends on what industry is in question. Their shares can be sold to collectives and individuals to create companies under mixed ownership.

This design of ownership reform holds the key to the success of economic restructuring. Once it is translated into reality, it will impart motivation, a sense of responsibility, incentive, and interest in our enterprises, and diversify ownership and management without sacrificing the leadership role and dominance of public ownership.

The Need for a Relatively Complete Market

5. Market can balance supply and demand with its self-regulatory function, but it also has limitations that can only be overcome with government regulation. However, this does not mean government can do it all, or that market is needed only when government is weak. In my opinion, the relationship between government and market should be interpreted in this way: Market enables the economy to regulate itself and coordinate supply and demand, but needs government regulation to make up for its shortcomings, such as its limited resource supply and incomplete economic information system. The bottom line for economic restructuring is that the socialist economy should be a market economy in the first place, and then a market economy supplemented by planning.

6. Market regulation coexists with government regulation. They supplement each other, but are not mutually interchangeable. They combine to form a dual mechanism, which, nevertheless, is not the combination of two separate elements. Government regulation must take market regulation as its starting point, and works merely to pick up the slack of market regulation. Market prices are greatly variable. Besides free prices resulting from complete competition, there can also be prices from incomplete competition; and state-regulated prices must be based on a wide variety of market prices although there can be discrepancies between planned prices and market prices. The causes and magnitudes of such discrepancies are subject to government regulation, which should still take market prices as its basis.

7. A relatively well-functioning market mechanism cannot be transplanted; it can only grow to completion by itself in an economy. In the past, it could not grow in this country because it lacked a salubrious environment, i.e., a socialist market economy. Today, it can grow and improve over time, as long as we are resolved to put a socialist market economy in place. Please note that I am using the term "relatively wellfunctioning" to describe my idea of a market mechanism. The market mechanism cannot become completely competitive the way things are in China under the current circumstances. We should be fully aware that our economy is limited by scarcity in resources, and that government regulation is needed to supplement market regulation.

8. A socialist market system should encompass four markets. First, a commodity market that entails a consumer goods market and a capital goods market. A real estate market should also be included, because commercial housing is an inevitable trend in our economic development. Second, a capital market which includes a securities market. Once the shareholding system is introduced, a securities market is needed; otherwise, share flow and trading will be out of the question. The securities market can be regulated, and specialized securities markets set up. Where conditions are immature, banks may act as intermediaries to issue and deal in stock shares, or work as brokers to mortgage stock shares or discount them for cash. Third, a technology market for payable transfers of research and development results. Fourth, a labor market, or service market. Having never been opened to free competition, our labor market is fragmented and differs across localities. Given labor's limited lateral and vertical mobility, the labor market can only grow gradually.

We have got to develop a unified commodity market in which nationwide circulation of consumer and capital goods is allowed. If such goods cannot be circulated nationwide, the reasons are more economic (such as high costs and low economic returns) than non-economic. The capital market referred to here should be unified nationwide as well. If capital cannot circulate across the land, it should likewise be attributed to economic causes, rather than government interference and other non-economic factors.

Raising Government Efficiency

9. Effective economic decisions, policy enforcement, and economic supervision are hallmarks of a highly efficient government. A government with little or no work efficiency is invariably crippled by legislation that is absent, bypassed, laxly enforced, or simply superseded by state power. An inefficient government plus an incomplete market can scuttle economic reform no matter how good the reform plan is. Therefore, to make economic restructuring a success, we must raise government efficiency without fail.

10. Government efficiency is more needed in economic regulation than in government intervention, more for indirect market control than for direct market control, and more for guidance planning than for central planning. We should be aware that managing the economy has become more challenging after economic restructuring came under way. The efficiency level of our economic administrators leaves a great deal to be desired. We must speed up

training to raise their overall quality and proficiency, for only thus can government efficiency be boosted effectively.

11. We should relinquish planned management if it is arbitrary and unscientific, and dismantle economic regulation if it is ineffective and arbitrary. In either case, we would let the market mechanism run its course. Thus, the kind of government regulation that is paired with market regulation should be scientifically viable and highly efficient. The dual mechanism does not mean market regulation and government regulation are both indispensable. Government regulation should be predicated on scientific feasibility and high efficiency. If we reject willful government intervention and bring the role of the market mechanism into play, at least we can boost the economy during fluctuations. The involvement of a bull-headed government can only inflict stagnation or setback on our economy—what happened in 1958 across this land was a typical case in point. We should learn to differentiate between sound and unsound government regulation. Sound government regulation is good in that it can overcome market failures; unsound government regulation can do nothing but nullify the self-regulatory function of the market mechanism. The market mechanism can strike a general balance between supply and demand and facilitate economic growth, even though it may take more time and is likely to cause major fluctuations in the course of it. If we can see the dual mechanism in such light, we are able to open up new horizons.

12. Administrative reform is a must if government efficiency is to be raised. The system whereby government officials are selected and appointed must be overhauled. We should evaluate the performance of civil servants within a framework that holds them accountable for the goals set for their tenures. It makes no sense that these people can only be promoted and not demoted. It makes little sense, either, that people can be both promoted and demoted. Of course, there should be both promotions and demotions, but only competent officials should be promoted and incompetent ones demoted—no exception should be made in this regard. Only thus can the government work efficiently, and institutional reform be speeded up.

Entrepreneurship and Socialist Entrepreneurs

13. China needs legions of socialist entrepreneurs as much as it needs entrepreneurship. Our entrepreneurs should have strategic vision, dare to innovate and create, be pragmatic and imbued with organizational and business

acumen. In economic restructuring, socialist entrepreneurs should be protected, and their talent given full scope. Without entrepreneurs and entrepreneurship, the economy will be sluggish even if the ownership system is transformed, and even if shareholding firms, enterprise consortia, and new-type state firms are established. As argued above, ownership reform holds the key to economic restructuring. But the next question is: Who are to run the restructured state firms, and to use their talent to inject life into these firms? None other than entrepreneurs. Without entrepreneurs, ownership reform can get nowhere. Entrepreneurship is essential to ownership reform. In the years of reform, we should never lose sight of the importance of entrepreneurs and entrepreneurship.

14. Socialist entrepreneurs do not come forth by doing the government's bidding, nor can they be groomed in a "greenhouse." Their destiny is bound up with the development of the socialist market economy and with the economic activity of their enterprises, where they come to the fore through competition. We should keep an eye on businesses in adversity, rural firms included, for these are where socialist entrepreneurs are likely to emerge. We should go to medium-sized and small firms and those run by farmers if we are to find socialist entrepreneurs. Because those who can emerge unscathed from unfriendly territories at least have the makings of an entrepreneur. "Socialist entrepreneurs are born of pressure." That line sounds realistic to us all. Entrepreneurs born of adversity are the only people who can bring a competitive edge to our firms.

15. Entrepreneurs and entrepreneurship are fruits of the market economy. The farther the socialist market economy advances, the more entrepreneurs will turn up, and the more impact entrepreneurship will bring. The burgeoning socialist market economy can provide a constant supply of entrepreneurs—this is more effective than putting a lot of factory directors or managers through advanced training courses. Without a market economy we will not be able to produce so many socialist entrepreneurs. By the same token, our university economics departments cannot necessarily cultivate entrepreneurs even though they are doing a fair job of instilling basic economics knowledge in students.

16. Enterprises must be allowed to go through a "metabolic process" in which the new supersedes the old. Ill-managed enterprises should call it quits or be closed down, phased out, or liquidated. For a certain percentage of enterprises to go bankrupt on a yearly basis is not the end of the world for the socialist economy. The platform for the socialist market economy should be

preserved for emerging, dynamic, and competitive enterprises. Market competition is a whirlwind that can dispose of outdated and inefficient firms and preserve competitive ones. But more importantly, it can level the ground for more enterprises to grow. Such is the process of innovation. Such is the way socialist consortia come to stay, and the way socialist multinational companies carve out a niche in the world market. Only in this way can our economy respond to the pressure of competition and brim over with vitality.

Economic Norms Based on Socialist Ethics

17. Social inequity spawns social instability, but social instability does not necessarily stem from social inequality. Income disparity may spur efficiency, but efficiency does not necessarily come from such disparity. In an objectively equal society, if the standard of living first rises and then drops, with increase outstripping decrease, the irreversible nature of consumption, income, and wages can also work psychologically to cause social unrest. In an objectively equal society, there are people who work harder and make more money than others, but there are also those who work less and are paid less. If those who make less money refuse to accept the fact that they do less than others and claim that they have been taken advantage of, they are likely to stir social instability. If the income gap exceeds a certain limit, it can affect efficiency and drive some people to despair and indolence. That is why in the socialist economy, the relationship between equality and efficiency should be handled properly. Equality, as we understand it, entails turning workers into owners of capital goods, equal opportunities for all and distribution according to work done. Efficiency, as we understand it, is also based on public ownership of capital goods, on equal opportunities, and on the principle of distribution according to work done. Only with this understanding in mind can the relationship between equality and efficiency be well handled.

18. From an economic point of view, despite its limitations, the market mechanism enables the economy to grow amidst fluctuations. From the perspective of social coordination, however, the limitations of the market mechanism are more pronounced, for the market itself cannot coordinate social development. We do not seek economic growth for growth's own sake. Rather, economic growth should be consistent with coordinated social development. Efficient government regulation is needed because its impact is both economic and social. The social impact of government regulation manifests itself in regulating income distribution while ensuring economic growth, an

impact that is mandated by the socialist goals for socioeconomic development. Thus, in the course of economic restructuring, progressive income tax, income-adjustment tax, and allowances for low-income families are needed, but should be kept within reasonable bounds to ensure economic growth and social harmony. At the same time, however, we have got to know that we cannot do without these taxes and allowances in securing economic growth and social harmony. This is exactly what economic reform is all about.

19. An important task of socialist cultural development is to foster new values. For instance, what is "equity"? What is "employment"? What attitude should we take toward the policy of "allowing some people to get rich first"? These questions should be considered in a new light, so that we can clarify the dos and don'ts in economic restructuring, and know what to strive for and what to give up. People tend to cling to things not worth their devotion. To change that habit calls for a change in values. We cannot make a sound judgment on economic restructuring without changing our values.

20. The concept of family and the small-time producers' belief in egalitarianism are at the core of the Eastern cultural tradition, whereas individualism is the nucleus of modern Western culture. The two are mutually conflicting. Those of us who live in a developing nation striving for modernization on the basis of traditional Eastern culture invariably find ourselves torn between these conflicting values. What we pursue is socialist modernization, and the problem confronting us is not so much to choose between the values of our traditional culture and the values of the modern Western culture as to go beyond these two cultures and explore new values that suit socialist ethics. This is a hard nut to crack, but we have to do it. In that sense, to change our values calls for an even more profound revolution than economic restructuring, a mission that cannot be fulfilled in just one generation's time. We have to be fully aware of the arduous and protracted nature of this mission.

Immediate Issues to Be Handled in Real Earnest

21. Extending lateral ties in the economy is a major immediate-term task for economic restructuring. Only by extending such ties can we unify our commodity market, gradually bring about a capital market, and lift the barriers resulting from the interference of central and local government boundaries. This task is of paramount importance. If we cannot promote lateral economic ties between firms and let them collaborate and exchange with each other in capital, labor, and technology, and if we do not allow one company to sell its

products on another company's turf, we can never build a workable market mechanism and break down the barriers between central and local government boundaries. This task is high on the agenda of the immediate round of economic restructuring. As we build on what we have accomplished so far to go on with economic reforms, the main thrust of our endeavor should be to extend lateral economic ties.

22. As things are today, excessive investment in infrastructure construction remains the number one headache in the Chinese economy. Overheated consumption funds can only take a second seat. This does not mean excessive increase in consumption funds should not be controlled, but that it is not our primary concern. Make no mistake about it, the consumers in our nation have money to spend in return for the material products and labor services they have provided. Income is always relevant to supply. If the control of consumption funds is overly tightened up, it can stifle supply and demand at the same time, and its side effects on economic development will be felt sooner or later. In regulating the economy, aggregate demand and supply should be properly controlled. On no account should we cut supply while curtailing demand. I believe premature consumption should be avoided, but there is no reason to say that China today is already in a period of premature consumption. Of course we should draw a lesson from other developing nations' experience and forestall the emergence of premature consumption. There are two telltale signs for premature consumption. One is an excessively low saving rate. By contrast, the saving rate in our nation is maintained at 30%, which is deemed a high level. The other is that the lion's share of scarce resources is overused by a new mode of consumption. For example, production will be affected if too much petroleum is consumed in everyday life. That scenario is yet to be experienced in this country. Clearly, there is no trace of premature consumption in China today.

23. Equilibrium is part of an analytical approach, and the starting point of economic analysis. Equilibrium itself is not the goal. Our goal is to achieve the Four Modernizations. The socialist economy always swings around an equilibrium point as it moves along. In that sense, we are not seeking balance for balance per se. Fiscal balance and credit market equilibrium can mean nothing if the economy stagnates. We have got to know that equilibrium can be maintained at a low or high level. Low-level equilibrium can be easily achieved by adopting a retrenchment policy. If, instead of going single-mindedly after curtailing demand, we do everything we can to stimulate supply, we can achieve high-level equilibrium, not to mention the fact that the economy

always advances while hovering around an equilibrium point, which is a sign of basic equilibrium whether demand outgrows supply slightly or vice versa. In China today, for demand to outgrow supply slightly is a preferred and realistic option, whereas it is unrealistic to expect that supply can slightly outgrow demand. That is why we should adapt ourselves to the current situation and learn how to run the economy under such circumstances.

24. Government policy stability and continuity should be maintained to set people at ease, especially those in the thick of economic reform. Policy volatility can mar government policy. Major economic unrest often occurs when firms and individuals hasten to take countermeasures upon sensing an imminent major policy change. For this reason, if we can foster a settled sense of economic stability in firms and individuals and keep them confident in government policy, we can take the edge off the impact of the shock waves that might come from economic restructuring, and carry out reforms in a healthy social environment.

Tentative Projections of the Chinese Economy

25. The leading position of the state sector in the national economy is not determined by its proportion of the nation's total number of firms or aggregate output value, still less by its shares in the key branches of the national economy. Rather, it is determined by its control of industries that are the lifeblood of the national economy, and by its shares in the output of crucial commodities. In the long run, there will not be many state firms, as most enterprises in this country will come under mixed or collective ownership. Moreover, the state firms referred to here are not the familiar old-fashioned type. Rather, they will be transformed into shareholding or holding companies that are publicly owned in the main, and some of them will belong to a certain enterprise consortium.

26. From a long-term point of view, there is no reason why mandatory plans cannot be abolished to make way for guidance plans as the one and only form of planning. Of course, there must be certain conditions to make it happen. One such condition is that key resources are no longer in short supply and that the disparity between demand and supply has been reduced. Another condition is that the government is efficient enough in running the economy, because it is more difficult to carry out guidance planning than mandatory planning.

27. Of the four economic policy instruments in use today—fiscal policy, monetary policy, price control, and wages—the decision-making power to

determine wages should be delegated to firms at the grass roots level. Central and local governments should use fiscal and monetary policies as chief economic regulatory means. Unless absolutely necessary, the use of price control as an economic lever should be minimized. Such is my idea of how to shape our long-term macroeconomic regulatory system. The State Planning Commission should take charge of drafting relevant long- and medium-term development plans.

28. The rural economy is probably where the Chinese economic landscape will change most dramatically. Farmland will devolve to the hands of skilled farmers. Farms will grow in size under a household responsibility system. Labor productivity will go up, and surplus labor force will be reallocated to rural firms. The countryside will be clustered with small towns, which will combine with large cities to form multilayered economic networks. Small towns will become cultural, educational, commercial, and recreational centers that also provide a complete array of community services. The improving Chinese standard of living will be benchmarked not by current cash-income growth but by increases in household wealth.

— A report to the Peking University "May Fourth" Symposium
April 25, 1986

· 4 ·

A TENTATIVE STUDY OF SOCIALIST OWNERSHIP STRUCTURE

I

Ownership reform stems, in the final analysis, from the requirement for developing a commodity economy in this nation. It also arises from the unchangeable position of companies as commodity producers. Whatever its form, ownership structure should contribute to the promotion of production. A monomorphic ownership structure is detrimental to the growth of the commodity economy, to the motivation of firms as commodity producers, and to the effort to make the most of the superiority of socialism. All this gives rise to the mission of hammering out a post-reform ownership structure.

Will the post-reform ownership structure include public ownership? The answer is in the affirmative: Public ownership will be included. However, the reformed public ownership will no longer be the same as it is today. There will be differences between the two.

Under the influence of the traditional economic mode, people believed that the only workable way to run public companies was to put them directly into the hands of government institutions. In the reality of socialist economic development, however, the drawbacks of this practice were becoming pronounced. Companies became appendages of the government, which held all the power over human resources, finance and materials, and kept a tight rein on them. A company's performance thus had no direct bearing on its economic gains, nor was it held accountable for its own economic losses. Such was the inevitable outcome of the direct government intervention of business management, in which public ownership was synonymous with the direct involvement of government institutions in corporate activity. This is why the main thrust of ownership reform should be directed at public ownership.

We should know that in a public company, both capital goods and products belong to the public. The public attributes of such institutions represent the people's fundamental, overall and long-term interests. Recognition of the public ownership of such companies means that they are engaged in production and management in the common interest of the entire citizenry. The issue here is: How can public companies manifest their public nature in production and management, and go about their economic activity truly in the interests of all the people? It should be noted that public companies are not an empty concept but entities in the thick of economic activity. Their public nature is embodied in the fact that both their managers and workers are responsible for the interest of the whole population in such activity. However, this responsibility does not mean that public companies can only be run by the government. Moreover, it should be noted unequivocally that, supposing the public nature of these companies could be manifested only under government management, those companies that are malfunctioning and riddled with malpractice cannot honor their commitment—rather, they can only betray the basic interest of the entire state and citizenry. Thus, in transforming public firms, we must understand their public nature in a new light. That is to say, their public nature should be reflected in the results of their economic activity rather than in being state-managed. To reform public ownership is neither to negate this form of ownership nor to change the nature of public companies. To reform public ownership is precisely to emphasize these firms' public nature through effective and fruitful economic activity.

II

An essential task of the socialist ownership structure is to meet the requirement of the developing socialist commodity economy that forms of ownership should be diversified. Ownership diversity means that a socialist society may have more than one form of ownership, both public and nonpublic. Moreover, capital goods need not come solely under public ownership but under a mixture of state, collective, and private ownership. In this mixed ownership system, public, collective, and private ownership are intertwined and infiltrate each other in a "you in me, me in you" situation. That is to say, the capital goods in a company may come under a mixture of ownership. The need for ownership diversity, including ownership mixtures, arises from the nature of labor in our nation at the present stage of development. Workers still care about their labor input—which differs in quality and quantity—and its economic returns out of the concern for their own interests. Furthermore, due to differences in working conditions, companies also vary in managerial performance and economic returns. Some may be more productive than others. The earnings from such extra output should be put at these firms' own disposal so as to spur their managers on to improve management. Diverse, mixed forms of ownership enable firms and workers to align themselves with production and management performance because this is where their own interests are at stake.

The existence of diverse and mixed forms of ownership is also relevant to our nation's present level of labor productivity. We know that a certain form of ownership of capital goods is determined by the development level of society's labor productivity. What forms of ownership should be adopted or allowed in a socialist commodity economy is circumscribed by the law governing labor productivity improvement. As things stand in our nation, productivity is relatively low and its development is uneven. This implies that, independent of man's will, diverse forms of ownership will be around for a long time to come while infiltrating or integrating each other inside a business.

In all, when designing a new national ownership structure, we should decide what kind of corporate ownership system is really needed. Such a decision cannot be detached from the requirements of the commodity economy and the restraints arising from the nature of labor and the level of productivity at the current stage of development. To advance the commodity economy, every company must organize its production and business as a producer, have the final say on production, supply and marketing, and strive to survive and grow through competition. The issue here is not so much "decentralizing power to companies" as "returning power to companies." Companies should have the decision-making autonomy that they deserve as commodity producers. The same is true with public companies. After ownership restructuring is completed, the government should put capital goods at these companies' disposal and allow them to handle the fruits of their economic activity. As to what form of ownership a company should adopt, it should be decided according to the merits of individual cases.

III

It is both necessary and workable to establish and develop shareholding companies in a socialist society. Socialist construction cannot do without colossal sums of money. Dispersed capital should be pooled, and the financial potential of all sectors tapped. To allow companies to issue stock shares helps pool money and meet the funding needs of production expansion. Public ownership of capital goods is the foundation stone of the socialist economy. Shareholding companies should be built on the same foundation. If a collectively owned company sells shares to its workers, its collectiveness will remain intact because it is formed with money raised from and by its workers. The fact that the shareholding system can operate for collective companies should not be a cause of concern. The issue here, rather, is whether public firms should be allowed to issue stock shares, and whether doing so will change their public nature. We must see it in perspective. It is wrong to insist that only collective firms can issue shares and to forbid public companies from doing so. The adoption of the shareholding system by public companies should not be judged from a traditional viewpoint.

If a public firm becomes a shareholding company, its shareholders may fall into three categories judging from the current structure of capital goods ownership: central government agencies, local government agencies and the company itself. If all its shareholders are in the public category, the company's public nature will not be affected. If the public firm raises funds from all walks of life, its new shareholders will roughly fall into three categories, excluding foreign investors: other local government agencies and other public firms, collective firms and workers. If all the new shares are sold to the first category of shareholders, the firm's public nature remains. If the new shares are also sold to the second and third categories of shareholders, the firm's public nature will acquire a collective element. No matter what happens, the enterprise remains publicly owned.

To determine who controls the use of capital goods, it is necessary to find out who are running the shareholding company, because the right to own capital goods and the right to use them are separated. The operation of such a company is controlled by its managers. Given that the shareholders of a socialist shareholding enterprise are workers or organizations that represent the workers' interests, then the managers elected by shareholders' representatives should also be regarded as the workers' representatives. In a shareholding company under public ownership, if the second and third categories of new shareholders have contributed more money than the old shareholders and the first category of new shareholders, the company is still in the hands of those representing public ownership. If the second and third categories of newcomers have bought more shares than the others but such shares are scattered rather than concentrated, the company is still under public ownership. In all cases, the company's public nature remains basically unchanged.

Even if a shareholding company is controlled by the second and third categories of new shareholders who have contributed more money while the shares held by the second category of new shareholders are not scattered, isn't the enterprise still a public socialist enterprise? Isn't the management of the company still in the hands of those representing workers' interests? Is there anything to be concerned about?

Now, a look at the superiority of the enterprise shareholding system. As the best option available for invigorating our companies, the shareholding system has at least three advantages.

Firstly, the shareholding system can fundamentally change the situation in which government administration is confounded with business management, and thereby turn companies into purely economic entities. Under this system, the general manager is held accountable to the Board of Directors, and the Board of Directors is responsible to shareholders, and thus the company can no longer be an appendage to a government department. The shareholding company makes its own decisions in compliance with government policy and economic legislation. In other words, the government can no longer interfere in the company's business, but can influence its economic activity by holding its stock shares. The economic relationship between enterprises and the government becomes one between paying and levying taxes, and the enterprises will have no problem in making their own business decisions.

Secondly, a shareholding economy works relatively more effectively in meeting the need to allocate production factors efficiently. The profit level of such a company is a signal that guides the shift of capital to highprofit fields, thereby rationally allocating capital and workforce, and raising capital utilization efficiency. The shareholding company can find a foothold in market competition and develop itself only if it can put its capital to best use, utilize it sensibly, and avoid decision-making errors and waste of money. Government departments may, through legislative and compensatory measures, attract share capital to the national economy's weak links and backward sectors in a well-planned fashion, and promote the rational allocation of productive resources from a macroeconomic perspective.

Thirdly, raising funds by selling shares helps pool idle money from non-governmental sources to meet financing purposes. Under the prerequisite that funds are raised from non-governmental sources and workers are allowed to buy shares individually, the surplus of personal consumption fund comes in the form of newly added share capital that cannot be withdrawn arbitrarily. For this reason, after the surplus fund for personal consumption is absorbed to buy company shares, it is unlikely for such money to be withdrawn from a shareholding company and spent in the consumer goods market. Apart from allowing individuals to buy shares, the shareholding economy can also use part of the profit at a company's dispensation as a major fund-raising source. By pooling idle money from localities and companies and spending it on construction projects that have a close bearing on the immediate interest of these localities and companies, the shareholding economy can also speed up development, and effectively create jobs for society, rural areas in particular.

IV

The practice of companies buying each other's stocks gives rise to a corporate stock-holding system under socialism. As an inevitable result of economic development, this system, also known as "participatory system," originated in an economic organizational form that emerged from the monopolist stage of capitalism, when a big corporation infiltrated other companies by buying their majority shares and getting them under control. The control through stock-holding and penetration into multiple companies eventually brought about a corporate system in which the general company branched into one level of subsidiaries after another. Under capitalism, therefore, the corporate stock-holding system is a tool with which large capital controls and manipulates small capital.

As a form of business management in society's large-scale production, the stock-holding system can be made to work for the socialist shareholding economy on account of the dual attributes of business management: its natural attribute determined by society's large-scale production, and its social attribute determined by the social system. In terms of society's large-scale production, socialism is identical to capitalism; in terms of social system, socialism is categorically different from capitalism. Thus a socialist society can adopt the stock-holding system by retaining its natural attribute and altering its social attribute.

In a socialist economy, a competitive and highly efficient company may use its after-tax profit to buy another company's stock shares. When it has become the other company's majority shareholder and thus taken control of it, it will run or reshuffle that company according to its own will. Because of the role of equity and equity-related interests, the scramble between companies for majority holding rights is bound to intensify. When that happens, it is a boon, instead of a bane, for every shareholding company on the scene, because it gives them a good opportunity to improve their economic efficiency. When products become highly substitutable, when the prices of consumer goods show a large degree of elasticity, and when the profits from those products that are being upgraded become unstable, illmanaged businesses will be in danger of being "taken over" by others if they fail to cope with the situation. When such a business is taken over, the buying company may buy its stock in a large amount by taking advantage of its declining profit rate and its shareholders' hasty disposal of their shares. In this way the new CEO turns it into a subsidiary, and goes further to overhaul its production, management and technology. This happens even in a monopolistic industry, where failing companies are in danger of a "takeover."

A small business that does not perform well may be taken over by its employees. These employees are scattered stockholders with a shared desire for their business to make a profit and grow, and their personal interests are tied to its gains and losses. When and where possible, they may pool their equities and act collectively to take over the business and reshuffle its management. When this happens, it is definitely conducive to the future success of the business.

V

A powerful large socialist enterprise under the shareholding system may organize trans-sectoral and trans-regional business, and, through multilevel share-controlling actions, establish multiple layers of subsidiaries to form a socialist corporate consortium or enterprise group. Several large socialist enterprises can foster different economic ties and combine themselves into a consortium or enterprise group. At the center of a socialist corporate consortium is the decision-making matrix—or holding—company. Under the parent company there are first- and second-layer subsidiaries which, rather than being mere branches or appendages, do business independently, make their own decisions, and bear the responsibility for their losses and gains. The matrix company exerts its influence through its control of stock shares. That is to say, the parent company carries out its business principle through its equity, thereby fending off the drawbacks of administrative intervention. This corporate management system, in which rights are both centralized and decentralized, helps set a company's business activity on a rational and efficient footing.

Some giant socialist enterprises may rise, and some others may fall in market competition. To put it another way, one giant socialist corporate consortium may grow in strength while another may fall into a decline. There is nothing odd in this phenomenon. A giant enterprise can stay competitive and at the top of the ranking chart only with sensible and effective development strategies, wise leadership and fine workforce quality. Companies or consortia are doomed, no matter how large they are, if they are no longer competitive, if their development stratagems are wrong, or their leaders and workforce are low in quality and proficiency. The shareholding system and the controlling shareholder system compel a company to readjust and save itself. Without such readjustment and self-rejuvenation, a waning company can only watch helplessly as its stock dwindles in value and its property rights become vulnerable to a takeover. Such a takeover, however, may give the company a new lease of life and return it to the ranks of competent competitors.

Under the stock-holding system, the relationship between banks and enterprises may change in one of two ways. First, specialized banks may convert themselves into commercial corporations under shareholding management, and allow businesses to purchase their stock shares to become their shareholders. Judging from the prospects of ownership reform in this country, it is not unlikely that businesses will hold stock shares of specialized banks and join their management. Second, demutualized banks may also participate in managing other businesses; and, as things stand at the present stage of development, the relationship between banks and businesses is more likely to change this way. We can assume that banks are not just loan providers. They are also stockholders of businesses and can run their own companies. After a bank gains control of a business' stock, the common interest resulting from this will bring the two sides closer. A bank that holds the stock of a large business can send representatives to join the latter in managing its funding, production and business operation.

Banks can also convert themselves into socialist banking consortia through their involvement in business. Such a banking consortium may work alongside a socialist corporate consortium to do business that transcends departmental and regional boundaries. At the core of this banking consortium is a central bank that functions as the holding company. The first and second tiers of subsidiaries to such a central bank are not its branches or affiliates; rather, they are economic entities that make their own business decisions and are liable for their own gains and losses. The holding central bank needs to influence the production and management of these subsidiaries by way of its equity. Moreover, the bank's involvement in business also helps improve its credit management because if a business applying for a loan has no idea about the risks involved, the bank providing the loan is liable for such risks. If the bank cannot recoup the loan it has issued in due time, or if the project invested with the loan falls through, the bank will bear the financial loss thus incurred. In a shareholding company established with a bank's participation, the outcome of business failures is borne by all partners, a fact that can galvanize the bank into improving its management.

VI

Mixed-ownership companies, as the name suggests, are economic entities invested jointly by public, collective, and private partners. Firms of this type allow for joint business activity under different types of ownership even in the absence of the shareholding system. However, demutualization of firms inevitably produces a large number of companies under mixed ownership. Enterprises under a single type of ownership will go on as usual, but the emergence of many mixed-ownership economic entities will be an inevitable trend in a socialist economy.

How to define the nature of such mixed-ownership companies in a socialist society? If a public or collective enterprise has increased its capital by raising funds through stock share sales, and thus obtained a certain portion of share capital from a mixed-ownership firm and controlled its management, this company should be regarded as a public enterprise. If such a mixed-ownership firm is not deemed public, what else should it be? Let us look into this matter more closely. If, say, an enterprise has been set up with funds raised by selling stock shares to both companies and individuals, such a mixed economic structure should be regarded as an economic conglomerate under a new form of public ownership, which is different from traditional types of public or collective ownership.

We regard this type of economic conglomerates as public enterprises because they are similar to collectives whose partners buy stock shares with capital goods or cash. They represent a brand-new type of public ownership enterprise, which not only identifies workers as masters of capital goods but also energizes itself by becoming an independent commodity producer that makes its own business decisions and bears responsibility for its own gains and losses. Such economic conglomerates are most likely to become the mainstay in China's future corporate ownership structure.

The emergence of mixed-ownership companies meets the demand to boost productivity in socialist economic development, corresponds with the reality of the country, and promotes the commodity economy. Such firms can grow in both rural and urban areas. Flexible in business operation, they can adjust their corporate sizes according to circumstances to accommodate the idle and the jobless and better connect rural and urban areas. The presence of such mixed-ownership firms challenges old public enterprises to improve their management and start ownership reform at an early date.

VII

Like mixed-ownership companies, small cooperatives represent another nascent form of ownership. Convenient and flexible, these small cooperatives differ from mixed-ownership firms in two ways:

First, the shareholders of a mixed-ownership company are enterprises and individuals, and state-owned companies may buy their way into it. By contrast, small cooperatives are formed entirely by individual shareholders.

Second, mixed-ownership companies vary in size, whereas cooperatives are generally small, even though it is possible for them to grow bigger and evolve into mixed-ownership companies. Nevertheless, cooperatives tend to remain small, at least in the formative stage.

Small cooperatives, being organized by individuals who buy their way into them, identify their workers as masters of capital goods. That is why they are seen as a new form of socialist public ownership. Their members own the capital goods, join in collective labor and management, and distribute their after-tax profit among themselves. Such earnings may be used to cover daily expenses or be converted into new stock shares. Members of such a small collective get paid for their labor as employees while earning a certain percentage of the tax-paid profit as shareholders.

Small cooperatives are especially suitable for businesses in retailing, handicrafts, community services and farm produce processing. Their members are engaged in collective labor, make economic decisions and share gains and losses. Whenever funds need to be raised, they put their heads together to decide the ceiling and floor for the money to be paid by every member according to a ratio between labor and fund. This way of doing things is entirely agreeable to the nature of small cooperatives.

It does not matter whether or not a small collective calls itself a "shareholding company." They represent the collective sector in the true sense of the term. They differ from shareholding companies precisely in that, instead of turning to society for financial help, they raise money exclusively among their members. They can become mixed-ownership firms if, someday, they start to raise money by issuing stock shares to the public.

To encourage individual workers to form their own small cooperatives by buying shares or converting their contribution of capital goods into shares, and to confirm the collective—i.e., public—nature of such cooperatives, is to respect both theory and practice. To accept the small cooperatives as public enterprises is for no other purpose than to recognize an established social fact that has to be accepted as such.

Small cooperative enterprises are often called "small collectives" or "collectives run by individuals." People may name such firms any way they want. However, when you choose to call them "small collectives," you are wrong if you think that small collectives are not as good as large collectives or that small collectives should be turned into large ones. When you choose to call them "collectives run by individuals," you are wrong if you believe that they are "informal collectives" or that they should be converted into public collectives. We must see cooperatives exactly as a form of collective economy as well as a form of socialist ownership that is highly flexible and adaptable to different levels of productivity and corporate scales. The cooperative economy does not necessarily need to develop itself into other forms of collective ownership, and there is absolutely no such inevitability either. The cooperative economy, other forms of collective economy, and the mixed-ownership economy each have their own strengths and applicable scopes, and should be allowed to exist side by side and develop together in the long run.

VIII

We may regard the adoption of the household responsibility system that links remuneration with output as the first step toward rural ownership reform. In this chapter, let me make some tentative study of the next stage of ownership reform in rural areas from the perspective of the national ownership structure.

Let us start with some background information about the next stage of rural ownership reform. We have to understand that, on the basis of initiating the household responsibility system, the rural economy is being restructured in transition to a large-scale commodity economy. Rural areas will adapt their production and processing undertakings to market demand, and provide large quantities of farm and sideline products. The advance of the commodity economy enables every farming household to enter the commodity market as both producers and business operators. Rural ownership reform should keep up with the burgeoning commodity economy.

According to the requirements of the commodity economy, the rural household responsibility system will be maintained for a long time in agriculture, forestry, fishery, and animal husbandry. However, rural production and businesses are bound to develop along specialized lines. That means some fields of production will operate independently and be specialized. On the basis of a division of labor and collaboration, farming households can freely collaborate with one another in different forms. The assets of such voluntary economic cooperation will be owned by the members, who will distribute the earnings among themselves according to work done. Part of such earnings, however, may also be distributed according to shares of capital or of capital goods. This will give rise to a large number of small cooperative farms (forest, fishing and animal farms included) similar to the small cooperatives described in the previous chapter. A creation of the broad masses of farmers in their production activity, these cooperative farms will play a major role in the future development of the rural economy. They represent a new type of collective economy, and a breakthrough from the old agricultural collective economy in which capital goods and labor are centralized. On the basis of household management, these farms can bring farmers' funds and production factors under cooperative management. The emergence of such farms is nothing short of another round of rural ownership reform that can fire the enthusiasm of the rural population for production and development.

In the course of developing a commodity economy, the issue of revamping the ownership of old rural enterprises will be put on the agenda. These rural enterprises, according to common sense, represent a form of cooperative economy run by farmers (and townspeople) with their own money, labor and technology. Although many of them are dependent on loans, they are supposed to repay such loans with nothing but their profits. However, in actual fact, these enterprises have changed their collective economic nature and evolved, to a certain extent, into local government-run businesses. Some local officials, holding the power to appoint or dismiss the managers of these businesses, are given to interfering in their business activity. Farmers can hardly benefit from such businesses because their profits are often manipulated by these officials. Such problems with the old rural enterprises can only be redressed through ownership restructuring—that is, to put an end to government interference in them and let farmers be their true masters.

I do not here deny the fact that many rural enterprises are doing perfectly well and that, in many places, local farmers are benefiting from them. Rural enterprise ownership reform is not directed merely at mismanaged enterprises. Of course, enterprises that do not perform well should be straightened out, and the best way to do so is to restructure their ownership. However, well-run rural firms need ownership restructuring as well. Now that rural firms are collective economic entities, they should not become appendages to grass roots governments and muddle along under government administration that is entangled in business management. We have got to restore them to their true beings as collective firms. If we limit ownership reform to poorly run enterprises, we must answer the question: If, someday, a local government comes into the hands of a new leader who has changed the old way of doing things, will well-run enterprises start going downhill? Is there any way to prevent this scenario from materializing? Clearly, all rural firms, large or small, good or bad, should have their ownership restructured. Only by starting from ownership reform can these companies' business problems be fundamentally addressed. As to which enterprises should be the first to engage in such a reform, this should be decided in light of actual production and management situations.

How, then, should rural enterprise ownership be reformed? The guideline is to liquidate the assets and check the accounts, and to distribute the stock to every member household. In this way, farmers can become shareholders who can impose their will on their companies through voting in elections and exercising their management rights. Major issues on income distribution will be settled by consensus. Apart from getting paid for work done, shareholders are also entitled to dividends allotted according to shares. Township governments are not allowed to run enterprises, and their power should be limited to guiding and helping farmers in business activity. New rural firms and cooperatives established by rural workers with their own money, and mixed-ownership firms are, without exception, new types of public enterprises. Farming households should also be allowed to run wholly owned enterprises that belong in the private sector.

Rural supply and marketing cooperatives should have their ownership revamped in two ways. First, large numbers of rural supply and marketing cooperatives at the grass roots level should be converted into independent cooperative firms. Only thus can they truly become supply and marketing cooperatives that make their own business decisions, function as independent accounting units, and take responsibility for their gains and losses. Their after-tax profit will be dispensed among members according to shares after a certain amount has been set aside as public accumulation fund and welfare fund. Second, supply and marketing cooperatives at and above the county level, including specialized companies and industrial and commercial businesses, should be transformed into mixed-ownership, shareholding companies that make their own business decisions as independent accounting units and are accountable for their own gains and losses. They will have the same organizational setup as other shareholding companies.

By putting the rural ownership system through the abovementioned reform steps, the relationship between township governments and rural businesses will undergo another round of profound changes comparable to those taking place upon the adoption of the household responsibility system linking remuneration to output. The mode of rural economic activity born of the Movement of Agricultural Collectivization (1954–1955) and particularly of the Movement of the People's Communes that began in 1958, should be totally abolished. Grass roots governments will become pure administrative institutions detached from everyday production and business. Institutions that subject the broad masses of farmers to centralized administration, that allow a tiny number of township and town government officials to impose their will on people's economic activity, and that have hindered the growth of rural commodity economy and kept the monolithic rural economic structure unchanged for long years, will eventually be consigned to the dustpan of history.

The economic role of grass roots township governments will be limited to guiding the rural commodity economy. Land management is part of that role. The principle that land is public property shall never be changed, but it should not prevent land from being used with compensation. It is also the mission of grass roots governments to prevent arbitrary requisitioning of farmland and bar the selling and buying of land. These governments should also find ways and means to help local farmers beat poverty, organize them in running businesses, and help these businesses solve problems. They will also have a "matchmaking" role to play, that is, to bring enterprises together for technological and economic collaboration. "Serving the people" should be the motto for local governments in steering the advancement of the rural commodity economy. The purpose of their administration is specifically to serve farmers' business activities.

IX

Proprietorship over capital goods is at the core of ownership. However, to interpret ownership merely as proprietorship over capital goods is a narrow-minded understanding of the substance of ownership. In a broad sense, ownership also encompasses the organizational form of production and the administration and management of production, apart from proprietorship over capital goods. This being the case, the ownership reform discussed in the foregoing involves not only changes in ownership of capital goods before and after the reform, but also changes in the organizational form of administration over production. The new socialist ownership born of the reform effort refers precisely to proprietorship over capital goods, to new organizational forms of production, and to new administrative and managerial systems over production.

The reformed socialist ownership system will not be singular but plural. It will constitute multiple forms of ownership and can be understood from the following perspectives:

In terms of capital goods proprietorship, it will encompass diverse forms of non-public ownership in the service of the socialist economy, with socialist public ownership taking the lead. Under public ownership, there will be enterprises owned by all the people, enterprises under mixed ownership, and cooperatives. Under non-public ownership, there will be private firms, foreign-invested companies, and equity joint ventures with Chinese and foreign investment.

Concerning the organizational form of production and the administrative and managerial system over production, enterprises owned by all the people and enterprises under mixed ownership can be run on their own or rented or contracted out to cooperative enterprises or individuals. Likewise, cooperatives can also be run by themselves or rented or contracted out by individuals.

This socialist ownership system is born of the need of the burgeoning socialist commodity economy. In a shareholding company under public ownership, dividends are dispensed among shareholders according to their shares of capital (or money paid for stock shares), and shareholders are investors who contribute to production through the shares they have bought. The money they have spent on shares is similar in nature to bank savings, and therefore, they also deserve remuneration in the form of stock interest. The stock shares invested in the economy contribute a lot more to the growth and overall interest of the socialist economy than to the shareholder's individual interest. Leased and contracted management serves to adapt public enterprises to the demand for boosting productivity, allocating production factors effectively under the current circumstances, minimizing waste in human, material and financial resources, and promoting production.

I deem it unnecessary to say anything here about the presence of private economy that does not belong in the public sector of the socialist ownership system. This is because the private sector exists to supplement the socialist economy and help create jobs and tax revenues. Self-employed workers rely on themselves in business activity. It is only normal for them to make more money through diligence and shrewd management. Given correct government policy, effective administration, and sensible education and guidance, the private sector can grow in the course of serving socialism.

To sum up, ownership reform will bring about a dual economic system. On the one hand, the national economy will contain hundreds of large enterprises that will grow into corporate consortia (enterprise groups), which, through multilevel investment, will bring about a network of second- and third-tier subsidiaries. These consortia will point out the way for the national drive for industrialization and technological progress. On the other hand, the national economy will have numerous small enterprises under cooperative, private or mixed ownership, which will form a close-knit network of collaboration while competing with one another. Their shared mission will be to address the problems arising from the reallocation of surplus rural workforce, farm and sideline product production and processing, from the efforts to raise rural residents' income and build small towns, and from everyday services for urban and rural residents. These two groups of economic entities will each follow a different course of development and coexist in a mutually complementary relationship.

— *Hebei Academic Journal*, issue No. 1, 1987

· 5 ·

TWO TYPES OF DISEQUILIBRIUM AND THE MAINSTREAM OF CURRENT ECONOMIC RESTRUCTURING

Differences of Resource Allocation in Equilibrium and Disequilibrium

In economics, disequilibrium is pertinent to Walrasian equilibrium. The latter is achieved under the assumption of a complete market and a flexible price system. Disequilibrium, which is a kind of equilibrium arrived at in the absence of a complete market and a flexible price system, is also dubbed "non-Walrasian equilibrium."

According to the theory of French economist Léon Walras (1834–1910), given that the market is complete and the price system flexible, given also that traders possess full information and prices adjust instantaneously with changes in supply and demand, then under a given price condition aggregate demand must equal aggregate supply, excess demand and excess supply do not exist, and the settlement of every transaction is guaranteed by an equilibrium price. No deals will be reached before equilibrium price is attained; only with equilibrium price can transactions take place. According to this theory, over-production, unsalable products, chronic unemployment, and inflation associated with excess demand will never happen.

The analysis of Walrasian equilibrium, alien to economic reality, had long drawn acute criticism from dissentient Western economists. In *The General*

Theory of Employment, Interest, and Money published in 1936, John Maynard Keynes (1883–1946) went out of his way to dissect the unemployment and other perennial problems in capitalist society. Nevertheless, up till the early 1960s Western economists' study of disequilibrium was partial and unsystematic at best. Their interpretations of Keynesian economic theory were categorically divided as well. Mainstream Keynes followers believe that Keynesian economics is still a theory based on equilibrium and that Keynes did not negate the Walrasian equilibrium theory despite the fact that he somewhat amended it. Some other interpreters maintain that Keynesian economics broke through the limits of the equilibrium theory and provided initial but systematic pronouncements on the disequilibrium theory. They back their argument by citing Keynes's belief that market mechanisms are not necessarily effective, and that market alone cannot totally coordinate trading activities, with the result that output, levels of employment and investment are subject to fluctuations, whereas overproduction, unemployment, and insufficient investment demand are commonplace under capitalism.

The disequilibrium theory has made substantial headway since the late 1960s. Studies of disequilibrium have indicated that under the condition of an incomplete market where prices fail to adjust demand and supply, economic forces will proceed from their respective circumstances to adjust themselves to the point where they are well adapted to each other and where equilibrium is achieved. Obviously, the equilibrium achieved by way of disequilibrium is not the equilibrium in a complete market but in an incomplete market; it is not the kind of equilibrium with zero unemployment and zero inflation rates, but with both unemployment and inflation in presence. In other words, disequilibrium is actually a form of equilibrium, but unlike the kind of equilibrium described in the Walrasian theory, it is the kind of equilibrium that exists in reality. Such is the connotation of disequilibrium.

If an economy is exactly in Walrasian equilibrium, the market will be highly self-restraining in resource allocation. The market's self-restraining role can be fulfilled smoothly through the changes in the actual and expected benefits of every microeconomic agent. When a microeconomic agent believes that a certain resource input will bring no benefit and decides to stop it, this microeconomic decision also measures up to the efficiency standard of society's resource allocation. If, on the contrary, the agent believes that a certain resource input is beneficial to itself and decides to increase it, its improved efficiency will also help boost social efficiency in resource allocation. Therefore, so long as the agent is sensitive to its own interests, its resource allocation will be adapted to market prices, and resources are bound to be channeled into efficient sectors, localities and enterprises and withdrawn from inefficient sectors, localities and enterprises. The market's self-restraining function in the process of resource allocation manifests itself in that it does not allow any ineffective resource input to last and enables resource allocation to automatically measure up to efficiency standards.

Two Types of Microeconomic Agents and Two Types of Disequilibrium

As my analysis of the market's self-restraining role in resource allocation indicates, the ability of the market to adjust and rectify excessive expansions and recessions in economic practice is closely tied with the full vitality of microeconomic agents participating in market activity. Economic equilibrium is certainly on the premise of complete market and flexible prices, but the vitality on the part of microeconomic agents is a more important and fundamental prerequisite.

Thus microeconomic agents can be divided into two categories: those with full vitality, and those without full vitality or totally lacking it. A microeconomic agent can be brimming with vitality because it makes its own business decisions and takes full responsibility for its gains and losses. Such a firm can choose the best investment opportunities and patterns of production and management, distribute its after-tax profit according to its own interests, and take investment and management risks on its own. Such a firm is an independent commodity producer and manager. Such an individual, in economic terms, is a trader that takes part in market activity independently. Any microeconomic agent that does not have these attributes invariably lacks full vitality or lacks it totally.

In equilibrium, microeconomic agents are certainly brimming with vitality and, on this basis, form a complete market. This point need not be repeated here. What I want to find out is this: Is it true that microeconomic agents invariably lack full competitive vigor under economic disequilibrium? To find the answer, it is necessary to divide economic disequilibrium into two categories.

Economic disequilibrium in the first category is marked by an incomplete market, inflexible prices, presence of both excess demand and excess supply, and restraints on both demand and supply, while microeconomic agents in the market are independent commodity producers that make their own business decisions and take responsibility for their gains and losses, and that have the freedom to choose their investment opportunities and modes of management and bear investment and business risks.

Economic disequilibrium in the second category is characterized by an incomplete market and inflexible prices, and more importantly, by a market filled with microeconomic agents that, instead of being independent commodity producers making their own business decisions and bearing their own gains and losses, neither have the freedom to choose investment opportunities and management modes nor bear the responsibility for investment and management risks. Such microeconomic agents have not shaken off their status as government subsidiaries or are bound hand and foot by their pre-capitalist ties.

If my division of economic disequilibrium stands, there is reason to believe that the disequilibrium in a capitalist economy belongs in the first category and that the disequilibrium in a pre-capitalist economy belongs in the second category. What happens in a socialist economy should be treated differently. Disequilibrium under a traditional and dual-track economic system falls into the second category because its enterprises have yet to shake off their status as government subsidiaries. Under the new economic system born of economic reform, enterprises become independent commodity producers that make their own investment and business decisions, and are liable for their gains, losses as well as investment and business risks. Thus the disequilibrium in the new economic system falls into the first category.

In the first category of disequilibrium, microeconomic agents are full of vitality. However, these microeconomic agents are in an economic disequilibrium. They make transactions in incomplete markets where prices are inflexible and information is incomplete and congested. Therefore, such vitality is limited by this environment. For instance, price rigidity makes it hard for these agents to adjust production in response to price signals, and wage rigidity also prevents them from optimizing their resource allocations. However, a microeconomic agent that has full vitality but is circumscribed by its environment is very different from a microeconomic agent that lacks full vitality. This is exactly the difference between the first and second categories of disequilibrium.

The Market's Self-Restraining Role in the First Category of Disequilibrium

The self-restraining role of the market in resource allocation can work effectively under economic equilibrium, that is, it may prevent any ineffective resource input from becoming protracted under two conditions. Firstly, the market is perfect and prices are flexible; and secondly, microeconomic agents can transact according to their own interests. The first category of disequilibrium furnishes the second condition because microeconomic units are already brimming with vitality. Its only problems are incomplete markets, inflexible prices, and an economy in which restraints exist on resource supply and demand. However, we ought to regard microeconomic agents having full vitality as a more important condition than having a complete market. This is because a complete market and flexible prices serve mainly to provide a friendly environment for the development of a commodity economy, whereas encouraging microeconomic units to regain their competitive edge helps solve problems in market participants' interests, responsibilities, incentives and motivations. Even when market is complete and prices are flexible, its self-restraining role in resource allocations will be sharply limited if microeconomic agents do not have full vitality, cannot take advantage of complete market and flexible prices to make transactions, lack aggressiveness and enthusiasm to sensibly allocate resources and raise their resource utilization rate, and cannot bear the economic losses incurred from improper resource allocations.

All this indicates that the first category of economic disequilibrium possesses the more important one of the two conditions that enables the market to play its self-restraining role, that is, the existence of microeconomic agents with full vitality. This condition is beneficial for the market to fully play its self-restraining role. Because these kinds of microeconomic agents can act in their own interests to make deals, their instinct can prevent them from putting their resources into ineffective economic activity and enable them to refuse ineffective, efficiency-reducing approaches of allocating and utilizing resources. Consequently, even though the market is still incomplete and prices are inflexible, and even though there are still restraints on resource supply or demand, in the process of resource allocations, the market can still follow the efficiency standard to adjust the allocations and combinations of resources, thereby avoiding protracted ineffective resource input.

Nevertheless, the first category of disequilibrium is still a kind of disequilibrium, under which resource input is still different from that under equilibrium. The impact of this category of disequilibrium on microeconomic agents' market transactions and patterns of utilizing resources manifests itself in three ways:

First, with an incomplete market and imperfect and frictional information access, microeconomic agents cannot obtain adequate and timely information, and a lot of information they have obtained is incorrect. However, they have no alternative but to make resource input and combination decisions under the guidance of such limited or even erroneous information. This is likely to bring low economic efficiency and cause resources to be allocated in violation of efficiency standards.

Second, with inflexible or rigid prices, the adjustments of resource allocation by microeconomic agents will be restrained. This is because price rigidity cannot reflect the degree of resource scarcity and the results of resource input and, therefore, they find it hard to optimize their choices of needed resources. If, under rigid prices, the microeconomic agents are unable to follow optimized resource allocation approaches, the waste or idling of resources in allocation processes can hardly be avoided.

Third, because of the restraints on supply and demand, resources are allocated on a short-term basis where demand and supply are unbalanced. This entails tougher competition for microeconomic agents. In the case of supply restraints, the microeconomic agents on the demand side face the problem of limited supply sources and have to input more to secure supply. By the same token, in the case of demand restraints, the agents on the supply side face the problem of a limited market and have to input more to reach their sales goals. The extra resources spent by these agents for either supply or sales purposes are a manifestation of an abuse of social resources, which means more resources have been consumed than economic equilibrium allows. This is a clear example of improper resource allocation.

The above-mentioned impacts of the first category of disequilibrium on microeconomic agents' transactions and utilization of resources indicate that, even though the market can still play its self-restraining role, its effectiveness is whittled down.

The Market's Self-Restraining Role in the Second Category of Disequilibrium

The two conditions—a complete market with flexible prices and full vitality of microeconomic agents—for the market to play its self-restraining role effectively in resource allocation are absent in the second category of disequilibrium. Thus the market's self-restraining role is greatly restricted in the process of resource allocation. This may be analyzed in two ways.

On one hand, the reason why microeconomic agents lack vitality is that they have not truly become masters of their own interests, that the fruits of their production are not directly and inevitably related to their interests, and that they are not held accountable for the economic losses resulting from their production, management or investment mistakes. In this way, they lack not only motivation and stimulus but also pressure and a sense of responsibility. They may become indifferent to opportunities that are obviously in their economic interests and help elevate their resource allocation efficiency. But at the same time they may willingly do things that are apparently detrimental to their own economic interests and that may aggravate their inefficiency in resource allocation. The market's self-restraining role is rendered ineffective when microeconomic agents are callous about boosting resource allocation efficiency, to say nothing of following efficiency standards to control the input and utilization of resources.

On the other hand, the reason why microeconomic agents lack vitality is not only that they do not care enough—or do not care at all—about their gains and losses in production and management, but also that their performance in production and business is subject to restrictions imposed by government departments—they have to do the government's bidding. For this reason, even if microeconomic agents care for their gains and losses in production and management and wish to readjust their input and use of resources, their status as government subsidiaries determines that they can not follow their own will, interests and principles. The market is thus stripped of its self-restraining role in resource allocation; there is nothing it can do no matter how unreasonably resources are allocated and how gravely efficiency is impaired.

The above analysis testifies that in the second category of economic disequilibrium, it is hard for the market to play a proper self-restraining role in resource allocation. This is exactly where the significant difference between the first and second categories of economic disequilibrium rests. In the first category of disequilibrium, the market's self-restraining role still works despite the constraints on it. By contrast, in the second category of disequilibrium, the market's restraints on ineffective resource input can hardly be made to work. Therefore, if efficiency in resource utilization declines due to insufficient resource input or inappropriate resource combinations, the market is unlikely to rectify it. Even if the market can send a warning signal about the widening gap between the demand for and supply of a certain resource, or about a drop in economic efficiency or a large price fluctuation, microeconomic agents are unable to receive it. Even if they can receive it, they cannot—or do not want—to adjust the destinations or combinations of their resource input. Maladjustment in resource allocation will thus prevail, and grow from bad to worse, with one of the following three possible outcomes.

Possibility One: The economic disarray caused by increasingly disproportionate resource allocation forces the government to intervene with non-economic means in an attempt to rectify it. Such non-market intervention, usually known as "rectification" or "policy readjustment," is not uncommon in the second category of disequilibrium. It should be noted that the government in this context refers to the supreme decision-making echelon. Only when this echelon has sensed the serious nature of such disproportionate resource allocation and resolves to "rectify" it or "readjust" its policy, can such non-economic means of intervention be applied. However, by the time the supreme power has discovered the seriousness of the problem and resolves to do something about it, a lot of time has been wasted, and the delay inevitably causes considerable economic losses.

The issue, however, comes down to how the supreme policy-making echelon "rectifies" the situation. Only when the policy-makers have fully realized that the emergence and aggravation of disproportionate resource allocation are caused by the second category of economic disequilibrium (i.e., incomplete market, inflexible prices and microeconomic agents lacking vitality), and only when they are determined to eradicate this category of disequilibrium, can the "rectification" effort reap real results. If the decisionmakers' desire is to reverse the disproportionate resource allocation by noneconomic intervention while leaving this kind of disequilibrium intact, the strains on resource demand and supply can only be relaxed temporarily at best, and the disproportionate resource allocation will become so protracted and complicated as to involve another round of "rectification" or "policy readjustment" after a certain interval. The ultimate result is that unsolved problems grow in number, obstruction become more and more stubborn, the "rectification" effort becomes more and more difficult, and the situation goes from bad to worse.

Possibility Two: When disproportionate resource allocation occurs incessantly and hurts the economy badly, while the government decides not to intervene with non-economic means, which means it will not work to reverse the disproportionate resource allocation, the situation will keep worsening. When the problems have accumulated to a point where the conflict between resource demand and supply comes to a head, the economy will suffer from "stagnation," "inflation," or "stagflation," and, in the worst scenario, be pushed to the brink of collapse. Only then can the market's self-restraining role in resource allocation come into play. That is, when the economy is teetering on the verge of collapse, microeconomic agents will be forced to seek a way out. Confronted with a difficult and almost hopeless situation, they have no alternative but to seek a solution on their own through transactions that serve their own interests (or the interests of their workforce).

In this situation, many trading activities between microeconomic agents for their own interests are underground in the second category of disequilibrium. The rapid rise of such an underground market may force those microeconomic agents to pay more dearly for closing deals to their advantage, thus further changing the direction of resource allocation. Nevertheless, the underground market is still a kind of market, where sellers and buyers may bypass the intervention by non-economic factors and allow transactions to be impacted by the scarcity of commodities and the prices determined by this scarcity (similar to the prices under incomplete competition). Under these circumstances, the market's self-restraining role in resource allocation can work so that sellers and buyers can reach deals under mutually acceptable conditions. In this way, the underground market contributes more or less to alleviating the difficult economic conditions and preventing disproportionate resource allocation from causing a total economic collapse. This seems ironical, but is most likely to happen in the second category of disequilibrium.

Possibility Three: When resource allocation grows increasingly more disproportionate and leads to economic deterioration, the government realizes that the problem is caused by economic disequilibrium and that such disequilibrium manifests itself not just in market incompleteness but, more importantly, in a lack of vitality among microeconomic agents. Thus the government sets about overhauling the economy institutions while taking steps to revitalize these microeconomic agents and gradually improve market completeness. Meantime, in this reform process, the government also adopts macroeconomic regulatory steps, coordinates these steps with market regulations, and strives to ease the strains on resource allocation, thereby directing and combining social resources more appropriately.

Possibility Three is undoubtedly the least probable. When the economy is in the second category of disequilibrium, there is inertia in the economy that will push it closer to Possibility One. Possibility Two is usually not what the government hopes for in the second category of disequilibrium, but it is very probably the economy's spontaneous reaction when government intervention fails and there are no effective methods to control economic chaos. Meanwhile, if the economy moves towards Possibility Two, this may also be caused by the government's ineffectiveness in dealing with severe disproportion of resource allocation and underground trading activity. Possibility Three, however, may become reality only when:

— severely disproportionate resource allocation and economic aggravation awaken the government to the necessity of economic restructuring, especially the need to revive microeconomic agents through such restructuring;
— microeconomic agents, while gradually putting an end to their status as government appendages thanks to the government's effective economic restructuring steps, become motivated to care more about their own gains and losses in response to internal incentive and external pressure;
— at the same time, with the adoption of appropriate macroeconomic regulatory measures by the government, disproportionate resource allocation has been alleviated and the market's self-restraining role has been brought into play;
— and finally, on the basis of results achieved by the government in economic restructuring and regulation, the economy has come under the dual regulation of the market and government, causing a gradual improvement in resource allocation.

Obviously, none of these preconditions can materialize easily. However, under the second category of disequilibrium, of the aforementioned three possible outcomes of lopsided resource allocation, only Possibility Three is worth striving for. If Possibility Three becomes the reality, the second category of disequilibrium will be converted into the first category of disequilibrium. If economic equilibrium is an unrealistic proposition, to convert the second category of disequilibrium into the first category is nothing short of a second best choice.

Possible Friction Between Dual Mechanisms in the First Category of Disequilibrium

Market and government mechanisms may work in accord on one occasion and fall into disarray on another in the course of economic development. Inconsistency between the two may well be unavoidable.

The friction that may arise between the dual mechanisms is an issue pertinent to economic disequilibrium. Given the fact that disequilibrium falls into two categories, we should bear each category's attributes in mind when looking into such possible friction. Let us first consider what may happen in the first category of disequilibrium.

The inconsistency between market and government regulation in the first category of disequilibrium is apparent in two ways.

Firstly, if there are both market and government mechanisms in the economy in the first category of disequilibrium, with the former playing a basic regulating role and the latter assuming a regulating role at a higher level, friction may arise between them when supply is in disarray with demand. In this situation, because of market incompleteness, the rise or fall in prices can only slightly ease supply or demand shortfalls, and price changes cannot entirely reach the goals of market regulation. If, at this stage, the government steps in to make up for the deficiencies of market regulation but its regulating steps are at odds with the intention of market regulation, the shortfalls may be eradicated, but market mechanism will be damaged. This is a reflection of the friction between the two mechanisms. In other words, in this situation, government mechanism can work only at the expense of market mechanism—at least to a certain degree.

How should we evaluate the inconsistency or friction between the two mechanisms? We can only evaluate them from their regulatory results. Is it necessary, and worthwhile, for the market mechanism to be damaged, if only to a limited degree? Of course it is always better to rectify the situation in which supply falls short of demand or outstrips demand through government regulation without causing any damage to market mechanism. In that scenario, the two mechanisms are well coordinated and free from friction. But things do not necessarily go that way in reality. Therefore, the inconsistency between the two and the damage caused by government regulation to market mechanism can only be evaluated from the regulation results. Only by such evaluation can we see if such inconsistency is necessary and worthwhile. However, no matter what happens, friction between the two is highly probable.

Secondly, contrary to the above proposition, market mechanism may also hold back government regulation in the first category of disequilibrium, due directly to an incomplete market, incomplete and untimely information, the failure of prices in regulating supply and demand, and constraints on resource supply and demand. For instance, on certain occasions when the government takes steps to regulate the allocation of resources, these steps may not reach the expected goals because of factors such as incomplete market and incomplete and untimely information. In this scenario, the government hopes to inform market traders of what gains or losses are to be expected from its regulatory steps, in the hope that they will follow their own interests to readjust the allocation and input of their resources. In the meantime, however, the market is also conveying, through its own channels, its information on gains and losses to these traders. As a result of different information accesses and incomplete and delayed information, market mechanism may either accord with the intention of government regulation, which is, of course, the best scenario, or disturb or restrict government regulation. Both possibilities are also reflections on the inconsistency or friction between the dual mechanisms in the course of resource allocation or economic operation.

To sum up, in the first category of disequilibrium, market and government mechanisms may, in their coexistence, be locked in a state of inconsistency, and frictions between them are possible, and, sometimes, even unavoidable.

Possible Friction Between Dual Mechanisms in the Second Category of Disequilibrium

The second category of disequilibrium is more serious in degree than the first category. Therefore, the possible friction caused by the coexistence of market and government mechanisms may be more acute than in the first category of disequilibrium. This can be interpreted in three ways.

First, the fact that enterprises are not independent commodity producers or have not put an end to their status as government appendages will hold up their efforts to organize production and input resources in compliance with the principle on market interest. Lack of market standards in evaluating enterprise performance inevitably corrodes the efficiency of these enterprises. In this situation, government regulation is unlikely to achieve its expected goals no matter what specific measures are adopted. The main reason for this is that market mechanism is distorted when enterprises are not functioning as independent commodity producers, and the friction between government regulation and the distorted market regulation thus becomes unavoidable.

Second, when enterprises remain government appendages, government regulation on the economy is distorted because the government, for lack of sufficient information on the economic interests of these enterprises, cannot guarantee that every regulation measure it takes is appropriate. Difficulties in coordinating distorted government regulation and distorted market mechanism is another cause of friction between the two.

Third, if supply and demand shortfalls associated with constraints on resource supply and demand occur in the second category of disequilibrium, what are such shortfalls' differences from those in the first category of disequilibrium? In the first category of disequilibrium, these shortfalls can be resolved by balancing the quotas through transactions in incomplete competition according to the market's priority or monopoly principle. The balance of quotas can also be realized through transactions in incomplete competition according to government principles of egalitarianism, goals, and history. No matter what friction this may cause between market and government mechanisms, it is still possible to balance the quotas so long as transactions are conducted in incomplete competition. However, the situation may change in the second category of disequilibrium. This is because enterprises are not independent commodity producers and cannot allocate and input their resources in light of their own economic interests. Thus both market principles regarding priority and monopoly and government principles concerning egalitarianism, goals and history will be distorted and lose their original meanings where enterprises are stripped of their independent interests and cannot transact to their own benefit. Transactions carried out in incomplete competition may not help balance the quotas, and supply or demand shortfalls may remain, or even aggravate. As a result, the friction between market and government mechanisms will be more acute in the second category of disequilibrium than in the first category of it.

Implications of Economic Operation in the Second Category of Disequilibrium

A clear message from the above analysis is that, on certain occasions, friction between market and government regulation mechanisms are unavoidable in the course of economic operation under either category of disequilibrium. Such is the limitation of the dual mechanisms.

In addition, the fact that friction exists to various degrees between the two mechanisms in the course of economic operation can only point to such a limitation, which means that under disequilibrium no economic operation can follow a perfect course. However, this is not to say the dual mechanisms are unnecessary.

It is worth noting that dual mechanisms will be unnecessary if the economy is in equilibrium and excess demand and supply are nonexistent. However, as we have seen, economic equilibrium is purely a theoretical assumption. In reality, the economy is always in disequilibrium of either the first or second category. The coexistence of dual mechanisms is no wishful thinking, but an objective reality in economic operation. Under economic disequilibrium, and when there are restraints on both resource supply and demand (that is, either supply or demand is in shortage), only by engaging both mechanisms can quotas be balanced through transactions in imperfect competition. Therefore, even though friction is unavoidable between the two mechanisms, the development of the socialist commodity economy will not be seriously held back so long as the dual mechanisms play their normal roles. Needless to say, the economy can run more smoothly in the first category of disequilibrium than in the second. In the second category of disequilibrium, if the friction between the two mechanisms is not handled properly but allowed to aggravate, the socialist commodity economy is bound to be seriously hindered. This further drives home the imminent importance of socialist economic reform to economic development, and the imminent importance of the full vitality of socialist enterprises to smooth economic operation. In other words, the less the economic disequilibrium is, the less serious the friction is between the two mechanisms. However, so long as the economic disequilibrium persists, such friction should never be overlooked even if they do not affect economic development and operation. We can minimize the negative impact of such friction if we see its existence in perspective and take steps to hold it in check.

In all, my analysis of the two categories of disequilibrium and the friction between the two mechanisms in the course of economic operations boils down to three conclusions on the current economic reforms in our country:

Conclusion One: We need to understand that our current economy is not in the first category of disequilibrium, characterized mainly by market incompleteness, but in the second category of disequilibrium, marked in the main by the fact that the market is incomplete and enterprises are yet to become fully vital. Therefore, enterprise reform should be the mainstream of the current economic restructuring, with top priority given to imbuing our enterprises with full vitality. Through this reform, the national economy should accomplish its transition from the second category of disequilibrium to the first category. As much as economic equilibrium is unattainable, it is feasible and worthwhile to shift the economy to the first category of disequilibrium.

Conclusion Two: If, instead of setting enterprise reform as the mainstream of the ongoing economic restructuring, we are bent on bringing the market to completion and decentralizing prices when the economy is still in the second category of disequilibrium and when our enterprises are yet to be fully energized, we will fail to achieve good results, the economy will be crippled, and the already imbalanced resource allocation will be even more imbalanced. The reasons are clear. Just as mentioned in the foregoing, the second category of disequilibrium tends to lock government and market mechanisms in acute friction. With distorted government regulation tangled with distorted market regulation, economic efficiency will be further eroded.

Conclusion Three: Based on the nature of economic disequilibrium, the second category of disequilibrium in particular, the macroeconomic administrative reform should, as part of the current economic restructuring, emphasize promoting the market's self-restraining role in resource allocation, and stress minimizing the friction between market and government regulation in the course of economic operation. If we fail to do these things in the macroeconomic administrative reform, the transition of the national economy from the second category of disequilibrium to the first category will be held back, and supply or demand shortfalls are bound to be exacerbated. This is because the role of government regulation in eradicating supply or demand shortfalls is limited where enterprises cannot make their own business decisions and bear the responsibility for their gains and losses. When enterprises cannot readjust supply and demand according to their own interests the way they should as traders, the balance of quotas the government hopes for will never be achieved. If the government's administrative measures are detrimental to the effort to motivate enterprises in business activity and guide them in readjusting supply and demand in light of their own interests, and if such measures are designed to make up for supply shortfalls merely by reducing demand or to keep supply and demand in temporary balance merely by direct input or distribution, the Chinese economy will continue to languish in the extremely counterproductive second category of disequilibrium.

— *Economic Reference*, issue No. 128, 1988

· 6 ·

RELATIONSHIP BETWEEN ECONOMIC REFORM, GROWTH AND INDUSTRIAL RESTRUCTURING

An unanswered question in our nation's economy is how to foster a congenial relationship in which economic reform, growth and industrial restructuring supplement each other, so that the economy can grow effectively in the course of economic reform, a new mechanism for resource allocation can be found through economic growth and industrial restructuring, and the traditional economic system can be converted into a brand new one.

This is no easy mission. The Chinese economy is in a state of disequilibrium. The market is incomplete. Resources are in shortage. Firms are yet to become commodity producers that are motivated by their own interests. Under these circumstances, if we rely mainly on market regulation to decide prices when our firms cannot pursue their own interests, and if the flow of production factors is still hampered by ambiguous property rights, we are courting two dire results. For one thing, prices will rise, market information will be distorted, and our industrial structure, instead of running on an even keel, will become even more lopsided to inhibit future economic growth. For another, if we count mainly on government regulation and allow the government to impose restrictions on prices and quotas on commodities, some industries may grow fast, but the development of other industries will be hindered. Economic growth may be maintained at a certain rate, but because firms are apathetic about improving their efficiency, the establishment of a new resource allocation mechanism will inevitably be delayed or encumbered. As a result, economic growth may only be achieved at the expense of efficiency, while the industrial structure will stay warped for lack of guidance from accurate market information. Such is the sixty-four dollar question for my fellow economists in this nation. This paper is a study of this question starting from a definition of the term "investment principal."

I

Firms are principals in economic growth and industrial restructuring. As the term "principal" is interpreted in the context of "investor," firms must be true interest principals before they can become efficient investors. To put it another way, they must possess independent interests and be concerned with such interests. They invest, and constrain themselves in so doing to achieve such interests. If, in formulating policies for economic growth and industrial restructuring, we regard firms as investment principals that have independent interests and are willing to be restrained by such interests, we can blaze a new trail in this field. If we take this as the starting point, corporate institutional reform will become the overriding issue, which entails establishing firms as interest and investment principals, and letting economic growth and industrial restructuring be conditioned and promoted by their investment choices, so as to attain the goal of coordinating economic reform, growth and industrial restructuring in simultaneous development.

Industrial restructuring entails reducing investment in some industries and increasing it in others. The industrial structure embodies both the output ratios and the input ratios between industries. Input circumscribes output, and the input-output ratio also conditions output. The proposition, "let firms become investment principals in industrial restructuring," means two things. First, we should permit firms to act in their own interests when choosing their investment destinations, or when deciding which departments need more investment and which departments need less, and thus to impact the output ratio between industries. Second, we should allow firms to act in their own interests when adjusting the input-output ratio, that is, controlling input and increasing output by raising efficiency. The second meaning is probably more important because only by turning firms into interest principals can they be highly motivated to boost output by improving efficiency. That is a more sensible way to overcome shortfalls in certain commodities when resources are in shortage and input is constrained by circumstances.

From another point of view, to convert firms into investment principals is to turn them into demanders for, or purchasers of, production factors. When a firm acts in its own interests to redirect its investment and modify the way it groups production factors, and influences the sales volumes of products supplied by other firms by adjusting its demand for production factors, it is actually impacting a certain industry's changes in output and scale and leading the way for industrial restructuring. For this reason, when a firm becomes an interest principal, it can in fact moderate industrial restructuring with both its input—resource input and input-output ratio included—and purchases from other firms. The rate of economic growth is ultimately decided by each firm's output growth rate. Economic growth and industrial restructuring are part of the same process once firms can maintain their output growth through industrial reform. When firms with independent interests become principals of economic growth, they also become principals of industrial restructuring.

II

When we regard firms as investment principals and put a premium on the role they can play in industrial restructuring through their investment and purchase choices, we must take into account the fact that they are engaged in economic activity under economic disequilibrium, and that the incomplete market and resource shortfalls invariably affect their investment and purchase decisions. In so doing, we will recognize the paramount role of the government in industrial restructuring. The greater the degree of economic disequilibrium, the more important the role of the government becomes in industrial restructuring.

The government is duty-bound to support non-profit investment projects, a duty that is directly related to its nature. Under no circumstances should the government shun its responsibility for this field of investment. This point is self-evident, and no more proof is needed. The question to be discussed here is what, supposing the market is incomplete and resources are in short supply, the government should do as the economic regulator to influence firms' investment and purchase choices, and further impact industrial restructuring and put it on a sound footing. A fundamental answer to this question lies in the government's capacity to balance its quotas.

Balanced government quotas are achievable through the goals principle, the principle of averages, or the principle of historical ratios. Because each of these principles is limited in its scope of application and has its drawbacks, the government should choose between them on the basis of study and investigation.

The goals principle guides the government to allot quotas for the limited resources to be sold to industries in order of priority and urgency. This way of distributing resources helps implement government goals for economic growth and economic restructuring, boosts growth in some industries and restrains it in some other industries. But it also poses some questions. Is the alignment of the industries in order of priority and urgency scientifically viable? Do the quotas measure up to benchmarks for resource utility efficiency? Is there any way to prevent industries from putting the resources allotted to them to other uses or reselling them for a profit? In a sense, the side effect of the goals principle is that it may give preference to industries and firms with low efficiency, to the neglect of truly efficient industries and firms whose efficiency may be curbed by resource shortages. In this regard, the balance of government quotas under the goals principle is maintained at the expense of resource utility efficiency unless measures are taken so that resources can be reallocated among industries, and firms can change their line of production.

The principle of averages directs the government to distribute resources equally among industries according to the aggregate demand of firms and the availability of such resources. This principle may become an impediment to achieving the government's industrial restructuring goals, as it serves basically to maintain the status quo of the industrial structure. However, from the perspective of sustaining economic growth, quota allocation under the principle of averages cannot go so far as to cause dramatic fluctuations in the economic growth rate. Moreover, judging from the supply and demand of daily necessities, the principle of averages helps maintain social stability when limited resources are distributed according to it. Under this principle, resource utility efficiency tends to drop, but such a drop is ascribed mainly to universal shortages in the supply of resources rather than to changes in the industrial structure (because, as a matter of fact, such a structure tends to remain relatively unchanged).

The historical ratios principle guides the government to allot resource quotas to be distributed among industries or firms in line with distribution ratios that have been followed for a long time in the past. This principle works in a way similar to the principle of averages, that is, by maintaining the status quo of the industrial structure and avoiding major fluctuations in the economic growth rate. However, it also poses some questions: Are the historical ratios—the cornerstone of this principle—reasonable or not? Is there any guarantee that the resources distributed to industries and firms are not put to other uses or resold for a profit? Now that it is impossible not to adapt historical quotas to reality, how can distribution quotas be reset when and where such a need arises?

It is thus clear that when resource shortfalls necessitate distribution quotas, the government is faced with the arduous task of attaining both economic growth and industrial restructuring goals without discouraging firms in business activity and hurting resource utility efficiency. Such quotas should be scientifically viable whether they are arranged in order of priority and importance, evened out, or according to established ratios. First of all, only with viable quotas can errors and conflicts be minimized while limited resources are dispensed. Then, no matter which principle is followed, everything should be done to forestall the resale of scarce resources from one industry or firm to another.

A compromise between these three principles may be reached to help balance distribution quotas under government regulation. Of the trio, the goals principle is relatively more conducive to the government's industrial restructuring goals; the historical ratios principle works better to sustain economic growth and minimize fluctuations in the economic growth rate; while the principle of averages helps more in reducing conflicts of interests and keeping firms motivated. To give full scope to the role of coordinated government quotas in industrial restructuring, we may as well take the goals principle as the guideline and draw on the historical ratios principle and the principle of averages when setting ratios for the distribution of scarce resources.

III

Economic growth amidst resource shortage is relevant to government quotas for distributing such resources between industries. If such resources are allotted according to the goals principle, economic growth is bound to take place in the course of industrial restructuring, whereas the economic growth achieved in the course of industrial restructuring is inevitably of a "tilting type," a byword for uneven economic growth.

The issue here involves judgment of the value of this type of uneven economic growth. Economic growth, whatever type it is, is attained in a realworld economic environment. We may regard this environment as the initial condition for economic growth. The economy invariably reaches a certain anticipated economic level after a certain period of growth, and we may regard this anticipated economic level as the condition for end-of-period growth. Whether the economy is balanced or not, economic growth cannot be evaluated without taking its initial and end-of-period conditions into consideration. If the industrial structure is well coordinated at both stages of economic growth, then balanced economic growth is obviously the ideal. In this case, uneven economic growth is probably unnecessary or even detrimental to the attainment of the anticipated goals for coordinating the industrial structure. However, when the current Chinese economy is at the initial stage of disequilibrium and the industrial structure is already gravely lopsided, to strive for balanced economic growth not only is unrealistic but also contravenes the task of restoring economic equilibrium through optimal distribution of scarce resources. Therefore, our judgment of the merits or demerits of disequilibrium in economic growth should not be estranged from reality.

Whether the government's anticipated goals for economic growth and industrial restructuring can be reached as a result of imbalanced economic growth through quota rationing is determined, first of all, by whether the government industrial policy is scientifically viable or not, and secondly, by the determination with which this policy is carried out. If the government relinquishes its industrial policy and allows the market to run the economy completely, economic growth may be achieved and the industrial system restructured only when the market is relatively complete and firms are operating in accordance with their own interests. Even so, progress in industrial restructuring may be tardy because it always takes numerous transactions in which resources change hands numerous times before the market clears (that is, through spontaneous distribution of scarce resources or spontaneous division of the limited market). Given the current situation in our nation, an incomplete market and the failure of firms to assert their own interests make it hard for resources to be spontaneously redirected, and the results of market regulation of quotas are not necessarily in accord with prescribed government goals for economic growth and industrial restructuring. Thus the government needs to formulate its industryprioritizing policy and proceed from this policy to achieve imbalanced economic growth under balanced government quotas.

This industry-prioritizing policy is, indeed, a tilted one. However, it should be noted that no leading industry can do without the assistance of several other industries that are themselves tied with even more industries. This being the case, if the government chooses to carry out such a tilted industrial policy, this policy can allot quotas for scarce resources among industries only according to how closely they are associated with the leading industry. Such a policy cannot be tipped in favor of only one or several industries to the neglect of the other related industries. That is to say, in economic disequilibrium, the bias of this tilted industrial policy should be kept within reasonable bounds if the government has no alternative but to count on quota rationing to bring about imbalanced economic growth and to concentrate resources on leading industries for industrial restructuring purposes. It should never be overdone. Otherwise, instead of spurring the leading industries, it may only sustain or aggravate the lopsided industrial structure.

As the above analysis indicates, the argument on economic growth is not about which is supposedly better, balanced growth or imbalanced growth. Given that the initial state of economic growth is characterized by a disproportionate industrial structure, the argument is unavoidably focused on the degree of imbalance in economic growth, that is, on the degree of bias of the tilted industrial policy. An over-tilted industrial policy is more harmful than an unbiased one in that it may exaggerate the already warped industrial structure. When the initial state of economic growth is characterized by a lopsided industrial structure, balanced economic growth may help maintain the status quo of the industrial structure and prevent it from further deterioration, even though it cannot completely redress its lopsidedness. This is a point the government should keep in mind when making its industryprioritizing policy.

Now the issue comes down to how the government applies its industryprioritizing policy and whether it can keep the prejudice of this policy within bounds. To find the answers, I deem it necessary to look into the roles of the corporate operational mechanism and price signals in the course of executing the policy.

IV

The industry-prioritizing policy is formulated and enacted by the government. Generally speaking, dystopian government behavior generates a disparity between this policy and the government's anticipated goals for economic growth and industrial restructuring. Because it is hard for the government to tilt this policy with absolute precision, something has to be done to restrain such a tilt. Such restraints do not come from the government itself but, in the main, from firms that are investment and interest principals.

If firms cannot put an end to their status as government appendages, and fail to base their investment choices on their immediate and anticipated interests, they can never react properly to changes in supply and demand if the government industrial policy becomes over-tilted. The lopsided industrial structure aggravated by an overly tilted industrial policy, as well as the growing deficiency in the supply of some commodities and the demand for other commodities, can be remedied only when the problems have come to a head and alerted the government. Enormous losses occur simply because the government cannot address the issues timely. And the consequence does not stop just there. Because the bias of the tilted industrial policy is related to the government's rationing of scarce resources, firms lacking constraints on their interests may profiteer by taking advantage of that policy. They may use the resources in short supply to produce commodities not badly needed on the market or engage in nonproductive profiteering activities. In that way, they can only exacerbate lopsided government rationing, instead of curbing it, thereby making scarce resources even scarcer.

If, contrary to the intention of the government industrial policy, the aforementioned phenomena occur, and if the government fails to pinpoint firms' lack of independent interests as the key to the problem, the government is likely to believe that all this was caused by unreasonable pricing or the double-track price system. That misjudgment may compel the government to abolish the double-track prices and decentralize them in an attempt to rectify the badly warped industrial structure and eradicate shortages in commodity supply and demand. Theoretically speaking, this way of doing things is not groundless, because correct price signals can direct the flow of resources to areas needed by the market, and firms' flexible reaction to such signals can lead them to shift production to commodities in short supply and their investment to weak links of the economy, thereby hastening the effort to balance the industrial structure. However, this behavior is totally disagreeable to an economy under disequilibrium. If the government chooses to do so, it can accomplish nothing but to further damage the industrial structure and drive the economy deeper into chaos. The central problem here is that firms that cannot make their own business decisions and bear the responsibility for their gains and losses cannot become true interest principals to play a part in industrial restructuring.

As the above analysis illustrates, the lopsided industrial structure characterized by resource shortage in the initial stage of economic growth is an established fact, and so are the incomplete market and firms' lack of independent interests. With resources in shortage, rationing is imperative either by the government or the market. The double-track prices mean both government and market are rationing the scare resources. Government quotas are realized according to the goals principle, the principle of averages, or the principle of historical ratios. If the government decides to replace doubletrack prices with sole market prices, government quotas must be lifted, and scarce resources put at the mercy of the market. Then the market can allocate resources on a "first come, first served" basis or in line with the monopoly principle. No matter which principle the market chooses, the fact that the market is incomplete, that firm property rights remain ambiguous and that firms lack independent interests will curtail price elasticity in both supply and demand. The economy will end up with two new prices, i.e., open market prices and black market prices. The price gap between open and black markets inevitably sends prices on one round of hiking after another. This is exactly what happens in the Chinese economy under disequilibrium, a situation that does nothing but aggravate the lopsided industrial structure.

If the government takes into consideration the fact that the economy is in disequilibrium and that firms are yet to become independent commodity producers, and if the government is mindful of its goals for effective industrial restructuring, it should never decontrol prices and abolish the double-track prices. On the contrary, the government, while going on with quota rationing, should define firm property rights, transform their operational mechanism, and rely on their self-restraints to prevent the industrial policy from being overly tilted.

V

When firms become investment and interest principals, they will be able to restrain themselves in investment and operation. This self-restraining ability, once linked with firms' operational mechanisms, will help prevent the government industrial policy from becoming overly tilted. This is because firms will be capable of adjusting the direction and amount of their investment under the guidance of their own interests. If the industrial policy is overly tilted towards a certain industry under the double-track price system, firms may react in two ways.

Firstly, they may accept market quotas, that is, to adopt market prices that are higher than government-mandated prices to produce commodities that accord with their interests and are in short market supply, thereby making up for supply shortages resulting from the government's excessively tilted industrial policy. Naturally, firms may run certain investment and business risks if they choose to react this way. As interest principals, however, they are not only entitled to do so but also willing to run such risks because risks accompany profits. Profits are enough of a motivation for them to take this course of action.

Secondly, firms may choose not to accept market quotas mainly because, proceeding from their own interests, they believe the market has so overpriced the resources as to expose them to excessive investment and business risks. Then the lack of government quotas invariably will prompt firms to change their business scale and scope by altering their line of production, stopping production, reducing output, seeking mergers, or setting up joint ventures. This will cause production factors to flow, and the resources to be regrouped, among industries or firms. As such flow and regrouping are driven by firms' own interests, it will help make up for product shortages resulting from the seriously tilted government industrial policy.

Both possible reactions to the government's tilted industrial policy help make up for product shortages resulting from that policy. Both reactions point to firms' intention to restrain themselves to curb resource misallocation caused by the overly tilted government industrial policy. Their selfrestraining action can also restrain the tilted government policy in another fashion. That is, when they react in either way, the market situation will change to a certain extent, thereby forcing the government to stop tipping the industrial policy overly in favor of certain industries and revise its overconcentrated quota plans.

For example, if firms react in the first way, that is, if they purchase capital goods from the market at prices higher than government-mandated prices to produce certain commodities in short market supply, it will increase the supply of the related capital goods, and reduce the prices of the commodities being produced. The government will receive a certain signal from these firms when it allots quotas on the capital goods and commodities in question. Upon discovering that its original quota plans—that is, the overconcentrated plans made under the overly tilted industrial policy—can no longer work, the government is likely to adapt those plans to the new market situation.

If firms react in the second way, that is, if they cope with overconcentrated government quotas through the flow of production factors and the regrouping of resources, the supply of certain commodities in shortage will be increased, and the market situation will be changed. When the government has received such a signal, it is likely to readjust its quotas in response.

It is thus clear that balanced government quotas can help straighten out the industrial structure only when firms have ended their status as government appendages and become independent commodity producers that make their own business decisions and bear the responsibility for their gains and losses. Only thus can time-consuming delays be avoided in addressing an industrial structure warped by inappropriate distribution of government quotas. On the other hand, if the government counts on abolishing the double-track prices to improve the industrial structure without overhauling the nature and function of firms, the result will be contrary to its intentions.

All this illustrates the essential relationship between economic reform, growth and industrial restructuring under economic disequilibrium. In short, if effective corporate institutional reform cannot happen in the first place, it will be almost impossible for the nation to achieve present and future economic growth and industrial restructuring goals.

— *Quantitative & Technical Economics*, issue No. 12, 1988

· 7 ·

LAYING A SOLID FOUNDATION FOR NEW CULTURE

The topic of my speech today is the relationship between economic reform, new public ownership and a new culture. In my opinion, when we clarify the relationship between these three things, we will gain a better idea about the significance of and prospects for the economic reform that has been going on in our country for a whole decade, and find it a lot easier to understand the trials and tribulations our nation has gone through in the course of it.

The Study of People

In studying economic issues we are obliged to face certain questions. What is the purpose of growing the economy? For whom do we provide products, labor, and service? Why should we turn out more and more products and provide more and more labor and service? These questions boil down to one: What is the purpose of production? Common sense tells us that production per se is not the purpose. Human beings do not live in the world merely as laborers. People do not come into this world to serve production—it is production that serves people. The purpose of production is for people to be better cared for and better educated. It defeats the purpose of production if we concentrate single-mindedly on offering more products while our standard of living and cultural and educational attainments remain the same, and if our people are not duly respected and cannot live up to their potentials.

Based on this plain and simple line of reasoning, we may define economics this way: Economics should not be limited to learning how to increase material wealth, but more importantly, it should study how to use the wealth created by people to meet their needs in their material and cultural lives. The highest level, or focus, of economic research is not material products, but people.

Based on this plain and simple line of reasoning, we can understand the meaning of the ongoing economic reform. Economic reform serves not merely to put the Chinese in possession of more products. More importantly, it is designed for them to achieve affluence and better cultural and educational endowment, and to be looked after, educated and respected as society's masters. From this perspective, it is clearly inadequate to argue for economic reform simply for the sake of economic reform.

We must admit that in meeting people's material and cultural needs and in facilitating all-round human development, there is a yawning gap between reality and ideal. Therefore, we have to accelerate reform—economic, political, and institutional reforms included—and cultivate a new culture. I believe that not only will our per capita national income grow nonstop with rising labor productivity, but our civic character will also improve vastly with what has been accomplished in growing the economy and cultivating the new culture, so long as we can ensure essential progress in reform and development, motivate our workforce unswervingly, and give full scope to the wisdom and talent of our people. Reform is exactly where China's hope rests.

New Culture Holds People in Due Esteem

Prior to the liberation year of 1949, an old culture, in which people's position and role were disdained, dominated this nation for understandable reasons. But how is it that the old culture remains so powerful after 1949? It is because it has carved out a new form of existence under a new situation and in a new economic environment.

It goes without saying there is a certain correlation between the old cultures before and after 1949. The old culture is anti-scientific and antidemocratic, whereas science and democracy are salient features of the new culture. Our predecessors had studied this a long time ago. Today, it should be recapitulated further on the basis of previous studies. The old culture is centered on divinity, whereas the new culture is focused on people. The old culture emphasizes power, whereas the new culture stresses knowledge. Because of its emphasis on power, old culture is based on the official standard; for its stress on knowledge, new culture inevitably takes people and science as its starting point. Superstition is the shared attribute of pre- and post-1949 old cultures, which never hold people in center stage. In the old culture, power is worshipped religiously and pursued relentlessly, and science, knowledge, and people are never respected. The reason why the old culture of yesterday lingers on and a new form of the old culture came to the scene after 1949 is precisely because of the old culture's intricate foundation in the Chinese economy of yore and its deep roots in feudalism. That is to say, because the pre-1949 old culture escaped elimination, the post-1949 old culture has been allowed to rear its ugly head. If we call the pre-1949 old culture "standard old culture" and the post-1949 old culture "remodeled old culture," what existed from the 1950s through the 1980s were two kinds of old culture, the "standard old culture" and the "remodeled old culture," and the period from the late 1960s through the mid-1970s was one in which the two old cultures apparently got mixed. The "remodeled old culture" has been weakened considerably since the Third Plenary Session of the Eleventh Party Central Committee in 1979, but this has not happened to the "standard old culture." In fact, it has reappeared in such forms as construction sprees of temples and lavish tombs and the spread of wasteful weddings and funerals. This indicates that, on the one hand, the independent old culture won't beat a retreat anytime soon even with progress in economic restructuring and reform, and, on the other, once the old culture infiltrates lifestyles and habits, it becomes pegged to people's economic abilities. When people are having trouble making ends meet, there is little they can do even if they truly desire to build temples and lavish tombs or indulge in pomp and pageantry. Of course I am not saying they won't get these things done by falling into debt. Generally speaking, people become thrifty when they are hard up, but when they are better off, the "standard old culture" will penetrate their daily life and spread among them in no time.

Obviously, we can never eradicate the old culture, not even the "standard old culture," by raising people's income alone. The old culture totally denies people's status as masters of society and is steeped in benightedness and blind obedience. It can be rooted up and give way to new culture only by developing both the economy and education and raising people's scientific and cultural endowment. The kind of education I am talking about here is not simply the imparting of knowledge and expertise but, more importantly, the cardinal mission of "modernizing people."

Make no question about it, without the "modernization of people" there will be no modernization of society, the economy, or science and technology. Without the "emancipation of people" there will be no emancipation of productivity. New culture is connected with "modernization of people" and "emancipation of people." Only by grasping this point can we capture the profound meaning of the cultivation of a new culture.

The Foundation of a New Culture

Why is the old culture so powerful and the new culture so weak in China? Because the new culture has yet to build up its own economic base. The pre-1949 old culture was based on an old economic system, but, during the period from the late 1950s to the eve of the Third Plenary Session of the Eleventh Party Central Committee, another form of old culture, the "remodeled old culture," found its foundation in the ossified commodity economy and the traditional form of public ownership which confounded government administration with business management, made officials act like businesspeople, dampened producers' enthusiasm for production, and robbed the new culture of its corresponding economic foundation. The landmark significance of the Third Plenary Session lies in the fact that it unshackled people from long years of "Leftist" ideology, emancipated their minds, and pointed out the way for building a socialist system conducive to productivity development. After that meeting, we have not only transformed the old economic system into a new one, but also repudiated old culture, the "remodeled old culture" included, and built a socialist new culture. The socialist new culture has found its foundation in a planned socialist commodity economy that embraces a new type of public ownership whereby government administration is detached from everyday business management, officials no longer act like businesspeople, and producers are highly motivated.

Only by observing the mission for economic reform alongside the building of the socialist new culture can we fully comprehend the greatness of what our nation has been doing over the last decade and understand the adversities and trials involved in the cause of reform. It is hard to replace an old economic system with a new one, but it is even harder to replace an old culture with a new culture. Reform entails readjusting interests. Old culture and old habits hold sway over people's outlook on personal interests, labor productivity, education, and way of life, while the old economic system spawns egalitarianism and rigidity in such assertions of interests as wages, employment, and welfare. Reform is bound to touch upon everybody's established interests. If four of someone's five established interests have improved, he may still have complaints about the one interest that has suffered and go on to blame it on reform, because he takes the improvement in his established interests for granted and believes that something must have gone wrong if one of his interests has been impaired even if such an interest is unwarranted. The result is that society abounds with complaints that stem from all sorts of conflicts of interests. It is thus apparent that without correcting people's outlooks on their interests, without loosening the rigidity of interests caused by egalitarianism and the old economic system, without breaking the bandwagon mentality concerning interests based on tradition, and without fostering new concepts of culture and interests, the road ahead for reform will bristle with impediments. If we have fully accepted this point, we can arrive at three conclusions:

First, "reform" contravenes not only a 30-year-old economic system but also three millennia of outdated culture and habits. Therefore, reform can never be a simple undertaking.

Second, reform has brought a lot of new interests to people, no question about it, but because it has broken or is ready to break the rigidity of interests under the old system, it has also deprived people of certain established interests. Thus reform is confronted with more impediments as people, oblivious to the new interests they have gained, are having misgivings about their lost established interests.

Third, rigidity in interests is uncalled-for, and some of the established interests born of such rigidity are detrimental to productivity growth. Both should be rectified, and reform should never be reined in because of it. We cannot afford to give up reform midway for fear of an unjustified rigidity in interests. Otherwise, our effort to develop productivity will be thwarted, and our hope for a prosperous economy dashed.

From a historical point of view, and from the perspective of our confrontation with the three-millennium-old outmoded culture, ten years are just a twinkling of the eye. But what has been achieved in reform over those years has been breathtaking. History will pass a fair and honest judgment on it.

The new culture is bound to prevail once it acquires a sturdy economic foundation, that is, a socialist commodity economy and a new type of public ownership. The inexorable pace of socialist economic reform alongside the socialist new culture is unstoppable.

The Hope of China

I have just dwelled on the issue of confidence. I believe everyone present in this auditorium feels the same. True, the national economy has hit some snags—inflation, "official" and "nonofficial" smuggling, corruption, education crisis, and whatnot. We should admit these facts. Whining and griping gets us nowhere. Only by accepting the reality, knowing the challenges and hardships of reform, and getting to the root of the problems, can we understand why reform is irreversible and why problems can be redressed in the course of reform. Given that economic reform is challenged by the 30-year-old system plus three millennia of old culture, traditions and habits, we know that the old system will not crumble on its own and the old culture, traditions, and habits cannot vanish overnight. Nevertheless, we must recognize that our nation will be doomed if we lose heart and allow ourselves to descend into complaint and despair.

My career as a university teacher on the mainland has brought me in contact with members of the younger generations in and out of class. Take, for example, the young people in their thirties today. Unlike the college students of the 1950s, who had wallowed in idealism for a period of time before and after they started work, and who were somewhat belated in their awakening to the stubbornness of the prevailing old culture, these 30-somethings had taken part in the "cultural revolution" in the name of "casting away the Four Olds"—old ideas, old culture, old customs and old habits—during their middle-school or college days. Their tragedy is that in the adverse current of "annihilating old culture in name and maintaining old culture in practice," they had inadvertently become new culture's saboteurs. Superstition, blind faith, ignorance, and extremism had driven them to put on red armbands and hold aloft the Little Red Book—Quotations of Mao Zedong. When they sang the Song of Rebels and came to blows, wielding cudgels and belts, they saw themselves as faithful enforcers of the May Fourth Movement spirit.[1] However, it did not take long for them to come to their senses. "Re-education" in the countryside, loss of schooling opportunities, and joblessness eventually drove home to them the harms done by the old culture, especially to themselves. A considerable number of them were participants in or supporters of the Tian'anmen Incident of 1976.[2] History is at once merciless and dramatic. All of a sudden, those hoodwinked by the old culture became its intransigent foes. Their minds were racing. How should the new culture be fostered? How could the new culture prevail in its long-term combat against the old? Having mulled over these questions, some of them ardently joined the cause of fostering the new culture. However, as the majority of the people in their thirties today lost their schooling opportunities in the decade-long chaos, their attitude toward the new culture being fostered nowadays is based more on personal demands and expectations than on in-depth theoretical analyses and explorations. Nevertheless, there is one thing they share with people of other age groups, that is, they know from personal experience that it is no mean task to phase out the old culture and phase in the new culture.

The situation with the 20-somethings of today is somewhat different in comparison with the 30-somethings. A 22-year-old college graduate may have been born in 1966, the year the "cultural revolution" broke out. A 30-year-old lecturer, assistant researcher, engineer, or PhD candidate may have missed primary school because all manner of schools were closed and stopped enrolment in 1966. They have just a faint memory of the "cultural revolution," or no memory of it at all. They started school in the wake of the "cultural revolution," and their development has been associated with the sensible policies adopted since the Third Plenary Session of the Eleventh Party Central Committee. They have learned new knowledge, and have been fortunate to live in the reform and opening years. They are the new culture's born pursuers and aspirants. Frequent contacts with the outside world, and concerns about China's economic and technological underdevelopment, have combined with the on-campus academic atmosphere to convert this generation of undergraduates and graduate students, teachers, researchers, technicians and engineers into spirited builders of the new culture. Undeniably, however, they are not without their limits. Because they are too young to adequately understand the reality of Chinese society, they know little about the stubbornness and strength of the old culture, and tend to believe that the building of a new culture will be nothing but smooth sailing. They probably believe the old culture will step down the moment the new culture goes onstage. This oversimplified way of thinking turns them into a different type of idealists from the youngsters of the 1950s. The idealists of the 1950s believed their task was to build the new culture now that the older generation had basically fulfilled the mission to destroy the old culture. The idealists of the 1980s may not believe this mission has been basically accomplished, but they are convinced that, with their active participation, it will not take long for the new culture to triumph over the old. Unrealistic idealism is likely to fuel impetuosity, agitation, and, in time of setbacks, pessimism, and despair. Logically speaking, as a blessed generation, the 20-somethings of today should be less prone to dark moods than people a little older. In reality, however, that is not true. Why? It is partly because of their scanty knowledge of the trauma involved in the cause of reform and partly because they cannot beat the old culture merely with knowledge (they are a generation of knowledge) and passion (which they certainly do not lack). The new culture cannot succeed before it builds up its own economic base.

Thus they start whining and griping. But what good can complaining do? They are disappointed, but can disappointment change things? Confidence, as always, is of vital importance, and therefore, we should never lose heart. No matter how difficult reform is, we have got to brace ourselves and stick it out. We are ready to take chances no matter what. Our fate is bound up with reform. That is why I told my Hong Kong hosts just before this meeting, "The hope of China lies in our confidence in reform and in building the new culture. If everybody has lost heart, reform will be doomed."

I believe I made that remark for a reason. Many of you sitting in this auditorium have been to the mainland more than a decade ago and have returned there for visits recently. Did you see big changes out there? Of course you saw colossal changes. The changes will become even bigger ten years from now, no question about it. Every one of us, those who are not confident enough included, must see the world economic situation and future trend in perspective, and put our home situation into perspective too. The changes that have taken place over the last decade are by no means small. Ten years ago, it was impossible for us to talk openly about our backwardness and the gap between China and other countries. We would not have been able to speak our minds about our country's economic issues. More importantly, those unscientific "supreme directives" would have remained the only theoretical support for solutions to those issues. Therefore, of all the impediments to Chinese economic development, the old culture must never be disregarded. Never had its impact been so ferocious as it was a decade ago. Having seen the changes over the last decade, I believe we should remain firmly optimistic about our future.

Science and Democracy Can Save China

When we see that the Chinese economy today is still trailing a long way behind many other economies in the world, an idea naturally comes to mind. Had we allowed the anti-scientific, anti-democratic old culture to prevail and manipulate our thoughts, we would have lost sight of how underdeveloped we were. We cannot but owe this awakening to the outcry of the ideological, cultural, and academic circles, and to our growing exchanges and connections with other nations. Today, everybody, or at least most of us, have come to our senses. A major reason why reform is an irresistible trend is because ideas of science and democracy have been gradually engrained in people's hearts. We have every reason to believe that if the socialist new culture, for lack of a corresponding economic foundation, is too weak to compete with the old culture prior to the birth of a new type of public ownership, it will no longer be weak and at a disadvantage in competing with the old culture once the new type of ownership comes to stay and the economic foundation becomes an reality. The new type of public ownership under conditions of a socialist commodity economy will support the socialist new culture, which, for its part, is inevitably conducive to the consolidation of such ownership. This relationship of mutual support and promotion will have a major impact on future changes in the Chinese economy. With the support of the socialist new culture, the Chinese economy will enter a new period of historical development.

How is it that the socialist new culture can play such a role? Why is it that the Chinese economy cannot score major progress without the support of the socialist new culture? Why cannot the new culture grow on its own and be consolidated without its economic foundation in the socialist commodity economy under the new type of public ownership? In-depth analysis of these questions will touch upon the issue of science and democracy. We emphasize that science and democracy can save China not just because of their role in economic development, but more importantly, because of their role in modernizing and emancipating people. If our workers and farmers can truly understand the damage caused to the economy and our own long-term interests by egalitarianism, life-long tenures, the egalitarian practice of everyone eating from the same big pot regardless of work done, rigidity in interests and the bandwagon mentality concerning interests, will the impediments to reform not be minimized? If our government functionaries can truly see that only by shattering the old system that put the economy at the mercy of administrative directives can the Chinese economy take off and the income of government functionaries and their families grow in pace with the income of the rank-and-file in the course of economic growth, will the commodity economy and the new form of public ownership not be built a lot faster? If, more than anything, the broad masses of people truly regard themselves as the masters of society under the ideological guidance of science and democracy, will corruption not be considerably reduced? As I see it, all these questions can be answered in the positive. Herein lies the inseparable bond between the building of a new culture and economic and political reform. In the course of fruitful economic and political reform, a new culture commensurate with the new type of public ownership can definitely be translated into reality.

It takes a considerably lengthy process to raise the quality of the entire citizenry. Perhaps only after our economy has become truly well developed, our people's income has risen vastly, and our lives have become really affluent, can our culture, education, science and public health be provided with enough development funds and cherished by the entire public, and our national character—cultural, moral, etc.—be considerably improved. We are not here to overestimate the role of the economy. Rather, this conclusion is based on the historical experience of countries in economic and cultural development. Perhaps a well developed economy is the only way for the fine accomplishments of traditional culture to be truly cherished and carried forward. We have come to realize that on no account should a nation lose its fine cultural achievements. Outstanding cultural attainments should stand the sifting of history and the test of time. Is it not because of poverty, low per capita national income, and underdeveloped productivity that we do not have enough economic resources to maintain and carry forward our finest cultural accomplishments? Perhaps only when achievements in economic development have become an established fact can they become the best rebuff to the "remodeled old culture" and its foundation, the traditional economic system, and traditional public ownership. If we can say that many people today hate the "remodeled old culture" from the bottom of their hearts and are utterly disgusted by the anti-scientific and anti-democratic arguments advocated by it, such hatred and disgust are based mostly on theoretical and ideological understanding, or are felt mainly from their experience with the poor and backward Chinese economy manipulated by the "remodeled old culture." As to the questions of what will become of the Chinese economy after the commodity economy is developed and the new type of public ownership established, what will become of the people's income and livelihood, and what new social pattern and atmosphere can the economy bring once it becomes commensurate with the scientifically and democratically based new culture, our answers today are more imaginative than factual. However, once all this has become reality, a reality in which the benefits of economic growth, productivity development, and brand-new public ownership can be keenly felt by hundreds of millions of Chinese, our answers will no longer be empty or abstract. Rather, they will become concrete and solid, and bestow faith and spiritual strength on people. By that time, those who cherish science and democracy will no longer believe in the "remodeled old culture" no matter what high-sounding rhetoric it may employ.

What Entrepreneurs Can Do

Once, during a conversation on economic reform and the building of a new culture in the mainland, an entrepreneur asked me: "The building of a new culture is the task of the educational, cultural, and academic circles. What can a businessman do for it?" What the man did not know is that entrepreneurs have an irreplaceable part to play in building the new culture. I told him that new culture can never prevail over old culture by relying on intellectuals alone. The new culture can strike root in the Chinese soil only when entrepreneurs join workers and farmers under the new public ownership in contributing to the growth of the commodity economy and repudiating outdated traditions, culture, and habits in the course of it.

Generally speaking, our entrepreneurs today are not only doing their best to foster the new culture during the years of economic reform, but are also fostering a corporate culture. Given that corporate culture is a branch of new culture, let me talk at some length about how to foster it.

Corporate culture is the cultural concept and values of a company, and an embodiment of the collective faith and cohesion of its workforce. There will be no corporate culture to speak of if a firm remains a government appendage and has no independent interests, and if its workers' interests are irrelevant to its business performance. For this reason, company autonomy in business activity and company responsibility for gains and losses, combined with the unanimity of interest between the company and its workers are necessary internal economic conditions for corporate culture. Whether such a culture can be fostered also depends on the company's external economic conditions—meaning that at least it should find itself in a competitive commodity market. If no headway has been made in developing the socialist commodity economy, if a company fails to foster economic ties with the outside world through competition, and if its business deals are entirely controlled by a mandatory plan and the firm serves merely as a processing workshop, it will have no way of fostering, among its workers, the norms of conduct and values centered on efficiency, competition, risks and other concepts, and its relationship with its workers will be deprived of a foundation upon which risks and interests are shared. The building of corporate culture becomes empty talk under these circumstances.

Corporate culture cannot be built in the absence of two pivotal economic conditions. The first is corporate transformation, meaning that companies must be converted from the old type of public ownership in which government interferes in business management, and become a new type of public companies that are independent commodity producers, so that they and their workers can be internally adapted to the requirements of corporate culture. The second is transformation of the corporate environment, which means companies must be given a competitive economic environment in which transactions are conducted openly and contractually, and which provides both opportunities and pressure for them to readjust their relations of interest with their workers and foster a new and congenial relationship between themselves. Both conditions indicate that the socialist corporate culture is an outcome of socialist economic reform and a fruit of the endeavor to develop the socialist commodity economy and establish the new type public ownership under such an economy.

Corporate culture, being a major component of the new culture, cannot be detached from it to stand alone. Therefore, to understand the conditions that the socialist corporate culture cannot do without, we must study the new culture as the cultural background of corporate culture. Science and democracy are salient features of the socialist new culture. Holding people in great esteem, being solicitous for and cultivating them are attributes of the new culture that distinguish it from the old. Corporate culture is out of the question if, in its business activity and management, a modern company turns a blind eye to its people's corporate position, initiative, enterprising spirit and creativity. Nevertheless, businesses are, after all, microeconomic agents of society, and the relationship between a business and its workers, and the interpersonal relations of the workforce are microcosms of society's interpersonal relations. Exchanges between people cannot happen in companies without a social atmosphere. Corporate culture can never be fostered or developed either, if society is still manipulated by the old culture, if anti-scientific, anti-democratic ideas that form the core of the old culture still hold sway, and if the practice of handling interpersonal relationships inside a firm in line with the interest principle is still being scorned.

In comparison with economic reform, it is a lot more difficult to transform the cultural sphere and allow the new culture to prevail. I am not saying economic reform can be free from obstacles and setbacks. Progress in establishing the new type of public ownership, for instance, is not smooth precisely because of a variety of impediments and difficulties in its way, not to mention the fact that the birth of this type of ownership calls for the repudiation of outdated values and the fostering of modern values, and involves revamping the relationships between company and government and between company and worker—in the latter relationship, workers are not nominal but actual owners. However, it is relatively easy to convince people of the fruitfulness of economic reform, as long as some progress has been made in developing the socialist commodity economy and fostering the new type of public ownership, and as long as economic efficiency has been improved and people's income raised. When such achievements become established facts, anyone wanting to gainsay the socialist commodity economy and the new public ownership will risk offending the masses of people who are beneficiaries of economic reform. By contrast, it is unrealistic to hope that a new culture—corporate culture included—will draw the same popular support. To build a new culture means to uproot outdated values, where the foothold of old culture is strong, and impediments come not only from society but also from people themselves. Although the positive results of corporate culture are apparent in a company's improved economic returns, people may still attribute them to economic reform rather than to cultural development. Furthermore, new concepts of employment, new principles for rewarding labor, new welfare standards, new interpersonal relationships, new consumer attitude, and new investment psychology are—because of their striking difference from old conventions—most likely to disconcert those deeply influenced by the old culture. Disharmony of this kind exists within and without any company. A clear message here is that cultural progress tends to encounter more obstacles than economic reform, and thus calls for more strenuous efforts.

Specifically, fostering corporate culture will promote economic growth in at least three ways.

Firstly, any firm that has come a long way in fostering its corporate culture invariably becomes a pacesetter for counterparts and gives them food for thought: How is that company able to cultivate an interpersonal relationship based on camaraderie among workers and mutual trust between workers and managers? How is that company capable of raising its economic efficiency so dramatically? Why can't we do what that company is capable of doing? Does the discrepancy between companies in fostering corporate culture reflect their discrepancy in institutional reform? While searching for answers to these questions, companies will set about exploring ways and means to speed up their own transformation. The pacesetter's diffusing impact will be spread to managers and workers. Once these people have seen the need for it, their institutional reform and their effort to build their own corporate culture will naturally pick up speed.

Secondly, the impact on the government of what a company has achieved in fostering corporate culture cannot be underestimated either. The government judges a firm's accomplishments in fostering corporate culture by searching for signs of improvements, such as whether corporate income and government revenue have increased simultaneously, whether its products are popular or not with the public, whether the strain on supply and demand has been eased, and whether the workers are happy with their jobs and motivated. If the government is impressed by what the firm has accomplished in fostering corporate culture, it will willingly summarize and disseminate the firm's experience. When and where necessary, the government will go on to study the causes behind that firm's accomplishments and, by comparing it with other firms, try to answer the question of why that firm can foster its corporate culture but the others cannot. Isn't it because that firm is successful in corporate institutional reform in the first place?

If the government does not want to stop at merely summarizing that firm's success and experience, it will set the firm up as a model to advance institutional reform in other firms. The importance of the progress made by that firm will not be lost on the government, but it is more important for the government to disseminate its experience and encourage more firms to follow suit in corporate institutional reform. Only thus can a few firms' success in cultural cultivation be used to drive the corporate institutional reform as a whole. This role of government cannot be replaced by individual firms.

Thirdly, from a cultural point of view, the impact of a company's success in fostering corporate culture is by no means limited to the company itself, its workers, and their families. In other words, the "corporate spirit" that embodies the corporate culture of a successful and influential company can shake old cultural traditions to the core. For instance, a company can send shockwaves through a system where egalitarianism still holds sway by boldly replacing absolute equality with a system whereby income is distributed according to effective work done or economic efficiency. Initially, those who believe in egalitarianism will be taken aback, but then they will gradually come to their senses. The established facts—such as the company's improved economic efficiency and workers' pay rises—will eventually change their attitude. By the same token, a company can also shock the public with a new interpersonal relationship that eschews traditional hierarchy and the established pecking order in the course of overhauling business management and fostering corporate culture. Such a shockwave will spill over the remnant influence of the hierarchical concept in society and further disseminate the new culture. The impact of the achievements in fostering corporate culture on social culture and values may be intangible, but should never be underestimated.

— A speech to Hong Kong Chinese Importers' and Exporters' Association
January 1, 1989

Notes

1. Narrowly speaking, the May Fourth Movement refers to the Chinese student demonstrations in Beijing on May 4, 1919, in protest against the government's yielding to the pressure of Western countries in signing the Treaty of Versailles. These demonstrations sparked national debates on why China was economically and politically weak and the role of traditional Chinese culture. The movement triggered the New Culture Movement of 1915–1921, in which intellectuals criticized Confucianism and advocated Western-style liberty, democracy and science. The May Fourth Movement Spirit is anti-tradition, anti-feudalism, and pro-new culture.
2. The Tian'anmen Incident of 1976 took place in Beijing on April 5, 1976, when thousands of citizens gathered at Tian'anmen Square to honor the memory of the late Premier Zhou Enlai, and voice their burning indignation against the Gang of Four.

· 8 ·

CULTURAL ECONOMICS

A Tentative Study

Peculiarities of Cultural and Art Products

Cultural economics is not concerned with the process by which cultural and art products are produced but with the economic issues pertinent to the production and reproduction of such products. Thus something has to be said about the attributes of cultural and art products. In terms of economics, they fall into two categories: those in the form of physical commodity, like audiovisual products, fine arts, books and periodicals; and those in the form of service, that is, labor services provided by cultural and art organizations, such as performance art. In comparison with material production, the production of cultural and art products is unique in that it is more individualistic and creative. Looking back, we may find nothing inappropriate with the way we categorize cultural and art products and interpret their peculiar attributes. However, if we probe the issue of cultural economics more deeply, we will know where the problems are.

If, for instance, a novelist or playwright comes up with a novel or a drama script, the first material form of his brainchild is a manuscript instead of a published book. This manuscript must be recognized and accepted by editors of a press or a journal before it turns into the book form and is sold on the market. Thus the material forms of cultural and art products we see on the market are a kind of "collective" product, that is, products brought into being "collectively" not only by authors but also by editors, printers, and the like. If we regard cultural and art products as commodities, and their supply-and-demand relationship as a market relationship, two "trading" processes will take place in reality: (1) trading between authors and publishers; (2) trading between publishers and buyers (readers and distributors included). The former trading process, in which cultural and art products are not ordinary commodities but special ones, is different not only from transactions over raw materials in the course of material production, but also from purchases of household handicrafts or farm and sideline produce by modern processing companies. This difference is one of the peculiarities of cultural and art products.

As to the labor services provided by cultural workers and artists, they are likewise a lot more complicated than those provided by ordinary workers or organizations in other fields. For example, if a cultural worker or artist renders his labor or service as directly as a street performer does to his audience, the issue becomes as simple as what happens between a labor supplier and a labor demander—a deal between the two parties concerned in any supply-and-demand relationship. Nevertheless, this is not the dominant way for cultural workers or artists to offer labor service today. As things are nowadays, an author sends his manuscript to a publisher first, and then the publisher publishes the book and sells it on the market. An actor, a singer, or a dancer has to be hired by a troupe or sign a performance contract with it, before the latter puts on singing or dancing performances and pays the performer a portion of the box revenue. In that sense, this form of "trading" takes place only once, not twice. This is to say, only when a performer is brought in front of his audience can his service be really delivered. When he is hired by, or signs a contract with, a troupe, he is yet to deliver his "commodity" (i.e., his service), while the troupe hires him or signs a contract with him based merely on his previous experiences or evaluation reports. However, even this manner of transaction in labor and service is different from usual, because the "buyer" of cultural and art products (or the labor and service in performing art) is not an individual but all the audience, and the supplier is in fact also a "collective," even though one main performer (i.e., singer or dancer) plays a pivotal role in it. This is another special attribute of cultural and art products.

Judging from the two "trading" processes or either one of them, cultural and art products are commodities of a special nature. But the issue does not stop then and there. Let us take another look from the social evaluation perspective of the use value of cultural and art products.

Social Assessment of the Use Value of Cultural and Art Products

Normative economics comes to mind at the mere mention of the social evaluation of a commodity's use value. We must accept that in material production, the use value of a commodity per se does not have an ethical attribute. Opium and morphine have some use value because, when used as commodities, they serve certain human needs—they may be either used in the pharmaceutical industry or bought by drug addicts. The production, sale, and use of commodities such as opium and morphine are strictly controlled because they are a potential bane to society and humanity. The same can be said of weapons and certain chemicals, such as cyanides: the problem here is not so much related to their use value but rather to the way people use them. To tighten up the control of the production and sales of weapons and certain chemicals is precisely to prevent them from being used for improper purposes.

As commodities, cultural and art products are at once similar to and different from the aforementioned material products. For instance, books, movies and audiovisual products about reactionary politics, pornography, murder or violence may have some buyers in the marketplace, but they are definitely poisonous to society.

Nevertheless, these cultural and art products are different in some ways from opium, morphine, weapons and certain chemicals. Opium and morphine are generally harmless when employed as raw materials for anesthetics—they become a public hazard only when abused by drug dealers and addicts. The same can be said of weapons and certain chemicals falling into the hands of criminals. It is thus apparent that the problem does not arise from these commodities' use value per se but from who uses them and what they are used for. As to books, movies and audiovisual products about reactionary politics, pornography, murder, or violence, however, the problem is not as simple as who uses them or what they are used for, because their use value is suspicious in itself—they should not have been produced in the first place. Once they are produced, their pernicious social impact becomes immediately evident. We can hardly believe they can be put to "normal use," unless they are used for special purposes by the public security bureau or the judiciary. But even in that case, there is no need for these departments to organize the production of these products. Therefore, there is no need, either, to subject this kind of cultural and art products to "restricted production and sales."

This is another peculiarity of cultural and art products based on a social assessment of their use value. Such products are different from material products in that, born of people's spiritual needs, they have normative connotations peculiarly of their own. These products are the brainchildren of those who created them. To become commodities, they also need the labor input of related people—editors and printers in the case of books, and producers in the case of audiovisual products—other than those who created them. They also need an intermediary "trading" process, so that they can be delivered to consumers. Their normative attribute is reflected in society's appraisal of their use value. The reason why the production and sale of books, movies, and audiovisual products about reactionary politics, pornography, murder, or violence should be banned under all circumstances is precisely based on their normative attribute, that is, public assessment of their use value. This is precisely why not only their publishers and editors but also their authors should be held accountable.

Economic Returns of Cultural and Art Commodity Production

Let me devote this section to another issue, the economic returns of the production of cultural and art commodities. Please note the concept I dwell on here is the "economic returns of the production of cultural and art commodities," not the "economic returns" of all cultural and art products and creative works. These are two different concepts. When someone composes a poem or creates a painting or sculpture but does not market it, does it have economic returns? I would say it has no economic returns at all. (It does have its social returns as far as it is appreciated or read widely. Such social returns can be big or small, positive or negative, depending on its merits or demerits, which I will deal with in another section.) That is why this section is focused on the economic returns of cultural and art products that have become commodities. Where there are commodities, there must be suppliers (sellers) and demanders (buyers), prices and markets. On the part of the supplier, it is about costs, net returns, and the motivation and conditions for reproduction. On the part of the buyer, it is about the degree to which such a commodity satisfies his purchase intention and its actual effects. On the part of an organizer or a manager of such economic activity, consideration should be given to a series of issues such as the adjustment of resource allocation caused by the production and sales of these commodities, the margin of growth in GNP and national income, and fluctuations in fiscal revenues and expenditures. None of these factors can be ignored when the economic returns of cultural and art commodity production is studied.

This field of study thus takes on a vast scope that is not limited to the costs and returns of commodity producers or the growth rate of GNP or national income. Simply put, the economic returns of cultural and art commodity production can be analyzed from at least six different angles.

1. Comparing the labor and earnings of authors of cultural and art products. Designed to observe an individual's economic returns by taking into account the peculiarities of cultural and art commodities, this is a rather laborious research topic. What an author—writer, painter, or actor—puts into a cultural or art commodity is undoubtedly complex labor, but its degree of complexity cannot be easily measured. Because of this, it is hard to set an objective benchmark for such complex labor, and even harder to quantify and gauge its quality and to pay for it properly.

2. The cost-benefit ratio of suppliers—publishing houses, performing troupes, audiovisual workshops, etc. Supposing the supplier lists his pay to an author in his wage cost, which also includes his pay to the staff members involved, this wage cost plus depreciation expenses and consumption of raw materials makes up the total cost. The supplier's economic returns are determined by the margin between the total cost and the returns, i.e., the sales income.

3. The economic returns of the buyers (users) of cultural and art commodities. This refers to such a commodity's end-consumers, not including intermediate buyers. The more a cultural or art commodity meets a buyer's need, the more satisfied he becomes, and the more he is convinced that the deal has brought considerable economic returns. It is true that people normally do not regard the degree of their satisfaction as a benchmark for economic returns. In fact, there is no criterion to measure such satisfaction. Nevertheless, so long as we regard economic returns as synonymous to "maximum gain at a certain expense" or "minimum expense in return for a certain amount of gain," we cannot deny that the "minimum cost principle" and the "maximum returns principle" are being followed by both suppliers and buyers in judging their economic returns. The reason why a buyer considers where to spend his money before he buys a commodity, chooses a seller when he is buying it, and appraises the results of the purchase after he has bought it, is because all these behaviors are directly related to his concern with economic returns.

4. From the perspective of government finance, the production and sales of a commodity or of a particular industry can change fiscal revenues and expenditures. The larger the growth in net fiscal revenues such production and sales can bring, the better its economic returns is believed to be; the smaller such growth is, the poorer its economic returns is believed to be. The same is true with the economic returns of cultural and art commodities.

5. Contribution to the economic growth rate is another benchmark for judging the economic returns of the production and sales of a single commodity or a certain industry. Economic growth rate is usually computed on the basis of the annual rate of changes in GNP or national income, a method that also applies to the economic returns of cultural and art commodity production. For example, the press and publication industry, whose output value is part of GNP, is in a check-and-balance relationship with other sectors of the national economy. We have reason to believe the press and publication industry has contributed a great deal to economic growth if its growing output value has led to considerable growth in the output value of related industries.

Of the above five perspectives, only the second, and the fourth are relatively easy for analysts, and the first, third and fifth are relatively difficult. Nevertheless, none of them is more difficult than the sixth perspective that follows.

6. From the perspective of resource allocation, the production of a commodity, or the commodity production of a certain industry, calls for an input of resources, while the results of production can change the aggregate quantum and structure of resources. This is true with both material production and the production of cultural and art commodities. Supposing the aggregate quantum of resources is limited and the resource allocation pattern fixed, adjustment can be made only through incremental changes in resources. Thus society must answer the following question when appraising economic return: Is the production of a commodity or the commodity production of an industry improving or deteriorating resource allocation? Improvement and deterioration are benchmarks by which to judge whether economic returns is positive or negative. The degree of improvement or deterioration is the benchmark for determining the degree of positive or negative returns. Such a conclusion is derived from theoretical analysis.

The snag lies apparently in evaluating the current pattern of resource allocation and in measuring the degree of changes in resource allocation. People may suggest that the disparity between aggregate demand and supply—or, to probe more deeply, the extent of shortage or overstock of some key commodities—could be employed as the criterion for appraising the pattern of resource allocation and the degree of changes in it. However, this criterion can be applied only to short-term economic returns, but far from enough for long-term returns. That is to say, the allocation of a certain resource may not be problematic in the short run, but may cause a lot of problems in the long run. Some of the problems are latent or obscure and seemingly harmless to the economy for the time being. But if the problems remain unsolved, they will emerge and become so acute as to hurt the economy sometime in the future. Only by perceiving the economic returns of the production of a commodity or the commodity production of a certain industry in this light, can we gain a relatively comprehensive understanding of the concept "economic returns." Despite the aforementioned snag, resource allocation can never be factored out when studying the economic returns of the production of either physical materials or cultural and art commodities.

When we gradually shift our study to resource allocation, especially to its long-term economic returns, we are bound to come across the most difficult issue, that is, how to measure social returns. This issue is particularly critical to cultural and art commodities. We have already touched upon this topic in our previous discussion about the social appraisal of the use value of cultural and art products.

Social Returns of Cultural and Art Commodity Production

In a certain sense, the long-term economic returns of the production of a commodity or the commodity production of an industry are consistent with its social returns. But social returns usually entail a broader meaning than economic returns, and can be directly linked with socioeconomic development goals. If the production of a commodity or the commodity production of an industry is conducive to socioeconomic development goals, we can presume that its social returns are high; if it is detrimental to socioeconomic development goals, we can presume that it has no social returns at all. Therefore, when analyzing the social returns of commodity production, we have to clarify what are the socioeconomic development goals and what benchmark should be employed to judge if such production is a boon or a bane to such goals.

Socioeconomic development goals are multiple, rather than single. For instance, we should raise people's income, but at the same time, we must avoid widening the income gap; we should meet people's growing demand for a better material life, but their demand for a better spiritual life should also be taken care of; and we should improve both the social environment and the natural environment at the same time. Multiple socioeconomic development goals indicate that it is not enough to develop material production alone—the production of cultural and art commodities also matters. When we talk about the social returns of cultural and art commodity production, we can never overlook the role such production should and can play in attaining multiple socioeconomic development goals.

Every socioeconomic development goal can be divided into sub goals to be attained in different stages. The goal of meeting people's spiritual need, for example, should comprise a variety of specific goals for different periods. When evaluating the social returns of the production of a certain art product in a certain stage, we may do it in comparison with the degree of people's satisfaction with that product in meeting their demand for spiritual life during that stage. Only thus can we see if its social returns are positive or negative and determine the margin of changes in such positive or negative social returns.

In the case of a socioeconomic development goal for bettering the quality of people's lives, after that goal has been divided into sub goals for different stages, we can also compare the social returns of a given cultural and art commodity with the projected sub goal for a better life quality in a specific stage. I think we can be sure about the applicability of this approach to assessing the social returns of the production of such commodities. Of course many details in this approach need to be hammered out through the concerted efforts of those interested in cultural economics.

In observing the social returns of cultural and art commodity production, the most complex issue is perhaps how to evaluate its role in enhancing people's ideological awareness or in corrupting their minds. Theoretically speaking, it is the same as the aforementioned social appraisal of the use value of cultural and art products. However, insofar as social returns are concerned, such a role needs to be evaluated. Nobody can deny that cultural and art commodities are playing such a role, but it is difficult to measure it. The difficulty lies in particular in the fact that people's minds can be nourished or corrupted by a host of factors—the production, marketing and utilization of these products are just a few of them. In evaluating the social returns of cultural and art products, we have yet to find a way to strip these products from the other factors that are playing the same role for an exclusive study. It is, indeed, another hard nut to crack awaiting future researchers.

— *Economics & Culture*, issue No. 4, 1990

· 9 ·

ENVIRONMENTAL PROTECTION AND COMPENSATION TO VICTIMS OF ENVIRONMENTAL DAMAGE

Two Kinds of Victims

Compensating victims is a major theoretical and policy issue in the economics of environmental protection. It is, therefore, necessary to clarify the definition of "victims" before looking into the issue. As a matter of fact, victims fall into two categories: (1) those victimized in the course of environmental damage; and (2) those victimized in the course of environmental treatment. There are both direct and indirect victims in each category.

Direct victims of environmental damage are individuals who lose health, property and the means to earn a living, make less money, whose lives are disturbed, or whose family relationships are upset because of the damage done to their living environment. They also include businesses that suffer losses in output, product quality, revenue and property due to environmental damage.

Indirect victims of environmental damage comprise mainly those individuals and businesses whose economic interests have been impaired by the financial and other losses incurred by the aforementioned direct victims—individuals or businesses—with whom they maintain close economic ties.

Direct victims of environmental treatment include businesses that are forced to close down, reduce output or relocate, and individuals working in such businesses. These businesses and individuals make less money as a result.

Such direct victims also include families that are relocated due to the needs of environmental treatment—their property may be impaired, their income may drop, and their daily lives may become disturbed or disorganized.

Indirect victims of environmental treatment comprise mainly those individuals and businesses who suffer economic losses due to their close economic ties with the direct victims (individuals or businesses) of environmental treatment who make less money because of it.

People and businesses become direct or indirect victims for different reasons.

They are victimized directly or indirectly because of the behavior of those causing environmental damage or those involved in environmental protection. The damage done to them differs in degree as well. Victims of environmental damage bear both economic and physical losses, and in extreme cases, their lives may be at risk. Victims of environmental treatment suffer mainly from losses in income or assets, and their lives may be disarrayed by a changed living environment, although few of them are physically impaired or have their lives threatened.

Victims feel differently about their miseries, too. Victims of environmental treatment may demand compensation because they have either felt or foreseen its adverse impact on their income. Victims of environmental damage may have found out either after damage was done to them or after they were told about it. Some of them may have been oblivious to such damage for a considerable length of time and thus failed to raise compensation demands.

To distinguish the two categories of victims helps research into the issue of compensating victims of environmental protection in the following ways:

Firstly, it helps clarify the nature of such compensation and the rationale behind it. Individuals and businesses must be compensated properly for the damage done to them either in environmental damage or in environmental treatment. However, the nature of compensation and the rationale behind it may differ with the causes of the damage done. The harm done to victims of environmental damage is caused by perpetrators, and, theoretically speaking, should be compensated by the same perpetrators—they may pay victims themselves or through the government. Although the damage done to victims of environmental treatment should be blamed ultimately on the party that has caused it in the first place, the victims, out of personal feelings, or by tracing such damage to its immediate cause, tend to blame the party—government agencies, businesses, social organizations or individuals—that undertakes to repair such damage through environmental treatment, and demand compensation from that party. Double compensation, which occurs when the party treating the damage demands compensation from someone who caused the damage, is out of the question if the environmental damage was done by the same party that treats it; otherwise, double compensation becomes the issue. Theoretically speaking, there are ample reasons to demand twofold compensation. However, whether or not such compensation can occur in reality depends on the circumstances.

Secondly, the distinction helps determine the way compensation is made. Once direct and indirect victims of either environmental damage or treatment are distinguished, it is easy to choose a proper way to compensate them. Those victimized in the course of environmental damage should be compensated by the responsible party, with compensation money dispensed directly and in full. Where double compensation is not considered, victims of environmental treatment should be compensated directly, indirectly or in both ways by the party responsible for the treatment. Such compensation may be paid entirely, partially or in both ways in the light of the actual situation.

Thirdly, it helps bring the role of the government into play in compensation, a role that is associated with the government's commitment to protecting the people's interests and the environment. That is to say, whether the damage is attributed to environmental destruction or environmental treatment, the government is duty-bound to do its level best to compensate victims. However, it should be noted that even though governmental decision-making mistakes may cause environmental damage, the real perpetrators are mostly businesses or residents, who are naturally accountable for compensation. In that case, the government's major task is to see to it that victims are properly compensated by the perpetrators.

The situation with environmental treatment is somewhat different. The government may either be the decision-maker for environmental treatment or its executor. Thus it may become the party either to directly compensate victims or to demand recompensation from those who caused the damage in the first place. If the party engaged in environmental treatment is not the government but businesses, social organizations or individuals, the government may handle compensation in one of three ways: (1) The government may guarantee that victims are duly compensated by the party engaged in environmental treatment. (2) When the party engaged in environmental treatment demands recompensation from the perpetrator of the environmental damage being treated, the government will make sure such a demand is met fully or partially according to the circumstances. (3) When the party responsible for environmental treatment can compensate victims only partially, and thereby fails to meet the victims' demand, the government will decide, according to the circumstances, whether the victims' demand should be met, and to what degree.

Fourthly, the distinction helps probe further into the issue of compensation in environmental protection. As is to be illustrated in a later section in this study, many difficult issues concerning compensation for victims of environmental protection remain unsolved in theory and in government policy. To address these problems, the two categories of victims should be distinguished in the first place.

Principles and Approaches for Compensating Victims of Environmental Damage

As mentioned in the foregoing, environmental damage is done by those held responsible for it, and should therefore be compensated for by them. But this is true merely in theory. In reality, the situation is a lot more complex.

First of all, who should be held responsible for environmental damage can be a controversial decision. Such a decision can only be made according to the actual situation. Take, for example, the waste water discharged by a paper mill situated in the upper reaches of a river which impairs the interests of dwellers in the lower reaches. In this case, it is easy to pinpoint the paper mill as the culprit and ask it to pay dwellers for the damages done. If in the upper reaches of the river there are several factories whose waste water discharges have hurt the townspeople living in the lower reaches, not only must the total responsibility for environmental damage be clarified, but the responsibility to be shared by all those factories should also be decided according to the amount of waste water each factory has discharged, thereby making it possible to address the compensation problem properly.

Nevertheless, we may also find ourselves dealing with the following scenario, in which acid rain has impaired the interests of the businesses and individuals of a certain place. Can we ascertain who caused such environmental damage? If the answer is yes, can we settle the amount of compensation money to be paid by the perpetrator? The same dilemma may occur again in another scenario, in which long years of soil erosion and vegetation destruction have drastically changed a region's climate, and resulted in alternating drought and flood that eventually hurt the interests of local residents. In this case, it is also difficult to identify the perpetrator and quantify the money to be paid as compensation. Clearly, only when both the responsibility of the perpetrator and the losses inflicted on the victims are clarified can the aforementioned compensation principle be followed. Otherwise, another way must be found to compensate the victims.

Then, in our study of compensating victims of environmental damage, we may also be faced with the complicated task of how to clarify the degree of damage and quantify the losses inflicted. In the previous section I dwelt on how to differentiate between direct and indirect victims. It should be noted, however, the economic losses inflicted on direct victims of environmental damage are not necessarily higher than the losses of those victimized indirectly by such damage. If, in that case, the perpetrator of environmental damage can only compensate direct victims, it raises the highly controversial question: should the indirect victims be compensated for their losses too? If the answer is yes, who is to compensate them?

Next, when it comes to victims of environmental damage, only businesses and individuals are counted as victims that deserve compensation.

Looking deeper into the issue, however, it is not hard to see that the state or local community is also a victim of such damage. This is because when an environment is destroyed, it means a loss in national assets and in the local community's stock of resources. This means those responsible for environmental damage, once verified, should compensate two groups of victims: (1) businesses and individuals whose interests are directly impaired; and (2) the government or the local community.

Based on the above analysis, and by taking into account the complex situation in reality, we propose four principles for compensating victims of environmental damage:

1. Those responsible for environmental damage should, once their responsibility is settled, compensate the direct victims appropriately; such compensation should be delivered directly and in full to make up for the victims' losses.
2. Apart from compensating the direct victims, those responsible for environmental damage should, once their responsibility is fixed, also compensate the state or the local community for the losses they have caused to national assets and to the local community's stock of resources.

3. If, after damage is done to the environment, for one reason or another the responsibility for it cannot be allotted to the businesses or individuals that have perpetrated it, and, as a result, if direct victims of such damage cannot be compensated directly, the direct victims may be handled with social compensation, an approach that will be dwelt upon a few paragraphs later.
4. If indirect victims of environmental damage fail to receive the compensation that they deserve after direct victims have been compensated by the perpetrator, the social compensation approach should also be employed.

After laying down these principles for compensating victims of environmental damage, we need to define the approaches to such compensation. If businesses and individuals are direct victims, they may be compensated in one of two ways: (1) they may be directly compensated by those responsible for the environmental damage; or (2) those responsible for the environmental damage may be asked to deliver compensation money to the government and the government then pays the direct victims. Furthermore, compensation for the government or the local community shall be paid in money by those held responsible for the damage done. If perpetrators of environmental damage who choose to compensate victims through the government are also obliged to compensate the government, the government, upon receiving all the compensation money, shall divide the money into two according to a certain ratio, retain one portion, and dispense the other portion among direct victims.

Now let us consider social compensation. As a kind of indirect compensation, it is administered to victims of environmental damage with funds raised from all walks of life. Social compensation can be dispensed in the following ways: (1) preferential loans that help victims boost production and thereby raise their income, or that help stricken areas restore and develop local economy so as to increase their per capita income; (2) employment guidance and assistance to victims or residents of stricken areas; and (3) technical assistance to victims or stricken areas. In other words, social compensation as an indirect way of atonement is not given directly to victims, but is delivered in such forms as loans, employment guidance and assistance and technical assistance to enable victims to earn more and thus make up for their losses incurred in the course of environmental damage.

The organization in charge of social compensation raises the money needed from all quarters, including fees paid by firms, donations from businesses, individuals and nongovernmental organizations, as well as government funding. The scope and amount of such compensation are decided in light of the organization's financial ability and compensation plans. Given that it is theoretically viable to compensate all victims of environmental damage, this form of social compensation is a wise choice. It goes without saying that many details for such compensation need to be further discussed and clarified.

Principles and Approaches for Compensating Victims of Environmental Treatment

The term "environmental treatment" in this study refers to the treatment of an environment that has been damaged to various degrees, for the purpose of mitigating the damage done or restoring the environment in the best possible way. This kind of environmental treatment calls for certain economic and technical measures, and will have a certain impact on the industrial, technological, employment and consumption structures in the areas concerned. The losses in income or other fields inflicted by environmental treatment on businesses or individuals are contingent upon adjustments made in the course of environmental treatment to local industrial, technological, employment and consumption structures. Therefore, our study of compensation to victims of environmental treatment cannot but be linked with these readjustments.

As pointed out in the previous section, compensation to victims should be paid by the party responsible for environmental treatment. This, however, is just the starting point of such compensation. There are more complicated issues to be addressed as well. It is, therefore, necessary to proceed from the starting point to look further into the whole picture.

Firstly, the state or local community should be regarded as the beneficiary of environmental treatment. If the losses incurred in the course of environmental damage to national assets and to a local community's stock of resources are the reason why the state or local society should be compensated by those held accountable for such damage, in the course of treating such damage the state may benefit from increases or mitigated losses in national assets, and the local community may benefit from increases or mitigated losses in its resources. Therefore, the government should pay a proper portion of compensation money to victims whether or not it is the party engaged in the environmental treatment.

Secondly, in the course of environmental treatment, on the one hand, some firms and individuals may suffer an income loss while others may enjoy an income rise through industrial, technological, employment and consumption restructuring—the former are victims of environmental treatment, and the latter beneficiaries of it. On the other hand, the income of some businesses and individuals will grow in a repaired or treated environment; thus they become beneficiaries of environmental treatment even without restructuring local industry, technology, employment, and consumption. The businesses and individuals that are beneficiaries of environmental treatment are duty-bound to pay a proper part of the compensation money to victims of environmental treatment.

Thirdly, as illustrated above, the environment needs treatment because it has been damaged. Perpetrators of this damage have the obligation to pay a certain amount of compensation money for a second time, this time to those victimized in the course of repairing the environmental damage. Such is the recompensation demanded of the perpetrators of environmental damage by the party engaged in environment treatment. Obviously, such recompensation can be realized only after the perpetrators of environmental damage are verified.

Lastly, it is necessary to take a close look at institutions that may engage in this kind of remedial environmental treatment, such as government institutions, businesses, and nongovernmental organizations. The environmental treatment conducted by government institutions is generally in the national or public interest through such forms as homeland management and treatment, natural resource preservation, economic development, and living standard betterment in a certain area. For this reason, these institutions usually regard compensating victims of environmental treatment as part of the cost. For instance, when the government evacuates families from an area for environmental treatment purposes, it routinely pays a relocation grant to compensate these families. Such a grant naturally becomes part of the environmental treatment cost. The environmental treatment conducted by a nongovernmental organization is often relevant to its public welfare goals. Thus the amount of money it pays fully or partially to compensate those victimized in the course of environmental treatment is in keeping with its welfare goals in the same way as its other environmental protection expenses.

The environmental treatment carried out by businesses is somewhat complicated by two possibilities. Firstly, a business sets about improving the environment of a certain place in order to expand production or upgrade technology; secondly, some businesses have caused certain damage to the environment of a certain place, and, because they are held responsible for such damage, they must treat it in compliance with law or government ordinance.

A business may also have both the responsibility for repairing the environment of a place and the need to expand production and upgrade technology. There is a difference between these two possibilities no matter what the causes. In the latter possibility, no recompensation is needed in the course of environmental treatment; in the former possibility, recompensation is a necessity. It is not impossible for that demand to be met as long as the responsibility for the environmental damage done previously can be clarified; otherwise, the business must take it upon itself to compensate victims of environmental treatment.

Moreover, compensation to be made to victims of environmental treatment is not handled the same way as that to victims of environmental damage. A party responsible for environmental treatment can only compensate direct victims—businesses and individuals that have lost part of their income because of environmental treatment. The funding for environmental treatment—compensation money included—is so limited that indirect victims, who tend to be large in number and wide in scope, must be omitted from the compensation list. This is because, unlike environmental damage, environmental treatment itself entails goals for improving environmental quality, restoring the economy of the area concerned and enabling it to grow. That is to say, while direct victims are compensated to a certain extent, indirect victims may benefit from local economic rehabilitation and growth resulting from environmental treatment, and increase their income even though they are not compensated directly by the party engaged in environmental treatment. It can be said that the compensation for indirect victims of environmental treatment is subsumed in the use and result of the environmental treatment funding.

Based on these observations, the principles for compensating victims of environmental treatment may be spelled out as follows:

1. The organization engaged in environmental treatment shall, in the course of it, compensate direct victims appropriately for their losses. Because environmental treatment can increase national assets or mitigate losses, and boost the local community's stock of resources or

reduce its losses, the government should bear part of the compensation cost.

2. As environmental treatment is in itself a process of restoring and developing the economy of a given area, its indirect victims will benefit from it in due course. Therefore, they may not be compensated where the funding for environmental treatment—compensation money included—is limited and the compensation scope is too wide.
3. Compensation occurring in the course of environmental treatment is part of the cost, and the compensation money is raised in different ways, including the money paid by the government and other beneficiaries, and the money paid by the verified perpetrators of the environmental damage being treated. This kind of compensation money will be paid only to direct victims of environmental treatment.

Now that the principles are laid down, what should be discussed next is the way compensation money is to be paid. Compensation to victims of environmental treatment can be paid directly, indirectly or in both ways. It can also be paid in full or partially. Of course, such compensation is meant for direct victims. Then, to be specific, how to go about direct and indirect compensation? Generally speaking, direct compensation is designed to make up for residents' property and income losses incurred in the course of resettlement, and may be paid by the government or the party engaged in environmental treatment. The other losses caused to direct victims of environmental treatment may be indirectly made up for. If workers will lose their income because their factories have to stop production or are shut down in the course of environmental treatment, it is better to compensate them indirectly—such as by shifting the factories to other fields of production or the workers to other jobs—than directly, such as by granting a living allowance to them. The workers of a factory that has stopped production or closed down may also get paid by insurance so that their living standards will not drop too much, but this form of help belongs under social insurance and therefore has nothing to do with compensation from environmental treatment. As to the term "partial compensation," it means that the losses incurred by victims of environmental treatment may be partially compensated for—they can be fully compensated for only when there is enough money to cover it. The reason for it is the same: environmental treatment itself is a course of restoring and developing the economy of the area involved, which is an intangible form of compensation for victims.

A Closer Observation of Certain Issues

Ultimate Bearers of Direct Compensation Costs

Those held accountable for environmental damage may be producers or consumers. If consumers are liable for such damage, they have no way of shifting their direct compensation responsibility to any other people—in other words, they are the ultimate bearers of direct compensation costs. Whether or not producers can shift such payment to others is determined by the nature of their products, market conditions, and their own financial situation. If the supply of their products outstrips the demand, or supply and demand are balanced while their products are in complete market competition and they must bear the responsibility for their own gains and losses, the producers must eventually pay direct compensation whether such payment is listed as production cost or not—they pay for it at the expense of their profit. That is to say, they cannot but be obliged to swallow the bitter pill of environmental damage.

In reality, however, the producers that are supposed to pay for direct compensation are mainly large and medium-sized state businesses that do not take responsibility for their gains and losses. Their profits inevitably shrink once direct compensation payments are listed as their production costs, even if their products are in complete market competition, their supply outstrips demand, or their supply and demand are in balance. However, such losses are not borne by these producers, but by the state. The absurdity here is that businesses are the culprits of environmental damage, but it is the government that foots the bill.

If a product is in short supply and the market competition for it is incomplete, and if there is no rigidity in its price, the direct compensation to be delivered by its producer, once listed as a production cost, is incorporated into the product's price. Buyers of such a product end up as the ultimate bearers of the direct compensation cost. If the buyers are consumers, they cannot shift such a burden to others; if the producer is the buyer of his own product, the issue returns to such premises as whether the supply of his product is in excess of demand or in balance with it, whether market competition for it is complete or not, and whether the producer is responsible for his gains and losses. At the end of the day, the likelihood is that consumers and the state will find themselves paying for such direct compensation.

As illustrated above, to deepen corporate reform and establish a corporate system that holds businesses accountable for their gains and losses is a must if producers held liable for environmental damage are to be made to compensate. It is also imperative to improve the market and bridge the gap between supply and demand. If we fail in this, it will be impossible to prevent consumers and the state from unwarrantedly becoming the ultimate payers of direct compensation.

Who, then, are the legitimate ultimate cost bearers of direct compensation to victims of environmental treatment? The answer is the government and those engaged in environmental treatment. Where recompensation is not an issue, the direct compensation paid by the government or nongovernmental organizations is listed as part of the treatment cost in expenditure—it cannot be shifted to consumers because it is not part of production costs. However, the situation is complicated when it comes to businesses engaged in environmental treatment. If a business improves the environment in order to expand production or upgrade technology, it tends to lump direct compensation payment with its environmental treatment cost as part of its production expansion investment. This investment is to be recouped over a length of time determined by its economic efficiency. But no matter how long the recouping period, the direct compensation payment will be eventually factored into the business's production cost. The situation thus returns to what has been discussed previously, where such cost is eventually borne by the state and the consumer if the business is not liable for its gains and losses, if its product is in short supply and market competition is incomplete, and if there is no price rigidity. If the business is liable for environmental damage and if its environmental treatment is designed to remedy such damage, in the natural course of events its compensation payment becomes part of its total environmental treatment cost. As a matter of fact, however, the business will seek to shift this payment, whenever possible, to the state and the consumer, a possibility that justifies the necessity to deepen corporate reform, straighten out the market and mitigate supply shortfalls.

Judging Full and Partial Compensation

The term "partial compensation" refers to the kind of compensation that falls short of making good the losses inflicted on victims of environmental damage or treatment. It is relevant by and large to the losses suffered by direct victims. Because the indirect victims of either environment damage or treatment are always scattered over a large area, their number and their losses cannot be quantified easily, whereas the amount of money available is too limited to meet their demand for "full compensation," even with the money raised by the local community counted in. Therefore, the compensation to indirect victims, if delivered, is considered partial.

Although direct victims, by contrast, may be compensated directly or indirectly, it should be noted that it is no easier to ascertain if an indirect compensation to direct victims is full or not. Indirect compensation is marked by two characteristics. For one thing, victims have to wait for a certain time to be convinced that they have been compensated; for another, its effect hinges on the work efficiency of those who make such payment and the approach they take—the same amount of indirect compensation payment may have different effects on different beneficiaries. These two characteristics indicate that whether indirect compensation is paid fully or partially is not determined merely by its amount.

This is exactly why I have focused my study of partial compensation on direct compensation to direct victims of environmental damage or treatment. Whether a direct compensation payment is full or partial can be calculated by comparing the amount of property and income losses inflicted on a direct victim with the amount of compensation money he receives from the perpetrator of environmental damage or the party engaged in environmental treatment. Compensation is deemed full if the two amounts match, and deemed inadequate or partial if the victim is underpaid for his losses. In this regard, it is easier to figure out the property loss than the income loss. Property loss can be pinpointed if its value is properly estimated, whereas income loss is somewhat complicated. Apart from wages and other fixed income, earnings from sales, rents and other activities should also be included; when all these figures are computed, the anticipated changes in output and price, depreciation rate benchmark, and the number of years involved should also be factored into the depreciation category. Because it is not uncommon for income losses to be over- or underestimated, compensation may be inadequate where payment cannot cover the total losses, or overgenerous where payment outstrips the total value of losses. Only with appropriate methods can such errors be avoided when evaluating a victim's property and income losses.

Because it takes time for indirect compensation to take effect, its benefit seems to be delivered to victims in a constant stream. Thus indirect compensation may also be regarded as something paid in installments. Direct compensation is different in that it is paid in a lump. If that lump sum payment is commensurate with the victim's property and income losses, it is full and the case is closed. If that lump sum is partial, the direct compensation in question can become full with follow-up installments of payment. Given that full compensation is the guideline for dealing with direct victims of environmental damage, payment in installments is feasible where the starting payment is not enough to cover a victim's losses.

Following the same guideline, compensation to direct victims of environmental treatment can be paid directly or indirectly, in full or partially. Full compensation may also be paid in installments.

Compensation for Irreparable Losses

That is covered by the full and partial compensations that have just been discussed is victims' property and income losses. However, victims' losses are often not limited to property and income. For instance, environmental damage may also impair its victims' health and blight their lives, and environmental treatment may also destroy its victims' lives and jobs. Full compensation payment can only make up for their property and income losses, leaving their other losses unaddressed.

The losses inflicted on victims can also be classified as reparable or irreparable ones. Generally speaking, property and income losses can be made good through full compensation. The damage done to victims' lives and health may or may not be compensable. This is because of the incomparability of people's grievances in daily life even if the degree of damage done to their health can be defined. Victims vary in lifestyle. Some prefer the idyllic country life of farming to dwelling in an urban apartment building; some like living with family members and dislike separation from their children. Even if they have been compensated in some ways for the changes of lifestyle caused by environmental damage or treatment, they may still see such changes as an irreparable loss. People's impaired health can be cured or incurable, but no amount of compensation is enough to make up for badly impaired health or lost life.

The situation becomes complicated once the compensation issue involves losses other than those in property and income. To start with, victims whose health has been impaired by environmental damage have every reason to deserve the same direct full compensation payment that they receive for their property and income losses. But this poses two questions. First, what kind of compensation for impaired health can qualify as being full? The answer remains elusive to this day. For the time being, we can only make do by referring to the way work-related injuries and deaths and traffic accidents are handled. Precisely because of the irreparable nature of serious damage to people's health, we have to enhance our awareness of environmental protection in the first place. Second, how should victims be compensated for their impaired health when and where the perpetrator of environmental damage is yet to be identified? Impaired health may be compensated for through the social compensation fund. But can such welfare fund be used as direct compensation in such cases? In other words, apart from indirectly compensating victims for their property and income losses in the form of credit and assistance in employment and technology, can the social compensation fund also incorporate the money raised from various quarters as direct compensation to pay victims for their impaired health? This is probably a feasible solution, provided such social compensation fund can reach a considerable financial scale and have secured steady fund-raising sources.

The mental disorder and discomfort caused to residents by lifestyle changes resulting from environmental damage or treatment can hardly be converted into economic losses. Therefore, this kind of loss cannot be covered with the full or partial compensation payments for property and income losses, nor is there a legitimate reason for these residents to demand the same full compensation as for impaired health. Changed lifestyle, indeed, is a hard nut to crack in this regard. Pending an effective solution, we may just leave the issue aside for the time being under the supposition that after being fully compensated for their property and income losses, residents will be gradually acclimatized to their changed living environment.

Furthermore, while racking our brains over how to compensate for irreparable losses, we should lose no time in finding ways and means to compensate for the irreparable losses inflicted on the state or society by the damage done to natural resources or the ecological environment. Let me call attention to three issues:

Issue One, if liability for environmental damage remains unidentified, there is no way for the state or society to be compensated for this kind of loss.

This is a bitter pill, indeed, for the state or society to swallow. The entire population will have to bear such losses ultimately.

Issue Two, even if liability for environmental damage has been defined and the perpetrator has compensated, the amount of money the government receives will most likely be a pittance in comparison with the actual damage done to resources and the environment. Thus the losses, too, will eventually be borne by the entire population.

Issue Three, even if the compensation paid by the perpetrator to the government can offset the estimated amount of losses inflicted by environmental damage, it is still not enough to make up for all the losses incurred by the state or society, because some of the damaged resources are not renewable and part of the damaged eco-environment can never be restored. Such losses will ultimately be borne by the entire population as well.

My observation of these issues drives home, from another angle, the need to tighten up environmental protection.

Compensation for Environmental Damage Resulting From Wrong Government Policy Decisions

Businesses and individuals have been the subjects of my analysis so far in this study when it comes to defining the liability for environmental damage. No mention has been made of the environmental damage resulting from wrong government policy decisions and the resultant issue of compensation to victims. As a matter of fact, there is no lack of cases in which faulty government policy decisions are to blame for environmental damage.

That may happen in two scenarios.

In the first scenario, economic growth goals are on the top of government agenda while environmental protection fails to get equal attention. The result is that environmental damage occurs and inflicts losses on its victims in the course of economic growth.

In the second scenario, the government, having seen the need to restore the destroyed environment of a certain region, makes a wrong policy decision, such as adopting unworkable treatment approaches and attending to one thing to the neglect of another. Thus new damage is done in the course of treating the damage, and local people and businesses are victimized as a result.

Let me dwell on the second scenario first, in which the government makes a decision on environmental treatment and goes on to carry it out. If it takes a policy misstep whose dire consequence becomes swiftly apparent, it may use its fund for environmental treatment—compensation payments included—to pay for the losses inflicted on victims. But if it takes a long time for the consequence to be discovered and for victims to become aware of the damage done, the fund will no longer be available by then to pay for the losses.

Now, about the first scenario, which may occur in the process of economic growth, where a faulty policy decision arises from the government's obsession with economic growth and neglect of environmental protection. The losses inflicted by this policy misstep may or may not be compensated for in the course of economic growth. Even if victims are compensated to a certain extent, such compensation tends to be belated and indirect, and limited to property or income losses. Whether such compensation is full or not is determined by the margin of economic growth and by how long it takes to pay it. In addition, this kind of belated, indirect compensation for property or income losses is often delivered to collectives rather than individuals. That is to say, the benefits—in the form of, say, income increase—of economic growth are there for all to share, but the fact that people's losses through environmental damage are different in degree can result in a discrepancy in income increase from economic growth. Those getting the highest increase in income are not necessarily the same people whose losses are the heaviest, while those suffered the most may end up getting the lowest pay rise. Therefore, collective compensation in the course of economic growth is limited to a point where it can only address part of the compensation problem arising from environmental damage caused by government errors. Furthermore, if environmental damage has hurt people's health, compensation cannot be delivered collectively.

Likewise, the state and society should be compensated for losses resulting from destruction of resources and the environment. Government decision-making mistakes committed in either economic growth or environmental treatment can inflict losses on national assets and local community's stock of resources. These kinds of losses—some of which are irreparable—can be borne only by the state or society, that is, by the entire population.

Wrong government policy decisions on environmental protection, and the consequent damage and compensation merit public concern not only because such damage often covers a vast area and its consequences tend to be grave and multitudinous, but also because it takes more time and effort to correct such mistakes. However, because the government is often not the actual perpetrator of environmental damage and the actual bearer of the compensation payment for it, the serious nature of the government's decision-making mistakes tends to elude public attention. This is why it is essential to step up the effort to put government decision making on economic growth and environmental protection on a democratic and scientific footing, and to attach equal importance to both economic growth and environmental protection goals.

— *Social Sciences in China*, issue No. 4, 1990

· 10 ·

COORDINATING ECONOMY AND ENVIRONMENT IN LESS DEVELOPED REGIONS

An old argument claims that the poorer a place is, the less mindful the locals are of the ecosystem, the more indiscriminate they are in land reclamation, logging, and mining, while having less money to treat the damaged environment and thus sinking deeper into poverty. Another oft-heard opinion puts it this way: When a place is poor, water, soil and air pollution are rare; but when the local economy is booming and the local standard of living is improving, the local rivers, soil and air are polluted too. Which argument holds water? Or are both of them reasonable? If both hold water, does it mean that the cause of environmental protection is helpless whether a place is rich or poor, or that it can be helped only when the place is neither poor nor rich?

In fact, both environmental economics and development economics are confronted with the same baffling paradox concerning the economic operational mechanisms for environmental preservation and for the development of less developed regions. Only by beginning our study from these mechanisms can these questions be answered.

Economic Operational Mechanisms Associated With Environmental Preservation and Developing Less Developed Regions

Society, whatever its type, invariably relies on an inherent impetus and employs the resources at hand to keep the economy going in the direction of certain goals. Defying all sorts of interference, it strives to reach these goals or approach them as closely as it can. The "economic operational mechanisms" is a general term for all the relationships society employs to go through this process. These relationships are inherent in society, rather than emanating from outside. Generally speaking, there are four operational mechanisms at work in the course of socioeconomic development.

1. Goals mechanism. How do goals and the system of goals come about? How are these goals aligned in such a system? The issues that should be studied pertinent to economic development are: What are the goals of development? What are the starting point and basis for these goals? Do the environment and ecological equilibrium belong in the goals system; and if yes, what are their positions in it?

2. Impetus mechanism. What are the sources of impetus? How is impetus produced? In what ways can impetus be obtained? If the ecosystem and ecological equilibrium are listed in the goals system, how can people be motivated to take the environment and ecological equilibrium seriously in the course of pursuing development and acquiring the impetus to do so? In other words, what is to be done to motivate people to be concerned with the environment and ecological equilibrium? How can the impetus for this motivation be made to last?

3. Resource allocation mechanism. What principle is to be followed in allocating resources? In what way should resources be allocated? How do self-restraints and restraints for and between resource allocation principals come about? How do these two kinds of restraints work? How are resources allocated in the course of economic growth or environmental protection in the context of the relationship between the two? What conflicts will occur between economic growth and environmental protection in the course of resource allocation? What is to be done to reconcile such conflicts? How should resource-allocating principles restrain themselves and each other in economic growth and environmental protection?

4. Interference elimination mechanism. How should we identify interference in the course of economic operation? How might we eliminate such

interference? If economic growth and environmental protection are mutually interfering, how can such interference be identified? How can we estimate the seriousness of such interference? Can it be disposed of spontaneously in the course of economic growth? What is to be done if economic growth itself cannot overcome such interference?

Each mechanism has its distinct attributes. The topic of this study is the socialist economy's operational mechanisms in relation to environmental protection and the development of less developed regions, but the focus is on how these come about under the old operational mechanisms compared with their progress under the new ones being established. The purpose is to prove that the question of whether the economic operational mechanisms are old or new can make a difference in environmental protection and the process and results of developing underdeveloped regions.

When we study and analyze these four mechanisms, we find differences between the old and new goals mechanisms and between the old and new impetus mechanisms, but such differences are not pronounced. Because both mechanisms are based on the same system of socialist ownership, it is impossible for categorical differences to arise from their old and new forms, despite the fact that the goals are aligned and prescribed somewhat differently and that there are differences in how the source for impetus should be understood and in the way such impetus is obtained.

However, our analyses and comparisons do reveal striking differences between the new and old resource allocation mechanism and the new and old interference elimination mechanism. It is the differences in these two mechanisms that are the principal factors behind the differences between old and new socialist economic operational mechanisms in the state of environmental protection and the course and results of developing impoverished regions.

Environmental Damage Under Old Economic Operational Mechanisms

Dynamically speaking, a less developed region may encounter two kinds of environmental damage in the course of development. One such damage may have already existed in the early stage of development, in the form of damaged forests, grassland, and vegetation, depleted mineral ores and soil erosion resulting from predatory exploitation of natural resources by local residents in a hasty bid to beat poverty. Generally, this is the only kind of environmental damage that less developed regions suffered before they began to develop industry. The other kind of environmental damage occurs in industrial development and in the form of water, soil and air pollution caused by the emergence of factories. Of course, the first kind of environmental damage may exist alongside the second kind in the stage of industrial development.

What is the relationship between these two kinds of environmental damage and the old socialist economic operational mechanisms? Let us begin our discussion with a study of the supply and demand in less developed regions.

Such a region is usually an entirely or basically closed economy. Its scanty or zero external connection indicates that it has little or no input and output exchanges with other regions, and that local demand basically matches local supply at a fairly low level.

Such a region is not immune to the first kind of environmental damage even if it is basically in seclusion. For instance, cooking fuel shortage may compel local people to fell trees indiscriminately. Shortfalls in grain supply resulting from low-yielding farmland may precipitate wanton land reclamation. Nevertheless, it should be noted that even if the first kind of environmental damage happens in a secluded region, its consequences may be limited. This is one of the characteristics of a closed economy. Of course, the first kind of environmental damage will not cease in such a secluded region because of poverty. If the local economy is under old socialist economic operational mechanisms, and if a shortage in basic means of living has prompted behaviors that are damaging to resources and environment, such behaviors can only be intervened with administrative steps because the region has no internal mechanisms to coordinate its economic growth and ecological equilibrium.

Nevertheless, regional seclusion is bound to give way in the course of economic growth. The input-output ties between a secluded place and the outside world will grow gradually even if old operational mechanisms are still at work. The development of one place not only boosts its own supply and demand but also is impelled by the supply and demand of other places. Disparity between places in the margin of supply and demand growth will compel them to restructure their economies and readjust their spatial distribution of human, material, and financial resources, thereby causing local resident income to rise to varying degrees. This unevenness between places in economic growth and resident income increase stems mainly from geographical locations, natural endowment, population density and resources, and is not decided by differences in economic operational mechanisms. In other words, in places where old economic operational mechanisms still hold sway in local economic life, local economic structural changes are not circumscribed by economic operational mechanisms, but by non-economic operational mechanisms.

Under the impact of disequilibrium between regions in economic and resident income increases, the first kind of environmental damage may go from bad to worse in less developed regions where the state of seclusion is collapsing and economic ties with other regions are growing. Such environmental deterioration cannot be checked by merely relying on administrative intervention under old economic operational mechanisms. Undeniably, the officials and citizens of such regions care about developing local economies and increasing local income, and are doing their best to deliver themselves from the quagmire of underdevelopment and destitution. But what should they do to quit poverty and achieve prosperity fast? Development hinges on industry, but industry calls for capital. Where shall the needed capital come from? Industry can be developed with state investment, but not every less developed region can procure state investment in local industry. If a region cannot count on industry to grow its economy and accumulate its capital, where else can it turn to for help? Under old economic operational mechanisms, it is rather difficult for a poor region to go from rags to riches. This gives rise to two possibilities. One is that even though the region's external economic ties are growing, it may find it hard to develop its industry for lack of capital; and even though its agriculture may grow to a certain extent, it cannot grow enough to obtain the capital it badly needs. Thus the region finds it impossible to overcome poverty, while its per capita income gap with other regions widens gradually as a result of its slow economic growth. In the other possibility, the local residents may, of their own accord or in an organized way, resort to excessive tapping of local resources and selling them to boost income, but despite their hard work, they cannot gain what they want, and become even poorer. Their efforts may have an adverse impact on their region and those of others and on both their present and future. There is no lack of such examples in the course of China's economic development.

Changing Economic Operational Mechanisms Is More Important Than Formulating Incentive Policies for Poverty-Stricken Regions

We should admit that in a less developed region, the speed of economic growth, the margin of increase in local resident income, and the degree of seriousness of damage done to the local environment and resources are closely associated with economic policy for a given period of time. However, these problems have more to do with economic operational mechanisms than with economic policy.

As illustrated in the foregoing, "economic operational mechanisms" is a general term for the series of relationships an economy relies upon for development. Some of these relationships are defined in legislation and statutes; the others are instituted in economic rules and regulations. Under a given economic operational mechanism, the promulgation and effective enforcement of a major economic policy will impact the condition and progress of economic operation one way or another, and thus yield economic and social returns. Such is the way government policy works. The impact of economic policy on a given economic operational mechanism alters the condition and orbit of economic operation to a certain extent, and goes on to affect demand and supply, and input and output, causing changes in local economic and income levels.

However, it is economic operational mechanisms, rather than policy, that play a more profound part in the development of a less developed region. They determine the course of economic operation. By contrast, if government policy is to play a role, it must influence these mechanisms and change them in certain ways. For instance, the government may grant tax exemption or reduction, financial subsidy, and low-interest or interest-free loans to a rather poor region, hoping to help it beat poverty at an early date. However, the beneficial effects of these incentives can be restricted if the prevailing economic operational mechanisms are detrimental to local economic development. This is because the financial subsidy, interest-free or local-interest loans granted to the poor region through preferential government policy are often not used as start-up fund for local development. Instead, they are frequently spent to cope with immediate financial woes, and are not enough to generate a local economic boom. That is why people often say it is essential to endow less developed regions with the "blood-making" function. "Blood transfusion," whether sporadic or long-term, can never put any population or region on the road to prosperity.

Given that the economic growth of less developed regions is predicated on the soundness of economic operational mechanisms, environmental protection and ecological equilibrium, by reason of their close relevance to economic growth, are also determined by such mechanisms rather than by economic policy. Economic policy alone is not enough to help poor regions overcome poverty. By the same token, it is not enough to rely on economic policy alone to help these regions maintain ecological equilibrium in the course of development.

This being the case, we need to learn what kind of economic operational mechanisms are detrimental to the economic growth and ecological equilibrium of poverty-stricken regions, and what kind of economic operational mechanisms can help these regions address these issues. Once we have found the answers to both questions, we will know what policy to take to curtail the economic operational mechanisms that do not work and promote the role of the workable mechanisms. Once sound economic operational mechanisms are chosen, less developed regions will be able to increase their internal accumulation and reinvestment, and limit environmental damage. On the contrary, if they allow old economic operational mechanisms to go on dominating local economic life, they can never beat poverty no matter how much external input or "blood transfusion" they can receive. In that sense, a less developed region can be likened to either a funnel or a reservoir, and investment from the outside can be compared to water. If such a region works like a funnel, it will remain in poverty because all the "water" it receives will drain away sooner or later. If, however, the region works like a reservoir in which all the "water" it receives is retained, and the "fish" raised in it thrive, then the local economy will keep changing for the better. In that case, even if investment arrives in one installment from the outside, it will have such a start-up effect that the entire "reservoir" will be energized. Thus, to develop the economy of a less developed region, the first thing to do is not to turn the region into a "funnel" but to prevent incoming investment from going down the drain. For this purpose, we have to replace old economic operational mechanisms with new ones, and turn local economies from "funnels" to "reservoirs."

Less Developed Regions' Internal Accumulation Mechanism

Capital investment is pivotal to the development of less developed regions. The issue entails (1) the source of capital, (2) the direction or structure of the capital, and (3) the efficiency with which such capital is used. In a socialist economy, the differences between old and new economic operational mechanisms in capital investment are striking in all three aspects.

Insofar as the source of capital is concerned, a region's internal accumulation comes from the accumulations of local businesses and residents. If the region is perennially poor, it may have no industry to speak of. Even if it has a few industrial firms, their accumulations won't amount to a lot, and the low-income local residents will not have large savings. This is a realistic problem, but what I want to prove here is that, no matter how much local firms and residents may have in their bank savings, it is imperative to procure their reinvestment. This is where a kind of internal mechanism is needed to attract local reinvestment in such a region. In my previous brief introduction to economic operational mechanisms, I have pointed out that we need to approach the issue from the perspectives of goals, impetus, resource allocation, and elimination of interference. I have also mentioned that between the two kinds of economic operational mechanisms based on socialist ownership, the differences between old and new goals and impetus mechanisms are not as important as those between old and new resource allocation and interference elimination mechanisms. The differences between the old and new internal accumulation mechanisms are actually those between the principle for resource allocation and the approach to it. Thus it is safe to say that the internal accumulation mechanism for a region is an integral part of the resource allocation mechanism for the entire society.

There are three reasons why the internal accumulation mechanism can work in less developed regions under the new economic operational framework but cannot do so under the traditional framework.

Firstly, resource allocation is realized through capital investment and reinvestment. The pattern of resource allocation is readjusted repeatedly due to structural differences between such investment and reinvestment. But how can capital investment and reinvestment be guaranteed? The answer is apparent: We must convince such investors that they can benefit from such investment and reinvestment. Herein lies the role of capital investment and reinvestment in guiding interests. It goes without saying that the benefits in question refer to relative benefits. As both investment and reinvestment inevitably flow to where gains are high, this gives rise to the price issue. Under old economic operational mechanisms, the price ratio is irrational. All a less developed region can provide are primary products. As the prices for resources are on the low side, the prices for these primary products are kept low as well, whereas the production and trading costs (transportation included) for the less developed region's products are on the high side. Not only will the region end up with a negligible surplus in hand, it will also be deprived of its fountainhead of capital for investment and reinvestment. Such a situation can hardly attract capital investment and reinvestment from within the region. If, however, new socialist economic operational mechanisms are set up, the price ratio will be rectified and the prices for resources will rise to an appropriate level while production and trading costs drop relatively, so that internal investment and reinvestment become an attractive prospect. A major lesson to be drawn from this is that if macroeconomic decision-makers are really resolved to help less developed regions to prosper, they should, rather than choose the "blood transfusion" method, focus on changing their economic operational mechanisms and gradually address their low resource prices and high production and trading costs. Only in this way can these regions be helped to formulate an effective internal accumulation mechanism.

Secondly, capital investment and reinvestment come from a surplus fund that can be broken down into consumption fund and savings, or consumption fund and investment fund converted from savings. Therefore, from the perspective of resource allocation, the issue involves the distribution of the surplus fund in the very beginning. An underdeveloped economy with low labor productivity, combined with inappropriate pricing of the primary products such an economy provides, results in a scanty surplus fund at the disposal of such regions. If, under these circumstances, a considerable part of the surplus fund is spent on consumption, what is left for investment can be negligible. If less developed regions are to be developed in real earnest, everything should be done to prevent irrational consumption expenses from eroding the internal accumulation fund that can otherwise be used for investment and reinvestment purposes. The term "irrational consumption" points mainly to consumer expenses not on daily necessities but on outmoded conventions and customs, as well as consumer expenses that go way above local productivity and resident income levels. Under old economic operational mechanisms, such "irrational consumption" can only be controlled by administrative means. This kind of control may be effective on the surface, but it can bring a problem: For lack of motivation for internal investment and reinvestment, potential investors—namely, businesses, urban residents, rural firms, and farming households—may choose to bypass administrative orders, thus forcing local government to tighten its control time and again. What is more, even if administrative control succeeds under old economic operational mechanisms in coordinating prices and costs by raising resource prices and reducing production and trading costs, such a balance may still be eroded by irrational consumer expenses, and the hopes of internal capital investment will still be dashed if businesses and people are not motivated to invest and reinvest. After new socialist economic operational mechanisms are established, businesses and people will have both initiative and motivation to invest and reinvest, and, with internal constraints in place to hold back irrational consumer expenses, internal accumulation will grow. Local governments, on their part, can make more use of economic regulatory means—tax rate and interest rate readjustments—that work a lot better than hard and fast administrative rules.

Thirdly, resource allocation includes investment and reinvestment, as well as grouping such investment and reinvestment. Given that investment and reinvestment are embodied in both value and material, when they come in material forms, they give rise to such issues as ratios and approaches for regrouping human, material and financial resources. Furthermore, taking the input-output relationship and the flow of resources between regions into account, investment and reinvestment also entail how to effectively integrate the resources of one region with those of another region so that their value and material forms can be well coordinated. We have to put less developed regions on the track of fast economic growth in a way that enables the resources of one region to be integrated with those of another region in the most effective way possible, and through such integration, to yield more internal accumulations. Of course, if a less developed region must rely entirely on the inflow of resources—financial resources in particular—to grow its economy, such reliance cannot help the region formulate its internal investment and reinvestment mechanisms, nor is it realistic in the current stage of Chinese development. However, as things are in this nation, less developed regions can find it very difficult to jump-start their economies without the inflow of outside resources. The issue here is how internal resources can be integrated with external resources. Under old economic operational mechanisms, local and inter-regional groupings of resources are seriously constrained by the lack of autonomy and flexibility on the part of investors and re-investors. If, under these circumstances, the resources of one place can still be integrated with the resources of another place, this is most likely to happen through administrative intervention, but such integration can be both ineffective and short-lived. If new socialist economic operational mechanisms are permanently instituted, investors, endowed with autonomy and flexibility, can act in their own immediate and long-term economic interests to choose ways that work for such integration. Whether a less developed region can integrate its resources effectively with those of other places determines whether it can acquire a sizeable internal accumulation and speed up increases in local residents' income. Therefore, in order to bring about such an efficient integration in resources, it is imperative to change the economic operational mechanisms through reform.

Capital Investment Structure and the Coordination Between Development and Environment

According to the analysis made above, the second aspect of the regional capital investment issue involves the direction and structure of this kind of investment. The capital invested is known as "capital inflow," while the sectoral structure of such capital manifests itself in the form of capital stock that is accumulated over a long period of time. Under old economic operational mechanisms, it is the government that decides the direction of capital investment. An irrational capital sectoral structure makes stock readjustment very difficult. A feasible way to cope with the problem is to regulate the capital flow, the amount of money to be spent on capital investment. However, for one thing, the capital flow is limited, and for another, once the capital flow is invested, such amount of money will become part of the stock. We may as well liken capital flow to "flowing water" and the stock to "still water." To turn capital flow into capital stock is like turning "flowing water" into "still water." If that happens, the capital's sectoral structure in a less developed regions will become lopsided, a lopsidedness that cannot be rectified, thereby making it hard to bring about a workable mechanism to facilitate internal accumulation and internal investment and reinvestment.

Moreover, given the continuous process it takes to boost development and improve local resident income in less developed regions, it is imperative to maintain stability in investment and reinvestment from within these regions. Such stability is unreachable under old economic operational mechanisms, because the reliance on administrative steps alone can deprive capital investment and reinvestment of the guidance of interests and make lasting integration of resources between regions impossible. As a result, investment proceeds in fits and starts and fails to ensure steady and efficient growth.

What, then, will happen under new socialist economic operational mechanisms? We need to ensure that the initiative for internal investment and reinvestment is in the hands of companies with internal accumulations and of urban and rural residents with bank savings. It should not be in government hands. Only when companies and individuals are willing to invest in local economic undertakings can we be convinced that an internal accumulation mechanism has taken shape. However, it is naïve to believe that an internal accumulation mechanism will become permanent simply because an old economic operational mechanism has given way to a new one. If, under new economic operational mechanisms, firms begin to make their own business decisions and urban residents are keen on investing and reinvesting, their investment direction becomes an issue. Where do they want to invest, in their own region, or in other regions with better conditions? If, under the guidance of their interests, they choose to invest somewhere else instead of their own region, less developed regions will have no guaranteed money for investment and reinvestment in development despite the fact that they have adopted new economic operational mechanisms. This is where government regulation can help. Financial authorities at various levels may set aside a certain amount of construction fund to maintain investment and reinvestment in less developed regions on a certain scale. Local governments may also set preferential tax rates so that funds can be drawn from nongovernmental channels to less developed regions to make up for their investment and reinvestment shortfalls. On the basis of raising funds from the state, regions, businesses and various walks of social life, a development fund may be established, and its money can be deployed according to a region's internal investment and reinvestment needs.

At this point, we need to consider how to enhance equilibrium between economic growth and the environment in less developed regions by putting capital investment where it is most needed in the course of development. If invested capital is structurally flawed and results in disequilibrium in the capital sectoral structure, how effectively can changing economic operational mechanisms work in coordinating development and environment?

It should be conceded that old economic operational mechanisms cannot solve these problems for reasons already explained in a previous chapter. Given that old economic operational mechanisms can neither foster internal investment and reinvestment mechanisms in less developed regions, nor remedy the lopsided capital sectoral structure through readjusting capital stock, their limits are apparent in tackling problems in coordinating development and the environment. Can the problems be addressed under new socialist economic operational mechanisms? This is a complex issue that merits in-depth study.

Theoretically speaking, the establishment of new economic operational mechanisms does not guarantee adequate market information, nor does it indicate that capital investment principals are assured of access to adequate and timely information. A good part of the information they obtain may still be incorrect and misleading when they make resource input decisions. As a result, resource allocation can hardly meet the demand for equilibrium between development and the environment. Furthermore, capital investors, whose economic behavior cannot be restrained by such a demand because of resource supply shortfalls, may most probably step up their exploitation of natural resources to make up for such shortfalls, thus making it even more difficult to coordinate development and environmental issues.

Obviously, the establishment of new socialist economic operational mechanisms does not mean that problems in between economic growth and environmental protection can be automatically addressed. In comparison with the situation under old economic operational mechanisms, internal investment and reinvestment are bound to increase considerably under new mechanisms. However, the questions of which region or industry should be invested with such internal capital, and particularly, whether it can be invested in environmental protection, and if so, how much can be invested in it—these cannot be determined merely by changing economic operational mechanisms. Two points are worth noting no matter what happens:

Firstly, more capital will flow into internal investment and reinvestment under new economic operational mechanisms than under old ones. For that matter, even though the establishment of new mechanisms cannot spontaneously bring about a balance between development and environment in less developed regions, it at least sets the financial stage for such a balance.

Secondly, under old mechanisms, because businesses were government appendages that could not make their own decisions and be responsible for their own gains and losses, their indifference to government steps to coordinate development with environmental protection often derailed such attempts. By contrast, new economic operational mechanisms can turn businesses into independent commodity producers that are mindful of their own interests and willing to adapt their behavior to government intentions when they assess the impact of government steps on themselves and seek advantages and avoid risks from these steps.

Thus we can arrive at the conclusion that even though a shift in economic operational mechanisms does not mean that capital investment will be automatically directed rationally and that environmental protection will receive more investment because of it, the new economic operational mechanisms can bring more internal investment and reinvestment, and enable businesses to act on their own interests to adapt their behavior to government regulation intentions. Thus it is more likely for development and environment to be balanced under new economic operational mechanisms than under old ones. From the perspective of capital investment or capital investment structure, this drives home the close connection between environmental protection, development of less developed regions, and changing the economic operational mechanisms.

Resource Utilization Efficiency in Less Developed Regions

Efficiency in capital utilization is the third issue pertinent to local capital investment. With a given amount of capital investment and a given direction or structure for it, capital utilization efficiency is the foremost factor in determining the level of regional development and of increases in resident income. Furthermore, capital utilization efficiency also has a direct bearing on the level of ecosystem damage, the development of the environmental protection sector, and the level of balance between development and environment.

Capital utilization efficiency is an identical concept to resource utilization efficiency. The economic resources put into development can be converted into capital if they come in money form. Therefore, the level of capital utilization efficiency is the same as the level of resource utilization efficiency. Resource utilization efficiency also represents the level of effectiveness at which resources are used. Effective use of resources means that: (1) all sorts of resources have been put to full use, without being left idle or to waste; (2) various groupings of resources are working efficiently, that is, they can yield the highest possible efficiency under the assumption that the other conditions remain unchanged; and (3) the results of using resources are exactly what is needed by society, or, in other words, the products, labor and services provided by grouped resources have become effective supply. In short, effective utilization of resources entails three aspects: full use of resources, efficient resource grouping, and results of such grouping that are welcomed by society. Only by taking these three aspects into overall consideration is it possible to judge if resources have been put to effective use and—if the answer is yes—how effectively they have been used.

Under old economic operational mechanisms, the effectiveness of resource utilization is seriously handicapped. An incomplete market, coupled with lethargic company performance, inevitably keeps resource utilization efficiency low, and ineffective supply of resources cannot be remedied with the economy's internal strength alone. In both scenarios, intervention in the economy can be effected only through non-economic government means. However, if economic operational mechanisms remain intact, problems will keep snowballing even if the government can reconcile the conflicts resulting from low resource utilization efficiency through non-economic means. When the problems come to a head, the conflict between resource supply and demand will be fully exposed. An economy in disarray invariably forces firms to seek the way out through underground transactions in an attempt to protect their interests as well as the interests of their workers. This may enable a few firms to somewhat improve their resource utilization efficiency, but for society as a whole, such efficiency will remain low and tend to be aggravated by such underground transactions. This is because the underground market may force firms to pay a high price if they want to turn such transactions to their favor, thereby steering resource allocation further from the right course.

Under new economic operational mechanisms, and with newly gained decision-making autonomy and flexibility, firms will become keener than before in pursuing the highest possible resource utilization efficiency because it is directly relevant to their immediate interests. The gradually improved market works alongside government macroeconomic regulatory steps not only to furnish favorable conditions for placing resources where they are needed and grouping them as reasonably as possible, but also to set the stage for universal improvements in resource utilization efficiency. Insofar as resource utilization efficiency is raised, it is both necessary and urgent to shift the socialist economy to new operational mechanisms.

Putting an End to the "Low Income—Ecosystem Damage—Low Income" Vicious Cycle

From the angles of capital investment sources, the direction of such investment, and capital utilization efficiency, I have just probed into the development of less developed regions and the balance between such development and environmental protection under old and new economic operational mechanisms. As a matter of fact, these three facets of capital investment are closely interrelated. Pivotal to these facets, moreover, is the question of how to establish an internal accumulation mechanism in less developed regions.

Such a mechanism is the foremost precondition for speeding up balanced development in these regions. As long as these regions can establish their own internal accumulation mechanisms and secure a constant flow of capital to invest and reinvest in local economies, they will find it easier to tackle their other problems. To put it another way, if the economy of a less developed region is like a funnel that cannot retain any water, using and distributing such water is out of the question.

In the course of balanced economic development in less developed regions, effective use of resources is predicated on the formation of local internal accumulation mechanisms. One of the reasons why residents of these regions do not value their resources and are given to tapping them wantonly is because in their effort to develop local economies and raise their income, they have no alternative but to consume local resources as much as they can. Only when they have developed their internal investment and reinvestment mechanisms can they cherish their resources and economize on them. Only then can these regions put improving their efficiency in utilizing local resources on the agenda. The same is true of integrating local resources with those of other regions. It is true that all the input of resources, local or otherwise, should be put to best use and grouped as effectively as possible, and that every effort must be made to put the fruits of such grouping on the market in the form of products and services. However, nothing is more important to these regions than putting an internal accumulation mechanism in place. Only with such a mechanism can developed regions be motivated for economic collaboration with less developed regions, can sustained integration of local and outside resources happen steadily, and can actual benefits be reaped from the economies of less developed regions. In the absence of such a mechanism, interregional economic collaboration cannot be made to last—in extreme cases, once happened, it can never happen again.

In developing less developed regions, particularly in coordinating their development and environment, we must not lose sight of the salient features of the issue of effective resource utilization. After an internal accumulation mechanism has been set up in such a region, the effort to put resources to effective use and to keep raising the resource utilization efficiency should never be slackened. That is to say, the arrival of the internal accumulation mechanism does not mean utilization of resources can become immediately effective. If effectiveness is overlooked in this regard, the accumulation rate will fluctuate even in the presence of the internal accumulation mechanism. If the accumulation rate is on the low side, it can do little to boost economic development in less developed regions. Therefore, these regions must do their level best to increase resource utilization efficiency when fostering internal accumulation mechanisms, so that their internal investment and reinvestment can yield more output and surplus. It must be pointed out that effective utilization of resources is not only connected with the economic operational mechanism but also affected by production technology. Efficiency in resource utilization varies with technical conditions. Under a given economic system, improved technology can boost such efficiency, increase the output of per-unit input, and put available resources to more uses. It can even help discover and utilize more resources. Such is the importance of steady improvement of production technology in less developed regions.

The cultivation of internal accumulation mechanism and the increase of resource utilization efficiency in less developed regions are subject to the enthusiasm of local businesses and residents (workers included). The cultivation of the internal accumulation mechanism, in particular, hinges on motivating capital-supplying businesses and individuals. For instance, the motivation of businesses as investors helps them reinvest more; the enthusiasm of residents (workers and farmers included) as bank creditors helps boost the savings rate and furnishes favorable conditions to convert bank savings into investment. In boosting resource utilization efficiency, it is essential to motivate every supplier of production factors, including capital and labor suppliers—managers, technicians, workers and farmers. Furthermore, the enthusiasm of those on the demand side is also indispensible to efficient utilization of resources, because the marketing of the fruits of resource grouping cannot do without them. Otherwise, the products may be stockpiled or become unsalable. Of course I am not saying that demand should be stimulated artificially, but that demand is elastic, and that if properly guided, rational demand often has room to expand. To motivate those who need capital is in fact to guide them to expand purchases properly while turning the supply from poor regions into effective supply. In this regard we have to see the fact that the demand of less developed regions for manufactured goods is circumscribed by their per capita income and small markets. Therefore, to put demand under proper guidance can help improve the resource utilization efficiency on both sides of the supply-demand relationship.

As efficient utilization of resources also calls for protecting resources and the environment, we should, in the course of opening up less developed regions, focus our attention not only on whether resources are fully utilized (so that none of them is left idle) and grouped efficiently, and whether the products of such grouping are needed by society, but also on the protection of resources and the environment. From a long-term point of view, negligence in resource and environmental protection inevitably leads to overheated development and damaged resources. This is a pivotal issue to the development of less developed regions, for it has a close bearing on whether these regions can be released from the "low income—ecological damage—low income" vicious cycle that can be overcome only by replacing "ecosystem destruction" with "ecosystem preservation." If this fundamental change can be effected, low income can be gradually turned into middle-level income and further to high income.

During a recent fact-finding tour of Fengning and Weichang counties in Chengde Prefecture, Hebei Province, I told my hosts that I often heard the old refrain about developing mountain economies: "You'd better live off the mountains if you live there."

There is nothing wrong with that saying, because mountainous regions cannot be developed without tapping local resources. It can be very difficult to jump-start the economy in such regions if local resources are left unused. However, the old refrain can also be misunderstood by those who think: "We have nothing to fear, now that we can live off the mountains." If that philosophy is taken for granted, then everything in the mountains will be used up before you have realized it. That is, when mountain resources are used up or ruined, the mountains will become so uninhabitable that folk living on them will have nowhere else to turn to for sustenance. For this reason, that old refrain may be reworded like this: "Nourish the mountains to eat off them." To make the mountains "eatable," you have to "nourish" them. This means to cherish mountain resources and tap them in a restrained way while conserving them and building up their stock. Nobody can succeed in developing a mountain economy if they are given to "eating off" the mountains and do not care to "nourish" them. Chengde Prefecture happens to be a mountainous region, but my remarks apply not just to mountainous regions but to every less developed region as well. Only by "nourishing" the "mountains" can they become a source of wealth. Only by "nourishing" the "water" can the "water" become a depository of wealth. A great deal can be accomplished when you are devoted to nourishing something. This is not merely about technicalities, but more than anything else, about economic operational mechanisms. For a less developed region to escape poverty and embark on the road toward prosperity, the only way out lies in coordinating economic development with environment protection, and in reversing the vicious cycle of "low income—environmental damage—low income" into the virtuous circle of "income increase—ecosystem protection—income increase." Both conversion and coordination can happen after old economic operation mechanisms have given way to new ones. Such is my conclusion.

—*Social Sciences in China*, issue No. 4, 1991

· 11 ·

COMPARATIVE ECONOMIC HISTORY AND THE MODERNIZATION OF CHINA

Addressing the Title With an Overview of Economic History

Economic history, as an academic discipline, studies the historical process of economic activity that involves the evolution of the economic system, the development of productivity as well as the interaction between the two. It is a hybrid of economics and history, as its name suggests. From the viewpoint of the history of economics, a lot has been said and written about past economic phenomena and issues, and many ideas have been put forth on the relationship between economics and history from perspectives ranging from mercantilism to classical economics. These efforts, however, were not systematic enough to give rise to economic history as an academic discipline. It was not until the late 19th century that economic history emerged in Western Europe as an independent discipline, thanks to contributions from numerous prominent European scholars. These included representatives of the German history of economics such as Gustav von Schmoller, Albert Eberhard Fridrich Schaffle and Karl Wilhelm Bücher, as well as their contemporaries James Edwin Thorold Rogers, Henry de Beltgens Gibbins, Arnold Toynbee and William James Ashley of Great Britain, Emile Levasseur of France, and Charles Franklin Dunbar, Henry Walcott Farnam, Gerald C. Gross and

Richard Theodore Ely of the United States. Economic history came a long way in Europe and America in the first half of the 20th century. Scholars like Werner Sombart and Ernst Wagemann of Germany, John Harold Clapham, Michael Moissey Postan and Richard Henry Tawney of Great Britain, Henri Sée of France, Eli Filip Heckscher of Sweden, Alfons Dopsch of Austria, Henri Pirenne of Belgium, James Walter Thompson, Mikhail Ivanovich Rostovtzeff and Abbott Payson Usher of the United States distinguished themselves with important works in their respective areas of this discipline.

Under the influence of various philosophical, historical, and economic thoughts, economists are divided in their outlook on such major issues as the relationship between theory and history, on the roles of geographical environment, population, and government in economic development, and on whether socioeconomic development is single- or multi-tracked, progressive, or radical. Many of their opinions on the history of humanity's economic activity, the metamorphosis of economic systems and the development of productivity may be blinkered or Euro-centric in their global overview of economic history, yet it has to be admitted that their achievements are valuable for later researchers, both in the collection and collation of historical archives on economics and in textual research on specific facts in economic history.

Comparative economic history as a branch of economic history mainly dwells on the similarities and differences between the economic processes of countries and regions in the world, and analyzes their causes and effects for a deeper understanding of the historical process of socioeconomic activity. In both genesis and development it is something of a latecomer in comparison with economic history. For a considerably long period of time after economic history was established as a field of study, many scholars—such as G. Schmoller, K. Bücher, W. J. Ashley, H. Sée, H. Pirenne, E. F. Heckscher and J. H. Clapham—made comparative studies of the economic history of different countries, yet their efforts were hardly systematic. Moreover, because of their research focus on the establishment of a certain theoretical model for economic history, they tended to sort out and arrange the economic historical facts and figures of different countries in compliance with this established model. In other words, limited by the circumstances of the time, none of these European economists lived to see comparative economic history maturing into an independent discipline—it was a branch of economic history at best.

The Rise of Comparative Economic History

It was not until the end of the Second World War, particularly after the mid-1960s, that the importance of comparative economic history came to be recognized by the academic world. This had something to do with the postwar world political and economic situation. Following the disintegration of the old world political order, and with many less developed nations embarking on the road of modernization, comparative studies of economic systems, economic growth, and economic policies caught on widely among scholars, thereby paving the way for the birth of comparative economic history as an academic discipline. Ragnar Nurkse, Simon Smith Kuznets, Walt Whitman Rostow, Alber Otto Hirschman, and other scholars who had made a name for themselves in their studies of economic growth, delved into comparative economic history and came up with groundbreaking discoveries and enunciations. Although these people, with the exception of W. W. Rostow, are not considered as economic historians, the important position of their works in comparative economic history can never be ignored. The advent and development of theories on human capital, institutional and technological innovation, political cycles, the long wave, the political market and public choices, either have provided new theoretical backing for the study of comparative economic history, or become vivid research topics.

The rise of econometric history, also known as cliometrics or new economic history, was yet another major factor that contributed to comparative economic history in its formative years. Econometric history first appeared in the late 1950s, and progressed swiftly after the mid-1960s. American economic historians Robert William Fogel, Douglass Cecil North and Stanley Lewis Engerman are its major representatives. These economic historians label past studies in this field "traditional economic history" for the reason that they have stopped at the level of historiography, fallen short of integrating economic theories with economic history, and failed to apply modern quantitative analysis in studying past historical events and economic development processes. Accordingly, they believe they have remedied all these deficiencies with their brand of new economic history. During the period from the 1960s to the 1980s, the new economic history caught the attention of the academic world and gave a major impetus to comparative economic history by coming up with a series of works on the histories of technological innovation, institutional innovation, railways, the southern US economy, the Western European medieval manorial system, historical calculations of GNP and labor productivity, and the historiography of business cycles. This great impetus manifested itself mainly in improvements in research methodology. As R. W. Fogel and S. L. Engerman point out in *The Reinterpretation of American Economic History* (1971), "When the data are very good, simple statistical procedures will usually suffice. The poorer the data, the more powerful are the methods which have to be employed. Nevertheless, it is often true that the volume of data available is frequently below the minimum required for standard statistical procedures. In such instances the crucial determinant of success is the ability of the investigator to devise methods that are exceedingly efficient in the utilization of data—that is, to find a method that will permit one to achieve a solution with the limited data that are available."[1] Besides the support from certain theories, improved research methods, quantitative methods in particular, are also sine qua non for the achievements made in comparative studies of the economic development processes of different countries and regions.

From a methodological point of view, both vertical and lateral comparative approaches can be applied in comparative economic history. Vertical comparative analysis refers to a study of changes that have taken place in different periods in one or several countries along the historical course of economic development, so as to discover the norms governing economic development. Lateral comparative analysis refers to a comparison of the economic situations in different areas of a country or in several countries over a certain period or at a given time, so as to illustrate the distinctive economic features of the areas or countries being compared. Choices of economic indicators and of years are pivotal to the success of vertical comparison. The older the indicators, the more fragmented the statistical data tend to be, and the more difficult the comparison becomes. Moreover, such a comparison can make sense only when different statistics are converted into something that can be measured with the same benchmark. As to the choice of years, arbitrariness must be avoided—the years chosen to represent certain turning points or historical periods in economic development should be solidly grounded. Only thus can convincing conclusions be derived from such a vertical comparison. As to lateral comparative analysis, apart from the above-mentioned caution in the choice of economic indicators and years (as well as the comparability of such indicators), due attention should be paid to the connection between lateral and vertical comparisons. This is because only by putting the two kinds of comparison together can the regular pattern of the economy's historical development be seen more clearly, and only thus can the deficiencies of statistics concerning a certain historical period in a certain country be made up for with an approximate value derived from corresponding data available for the same historical period in another country. This drives further home the significance of quantitative analysis to the rise of comparative economic history.

Comparative Economic History and Studies of Modernization

The modernization issue has been drawing the attention of international academia as a major research topic since the end of the Second World War. Both development economics and comparative economic history have studied it, but the former has distinguished itself by approaching the topic more from the perspective of economic history, that is, by comparing the historical processes of socioeconomic development. To put it more exactly, development economics studies the mode and policy of economic development by leaning heavily on the allocation and flow of production factors, the relationship between saving and consumption, the roles of market mechanism and government functionaries, the relationship between sectoral and regional economic structures as well as between economic development and technological innovation, and the internal-external balance in the development process. Although development economics also links the modernization issue with the roles of institutional, cultural and other factors, it puts a premium on the present situation instead of on historical summary. By comparison, comparative economic history has a different focus in modernization studies.

As a branch of economic history, comparative economic history not only is devoted to historical economic development, but also explores issues with more extensity and profundity. To name just a few: How important are the roles of traditional culture, religion and ethics in the historical process of socioeconomic development of different countries or regions? To what extent can the differences in socioeconomic history between countries (and regions) be interpreted in light of their differences in traditional culture, religion and ethics? Both questions, however, fall into the category of comparative economic history rather than development economics. To cite another group of questions: What are the implications of the Asian mode of production? What is the economic difference between Eastern and Western pre-capitalist societies? How did such a difference come about, and what is its relationship with the later capitalist economic development? What conclusions can be arrived at if the role of geographic environment in economic development is belittled or exaggerated? Can such conclusions stand the test of science? These questions are, likewise, concerns of comparative economic historians, and rarely dwelt on by development economists.

Modernization entails a process of sustained economic, social, political and cultural development, with economic development as the driving force behind it. The academic world is widely divided as to when worldwide modernization was started. It is dated back variously to the scientific revolution of the 16th and 17th centuries, to the industrial revolution towards the end of the 18th century, or to a more recent date. The consensus, nevertheless, is that the hundred years beginning from the late 19th century constituted the modernization stage in the socioeconomic development of human history. Therefore, no research into modernization can be complete without summarizing the experiences and lessons of all nations in their economic development during those years. It goes without saying that modernized nations need to sum up their historical experiences so that they can address, with appropriate countermeasures, the socioeconomic problems arising from economic development. Nations that are striving for modernization, too, find it necessary to summarize their own experiences and those of others in economic development over the years. Without such summary, they may go astray or repeat other nations' mistakes in their modernization drive. In that sense, the study of modernization is synonymous with comparative economic history. More than that, because comparative economic history can prepare conditions for in-depth modernization studies, it is, indeed, an indispensable branch of foundational research for the latter.

In a comparative study of the relationship between tradition and modernization featured in the book *The Modernization of Japan and Russia* (Cyril Edwin Black et al, New York, 1975), I have discovered a typical example to illustrate the collaboration between comparative economic history and modernization research. C. E. Black and his co-authors chose to compare the Japanese modernization process with that of Russia precisely because the two nations, each with a heritage different from that of Western Europe, were seeking modernization and adapting it to their respective traditions. According to the authors' observations of modern economic history, Japan and Russia share a distinguished feature in their modernization processes in that they have both succeeded in preserving their traditions. However, such traditions are no longer the same as they were—they have been adapted to modernization. What the authors are saying is that, firstly, modernization is not the same as "Westernization" or "Europeanization"; secondly, these two terms imply that Western or European institutions and values are indispensable elements of modernization, as if other nations could only adopt Western or European values and institutions at the expense of their own heritages; and thirdly, as the Japanese and Russian experiences indicate, modernization can in fact be realized only when it is adapted to local traditions. Only by making the most of its past accumulations of wealth can a nation achieve success in its modernization effort and choose the best modernization strategies. Otherwise, all such effort will prove worthless.

This comparative research in economic history by C. E. Black and others tells us that the present cannot be torn away from tradition and that any type of successful modernization is necessarily the unification of tradition with modernization.

Why Comparative Economic History Catches the Fancy of Chinese Academia

Since the 1980s, a wide spectrum of Chinese society has shown great interest in the issue of modernization, an interest that manifests itself in its concern not only for the approach to Chinese modernization and its prospects, but also for the modernization processes of many other countries and regions. The reason why studies of socioeconomic development strategies—or modernization strategies—have deeply interested Chinese academia is because such strategic studies are of paramount importance in that they take place against the background of summarizing the experiences and lessons of other countries' modernization drives, and that their successes and failures are closely related to China's future development and the institutional and development modes the nation is going to adopt. Many scholars have joined in such studies since the beginning of the 1980s. We have every reason to believe that these scholars' ever-increasing attention to comparative economic history is inseparable from the tangential and circumferential research on socioeconomic development strategy at that time, an inclusive summary of empirical results from the modernization process in fellow countries.

A thought of far-reaching influence has run through Chinese research into comparative economic history: What matters for socioeconomic development is not economic growth alone, but—at least mainly—coordinated economic and social development. For a long period of historical development, the role of industrialization has been over-estimated. That is why the traditional development strategy adopted since the late 18th century always emphasized the growth of gross national product to the neglect of the costs involved; stressed industry, heavy industry in particular, to the neglect of agricultural development; favored investment in technical equipment over investment in human resources; and went blindly after abundant supply of consumer goods while ignoring the uncertain aftermath of such an abundance and the resultant changing lifestyles. In a word, coordinated socioeconomic development is more important—and worth the effort of less developed countries—than single-minded pursuit of economic growth.

Such a thought naturally gives rise to the following statement when evaluating the Industrial Revolution: the industrialization that swept across the West from the late 18th century through the 19th century was about revolutionizing production technology rather than about emancipating and developing intellectual resources. It was not until the 20th century, or as late as the mid-20th century, that this resource gained the attention it deserves. In other words, it was not until very late that investment in education was given proper consideration in association with modernization. This is a good lesson for all developing nations in pursuit of modernization. If China ignored this lesson drawn from comparative economic history and followed the example of some countries in the 18th–19th centuries in regarding human beings merely as tools and appendages to machines and came tardily to emancipate and develop its intellectual resources, its modernization process would definitely be delayed, and the widening gap between the economy and culture would become a heavy price to be paid for modernization.

It need be pointed out that China was not immune to the worldwide "Weber fever" of the 1980s, when some scholars in this nation were drawn to the German sociologist and economic historian Max Weber's theories in their studies of the crux of the modernization issue from a comparative research perspective. The spread of Weber's theories in China stemmed from the problems the nation had come across in its modernization drive and from the Chinese desire to learn from other nations' experiences and lessons in this regard. Comparative economic history posed the following questions: Why did the Industrial Revolution follow different courses in different countries and regions? Which factors precipitated the industrial revolution in one country after another? What was the most important of all these factors? Scholars of comparative economic history may list a host of factors that might have facilitated or hampered the industrial revolution in a given nation, such as the formation of capital, market, labor and its quality, technological progress and government policy. However, one may doubt if industrial revolution could take place by way of capital, market, labor, technology and policy alone. True, these factors are indispensable, but they are not sufficient to bring about industrial revolution. We have to delve into social structure, culture and ethics and look for the other factors that might have stimulated or hindered industrial revolution. In his works Weber made a point of integrating economic history with cultural and institutional histories. That is a basic reason why his theses have drawn the attention of scholars studying the issues pertinent to modernization.

Weber's ideas are, without doubt, controversial, but even his detractors have to concede that his ideas are quite illuminating. One of his revelations is that industrial revolution cannot take place in a nation that, despite having prepared the essential production factors, is ill prepared ideologically and ethically—meaning that the nation still lacks the social environment and mental driving force that are essential to industrial revolution or economic progress. In other words, there is a subtle spiritual force behind the industrial revolution that drives people to explore the unknown and run businesses in return for economic results. Furthermore, in Weber's own words, industrial development is also a process in which interpersonal relationships are readjusted, for the interpersonal relationships prior to the industrial society—such as the hereditary hierarchy, clannish rule and vassalage fealty—are detrimental to industrial development. For example, even though the Roman Empire in its heyday had no lack of needed capital and labor and its market was wide enough, industrial revolution in the modern sense of the term did not take place in that empire because its social structure, institutional scope and the interpersonal relations based on it were hostile to industrial development. Take Italy for another example. That country had acquired adequate capital and developed a wide market during the 14th–16th centuries, but its social structure, institutional environment and interpersonal relations rendered an industrial revolution improbable on its land. In those years, the Italian economy was not matched with a compatible social enterprising spirit, and as a result, the nation's accumulated wealth was channeled into nonproductive undertakings and failed to fuel technological and industrial growth. Weber's expositions in this regard drive home not only what comparative economic history means for modernization research, but also that society, culture and ethics must be studied extensively if we are to deepen our study of the modernization issue. Hence it is justifiable for Weber's Chinese followers to believe that his revelations pertinent to China's modernization lie in his methodological approach rather than in his theories *per se*.

A Historical Comparison of Economic Fluctuations

A nation is likely to suffer economic fluctuations in its pre-modernization period. Such fluctuations, however, are either caused by non-economic factors such as war, natural adversity, pestilence, or influences from the outside world. This being the case, pre-modernization economic fluctuations tend to evade the attention of comparative economic history researchers. But this is not the case when a nation has entered its modernization period. In the modernization process, economic fluctuations may be caused by internal and economic factors and show certain regularity. For this reason, the historical comparison of economic fluctuations has become a new topic for studies of the Chinese style of modernization.

British economist John Hicks's work *A Theory of Economic History* (1969) is of great utility for its reference value to Chinese researchers in this field. Like American economist and political scientist Joseph Alois Schumpeter, Hicks is interested in mounting a descriptive theory of socioeconomic history rather than specific elaborations on a certain period involved in a certain research topic about economic history.[2] In Hicks's view, it is understandable that quantitative changes in gold and silver can lead to fluctuations in prices within a secluded economy (for example, what it was prior to the Industrial Revolution). Even under the gold standard system, quantitative changes in a currency can still be counted as a reason for fluctuations in prices and the economy. However, in the 20th century, because the metallic basis of the currency was weakened, economic fluctuations could no longer be interpreted according to the amount of the currency, nor could it be simply ascribed to the adoption of a certain currency policy. The issue had to be seen in a new light. The cycle of economic growth and recession had to be probed from the perspective of the interaction between internal investment, savings and consumption. Moreover, the process of economic fluctuations could be illustrated by reference to the role of commerce, the supply of and demand for labor as well as the scope of market. That is to say, different research methods had to be applied to the history of economic fluctuations in the pre-industrialized society, during the Industrial Revolution and after the mid-20th century because each of these periods had its own peculiarities. According to Hicks's pronouncements in *A Theory of Economic History* and other works like

A Contribution to the Theory of the Trade Cycle, *Journal of Economic Perspectives* and *Crisis in Keynesian Economics*, economic fluctuations are not uncommon in a modernization process, and pose no hindrance to economic growth—fluctuations are merely a temporary setback or slack in the historical course.

Obviously, researchers of China's modernization will not rest contented with Hicks's theoretical presentation of economic fluctuations. But so far as methodology is concerned, historical comparison (Hicks's cycle analysis included) is still useful. In the 1980s, despite a divergence in opinions, scholars were basically unanimous on two basic conclusions in their analyses of the process and causes of the cyclical fluctuation of the Chinese economy over the previous 40 years. Firstly, economic fluctuations are unavoidable in China because, like other economies that are modernized or being modernized, the Chinese economy will never be in a rectilinear motion. Secondly, the causes of economic fluctuations in China's modernization drive are internal in the main, while the impact of the world market is secondary. However, scholars are strikingly divided on the causes of the fluctuations, the duration of each fluctuation, and the intervals between them. For example: Which is a more important cause of the fluctuations, the amount of currency or commodity demand and supply? Should the modernization drive be focused on investment or attach equal importance to investment and consumption? Which sector is more accountable for causing fluctuations, the agricultural sector or the construction industry? Which is more of a factor in the changing process of fluctuation: finance or banking, planning or market? With their own distinctive features, the economic fluctuations in China's modernization process can be analogized neither to those in Western and Southeast Asian countries, nor to those in the former Soviet Union and Eastern European countries. All this merits continued and in-depth study, for which comparative economic history may offer more support.

In historical comparative research, economic fluctuations are invariably connected with the economic system. If changes in the volume of investment or the growth rate of investment are regarded as a major cause for economic fluctuations in the modernization drive, this poses another question: Are changes in investment not related to a certain economic system? By the same token, if changes in the volume or supply of money are regarded as a major cause for fluctuations, are not these changes, too, an outcome of a certain economic system? From a macroeconomic point of view, changes in investment and money supply have different causes and effects under different economic systems, a fact that has a great deal to do with fiscal, monetary, and planning systems and market structure. From a microeconomic point of view, changes in investment and money supply are also directly linked with the corporate system. For example, whether a business is a true investor and stakeholder that makes its own decisions, whether it is sensitive to changes in credit and interest rate, and whether it is motivated by its own interests to seek technological progress and reduce its share of the money flow are inseparable from the changes in investment and money supply. All these indicate that comparative studies of economic fluctuations are, as a matter of fact, concerned with comparing the causes and effects of fluctuations under different economic systems.

When it comes to comparative research on economic systems, Chinese modernization scholars tend to hold one of two opinions:

Opinion One: China's economic system is highly comparable with those of the former Soviet Union and Eastern European countries, historically so with the former Soviet economic system in particular. The analogy between the Soviet economic system over the 70 or so years since the Russian Revolution of 1917 and the Chinese economic system over the last 40 years is quite manifest in some historical periods. Thus the historical relationship between the economic systems of the former Soviet Union and Eastern European countries and their respective economic fluctuations can serve as a reference for studies of the economic fluctuations that have occurred in the modernization process of China.

Opinion Two: In terms of GNP per capita and the percentage of agricultural population in the total population, the Chinese economic system is more akin to, and considerably more comparable with, some other developing countries insofar as socioeconomic structure, market organization and price system are concerned. These developing countries are susceptible to economic fluctuations on their road to modernization due to lopsided industrial structures and shortfalls in resource supply, or due to the unsalability of primary products and decreases in residents' income. Because these countries' fluctuations are relevant to a great extent to the problems existing in their economic systems, it is necessary to make historical comparisons between the Chinese economy and those of the developing countries if economic fluctuations in the course of modernization are studied in the context of economic systems.

The above two opinions are both reasonable and not incompatible to each other. As seen from the perspective of its economic system, fluctuations in China's modernization process are similar not only to those in the former

Soviet Union and Eastern European countries but also to some other developing countries.

Deep-Seated Issue: Traditional Social Structure as a Brake

Historical comparison of economic systems brings to light a deep-seated issue, that is, whether or not the traditional social structure acts as a brake on the modernization process. If the answer is yes, how serious is that role? And how can it be mitigated? It is precisely because Alexander Gerschenkron and Umberto Melotti have dwelt on all these questions and come up with unique explanations that Chinese economists are drawn to the former's works on comparative economic history and find the latter's study of the Third World and multi-linear mode of growth enlightening.

Gerschenkron's view is that the retarding role of traditional social structure is reflected in its constraints on the supply of production factors, which is a major hindrance to the progress of underdeveloped countries. He thinks that large-scale industrial development in Russia and Balkan countries has been shackled by traditional social structure in comparison with Western Europe. But it is noteworthy that while Gerschenkron acknowledges the existence of the braking effect of traditional social structure in modernization, he also stresses that underdeveloped countries may find themselves at a relative advantage once they are resolved to achieve modernization. In this regard, he employs two terms: the "advantages of a latecomer," such as the traditional social structure's low labor cost; and the "disadvantages of a latecomer," such as the yawning gap in technology between underdeveloped and developed countries. He also points out that the advantages and disadvantages are coexistent and mutually convertible. An underdeveloped country can overcome its disadvantage if it can make the most of its advantages, including low wages. If an underdeveloped country lets the opportunity slip through its fingers, its latecomer advantage may fail to play a role and its modernization process may be delayed, just like a man who, having missed a bus, has to wait for a long time before catching the next one. Because good opportunities are rare, a "major outburst" in economic development—akin to a sprint at the finish line of the industrial revolution race—is not only necessary but also beneficial to nations under the heavy influence of a deep-rooted traditional social structure.

For his part, Melotti elaborates from different perspectives on the retarding role a traditional structure plays in the modernization of underdeveloped countries. As he sees it, the vast land area of these countries (mainly in Asia, Africa and Latin America) is studded with numerous village-sized economies that have evolved into a stable but self-enclosed and self-sufficient economic setup that ties producers down to the narrow activity scope of their lands. The economic development and social structural changes are seriously held back as a result. But how is it that Japan, of all Asian countries, made its modernization drive a success after the Meiji Restoration? Is the political factor alone enough of an answer to that question? In answer to it, Melotti points out that despite its distinctive Asian characteristics and its differences from European countries, in its pre-Restoration years Japanese society did not attempt to nip capitalism in the bud the way the other Asian countries did socioeconomically. The reason why post-Restoration Japan wasted no time in embarking on the capitalist track of development was not because of any external factors but because of the salient features of its innate traditional social structure.

For researchers of the Chinese way of modernization, Gerschenkron and Melotti have provided valuable references to the retarding role of traditional Chinese social structure in modernization. As a matter of fact, research on that role is highly relevant to the design and progress of the nation's economic restructuring and political reform. In this regard two views are prevalent among Chinese researchers.

One view holds that haste makes waste, given the nature of the fabric of traditional society and the difficulties it poses, and that only by pushing political and economic reforms one step at a time and coordinating reform with development can progress be made in the modernization drive and gradual changes brought to the traditional social structure.

The other view maintains that, bearing in mind the retarding impact of traditional social structure, modernization cannot be sustained without breaking up this structure or at least blunting its impact considerably, and that economic and political reforms should be sped up, since slowly progressing reforms can only prolong the survival of the traditional social structure and allow it to go on holding back the modernization process.

A compromise between these two views suggests that economic restructuring should be accelerated and political institutional reform conducted in a progressive way. In other words, once economic restructuring and economic development make some headway, political reform will go more smoothly and become more acceptable to the public because it helps minimize the shock wave emanating from the ensuing reshuffling of the traditional social structure.

Although divided in their opinions on the relationship between development and traditional social structure in the modernization process of different countries, Chinese scholars of comparative economic history see eye to eye on the fact that the traditional social structure does have a retardant impact on the nation's modernization drive. They see this as something that cannot be tampered with carelessly, and unanimously suggest that prudence be applied when countermeasures are chosen. Ours is socialist modernization. Therefore, improving and developing the socialist system should be the ultimate goal for economic restructuring and political reform, and the steps to be taken should be socialism-oriented as well. In their modernization studies Chinese scholars of comparative economic history are, indeed, sober-minded on this issue.

Global Diversity in the Modernization Process

Comparative research on the relationship between traditional social structure and modernization inevitably leads to another major issue as to whether modernization is single- or multi-tracked on a global scale. Historical materials on economic history have indicated that the Western European model of social development and its approaches to industrial revolution are not necessarily appropriate to the modernization process of developing countries. This issue can be traced back to some other questions: What did a typical feudal society look like? Where did it occur, in Western Europe, the East, or China specifically? The assumption that all Western European, Eastern and Chinese feudal societies were, without exception, typical ones may not be incorrect. In a word, there are a host of topics that are open for discussion, and the divergence of opinions can never evaporate into thin air overnight.

Shortly after the end of the First World War, Oswald Spengler pointed out in his book *The Decline of the West* that human history was about none other than the spontaneous rise and fall of civilizations, and that every civilization runs its own course, emerging and perishing on its own. His study of the rise and fall of civilizations convinced him that there is no cause-and-effect relationship in history, and Western civilization will eventually meet its demise along the same course followed by ancient Egyptian, Babylonian and Mayan civilizations. Spengler was able to broaden the vista of comparative history by eschewing the unilinear theory regarding Western Europe and embracing diversity in historical development, although his denial of the norms of historical development, his neglect of the successive and continuous nature of history, and his indifference to the intrinsic relationship between civilizations are open to question. Later, in his work *A Study of History*, Toynbee developed the theory on diversity in historical progress, believing that all civilizations are parallel in their development but each follows its own course of rise and fall. He maintained that civilizations are not isolated but interrelated: If a demised civilization can give birth to—or influence the rise of—a second generation of lasting civilization, it is evident that one civilization's fall is probably the starting point of another. True, Toynbee somewhat exaggerated the role of religion in his dissertations on human development and the rise and fall of civilizations; but like Spengler, he also stressed the multilinear development of history and maintained that civilization is multi-centered instead of having only one center. Such a proposition was accepted by most of his fellow history researchers.

Nevertheless, Spengler and Toynbee were general historians and historical philosophers, not economic history scholars. Though they touched upon many issues pertinent to economic history in their works, they never delved into the historical process of economic development and changes. As Hicked commented in *A Theory of Economic History*, "… the grand designs of a Toynbee or a Spengler, the makers of historical patterns which have more aesthetic than scientific appeal."[3] However, there is no denying the inspiration of comparative studies of civilizations to comparative economic history as an approach to historical philosophy or historical research. We may not accept Spengler's historical pessimism or condone Toynbee's belief in religion as the driving force behind the rise and development of civilizations. Nevertheless, we are obliged to admit that the influence of traditional social structures and concepts is comprehensive, and works on a civilization or a regional economy in many ways, resulting in differences in civilizations, regional economic activity and development modes.

Studies of diversity in socioeconomic development and modernization often put scholars of comparative economic history in mind of two questions: Would Eastern traditional social structures have crumbled without the invasion of the Western forces? Can Eastern nations accomplish industrial revolution and embark on modernization by their own bootstraps? The traditional social structure in Eastern countries was a powerful constraint on their economic development, and no amount of war, social unrest and dynasty substitutions in ancient and medieval times could change it substantially. Economic booms, long or staggered, did occur in the East in those times, but they stood no comparison with the economic development or industrial revolution of modern times. On the surface, Western inroads are directly related to the disintegration of traditional social structures in the East, as if without the former, the latter would not have happened, or without the latter, there would not have been industrial revolution or modernization. Though some people accept this deduction, the issue remains unsettled, and the dispute continues.

Scholastic opinions vary as to whether the disintegration of traditional social structure resulted from external forces or not. One opinion that may be of high reference value for studies of the Chinese modernization process has this to say: the inroads of external forces could only destroy the surface of the traditional social structure—its collapse was caused by internal forces alone. An early case in point in this regard is Latin America, where Spanish invasion and occupation did not cause the local socioeconomic structures to crumble. A more recent example is India, whose deep-rooted social structure survived the invasion of British economic forces till the mid-1940s. In that country, cities and rural areas were two different worlds. If capitalism was able to make some headway in cities, the traditional social structure remained intact in the vast rural areas. A third case in point is South Korea: Why was the South Korean economy able to grow rapidly, beginning from the 1960s when the disintegration of its traditional social structure picked up speed, while its economy had lagged behind for a long time earlier as it kept its original social structure under Japanese rule before the Second World War? Is it not the case that the destructive factor came mainly from within the country? These examples show that it is prejudiced and superficial to assume that without foreign invasion there would not be the collapse of traditional social structure and the advent of industrial revolution and modernization in the East. Without dissecting the deep-seated structure of traditional society or putting a premium on studying the role of internal forces within that society, there will be no way to account for the actual disintegration of traditional social structures in the East and the diversity in both world history and the modernization process. Of course, this is not to deny the role of the invading forces from the West in the collapse of the traditional social structures of the East. Instead, it is to say that the role of internal forces should be given center stage in studies of the modernization issue, including the relationship between the disintegration of traditional social structure and the process of modernization.

Disequilibrium in the Modernization Process Within a Country

The imbalanced nature of the modernization process has come to the attention of almost all researchers of comparative economic history in their study of different countries. This valuable finding virtually gainsays the assertion that countries follow a unified mode of modernization. In this respect, Sidney Pollard's hypothesis has attracted the notice of comparative history researchers in China.

Pollard points out that the study of European industrialization should be based on the innate laws of industrial development instead of on country-specific modes, and that the industrialization process looks like an outbreak of a skin rash epidemic. At the very beginning, new industrial cities emerge in a country like a rash of clustered spots in the human skin in varied quantity and density, some of which grow more densely clustered into an inflamed patch while others remain sparsely scattered after a certain period of time. Therefore he believes that studies of the industrialization process should not be based on countries but on regions, that is, by regarding the distribution and proliferation of the "red spots" as signals of the industrialization progress. As he puts it, "It is the argument of this article that the industrialization of 19th-century Europe was a single process and had an economic logic of its own. Like an epidemic, it took little note of frontiers, crossing them with ease while leaving neighboring home territories untouched."[4]

Pollard's "red spots" hypothesis helps decode the imbalance in the modernization process between countries and in a given country. It also indicates that such imbalance does not impede the efforts of countries or of regions inside a country to form an economic body. According to him, during its period of industrialization Europe was an integral community and so was the European market, and no European country could do without this community in industrial development. The industrialization of one region often has a major impact on other regions with its capital, labor, technology and import and export commodities. But the impact of the latter on the former cannot be overlooked either. When one region makes the first step toward industrialization, it brings development opportunities to other regions. Although these regions are a step later, such opportunities still put them at an advantage over the neighboring regions that are relatively more backward.

Modernization researchers may draw inspiration from Pollard's assumption. For instance, at a certain point of time, China has a number of industrialized cities and towns scattered in various provinces. They look like "red spots" on the Map of China, but at the same time, every province still has large areas in which not a single "red spot" can be seen. Thus, the differences between the provinces—or rather, the disequilibrium between them in industrial development—find expression in their differences in the number, density and size of the "red spots." In modernization studies, we should figure out the reasons behind these differences in those regions, the diffusion trend of the "red spots" as well as the relationship between them in different provinces.

Pollard's assumption and regional research method are valuable to studies of Chinese modernization and unbalanced regional development in economic history. For example, they may help ward off over-simplified conclusions in studying the regional distribution of large handicraft workshops with hired labor in the Ming and Qing dynasties and modern factories of the late 19th and early 20th centuries.

Comparative Research on Economic History Yet to Be Deepened and Widened

As mentioned earlier, comparative economic history is a relatively young academic discipline. In China, it did not begin to gain the importance it deserves until recently. It is drawing more and more researchers in this nation, but that is not reason enough to say that comparative economic history has come a long way in this nation. As things stand here, studies in comparative economic history are mainly centered on modernization, leaving many other important issues untouched or merely briefly mentioned. Insofar as methodology is concerned, the new economic history methodology has not had any influence on China so far. A few scholars have employed the econometric approach in their historical studies into recent decades; but their results have been obviously restricted by the lack of historical data for one thing, and by the institutional hindrance to Chinese economic development for another. But this does not mean that the econometric approach is not applicable to the study of Chinese economic history at all. With economic history and comparative economic history gaining steady ground and depth, the prospects of econometrics are becoming brighter in this nation. We have got to be patient, for it takes time to explore how to incorporate the institutional factor into the econometric study of Chinese economic history.

Discussing the relationship between economic history and economics in 1985, Robert M. Solow wrote in the *American Economic Review*: "A modern economy is a very complicated system. Since we cannot conduct controlled experiments on its smaller parts, or even observe them in isolation, the classical hard-science devices for discriminating between competing hypotheses are closed to us. The main alternative device is the statistical analysis of historical time-series."[5] His statement is reasonable in that the historical statistics method would be the best choice wherever other physical and chemical types of scientific experiments failed in the study of socioeconomic events. But queries on its effectiveness arise. Supposing the process of economic development and many historical facts are yet to be clarified, to what extent can a historical statistics method account for the issues even if it can be made to work? In the face of fragmented historical data and inaccurate figures concerning certain years, how can we guarantee the effectiveness of this method? We have no intention to play down the value of this method. We just want to point out that in quantitative studies of the Chinese economic history, only by collecting and collating historical data, and by weeding through falsehoods to fill in the blanks with nothing but authentic data, can full scope be given to quantitative analysis in studies of Chinese economic history.

As to the relationship between economic history and economics, Solow also points out: "So the economic historian can use the tools provided by the economist but will need, in addition, the ability to imagine how things might have been before they became as they now are."[6] His mention of "imagination" in this context is quite thought-provoking. It turns out that this view is shared by many other new economic historians. Thus a hypothesis is turned into a tool in the hands of analysts of economic history. For example, R. W. Fogel studied the historical role of the American economy by assuming that the American continental railway did not exist at all in 1890. R. W. Fogel and S. L. Engerman also began their research on the slave economy in the southern United States under the assumption that there was no Civil War in 1861–1865, and then went on to discuss the prospects of plantation economy. No wonder in a journal review of Frederic C. Lane's thesis, "Role of Government in economic growth in Early Modern Times," Douglass Cecil North and Robert Paul Thomas make this statement together: "The most crucial ingredient in comparative economic history, or any other economic history for that matter, is the development of imaginative theory."[7] By the term "imagination," we do not mean groundless or wild guesses, but academic inferences based on facts and achievements in comparative research on economic history. Only this kind of "imagination" can be academically valuable.

Why so much ado about "imagination" in economic history research and its relevance to comparative economic history? The reason is apparent: Combining vertical and lateral comparisons in economic history makes it possible to use the development process and socioeconomic problems of one country to speculate on what problems another country might encountered in about the same stage of development. Such is one of the ways in which economic historians may bring their imagination into play. "History may not repeat itself, but it does rhyme a lot," as Mark Twain puts it. As to a particular economic period in a certain country or region, speculations based on comparative research into economic history are bound to be more accurate than mere wild guesswork. In this regard, researchers in this nation have a great deal of work ahead of them. The more solid the studies in comparative economic history are, the more fruitful such studies become, and the more convincing the inference from an economic process—the estimation and evaluation of problems to be confronted in the modernization process included—tends to be.

(*Translated by Ren Xiaomei*)
— *Social Sciences Front* bimonthly, issue No. 1, 1993

Notes

1. Fogel, Robert William and Stanley Lewis Engerman (eds.) (1971), *The Reinterpretation of American Economic History*, New York: Harper and Row, p. 8.
2. Yining, Li (1989), "John Hicks's Research on Economic History," *Reading*, issue No. 5, pp. 29–34.
3. Hicks, John Richard (1969), *A Theory of Economic History*, Oxford: Clarendon Press, p. 2.
4. Pollard, Sidney (1973), "Industrialization and the European Economy," *The Economic History Review*, New Series, Vol. 26, No. 4, p. 648.
5. Solow, Robert M. (1985), "Economic History and Economics," *American Economic Review*, Vol. 75, No. 2, Papers and Proceedings of the Ninety-Seventh Annual Meeting of the American Economic Association (May 1985), pp. 328–331.
6. Ibid, p. 331.
7. North, Douglass C. and Robert Paul Thomas (1975), "The Tasks of Economic History," *The Journal of Economic History*, Vol. 35, No. 1, p. 19.

· 12 ·

GROWTH AND FLUCTUATIONS IN ECONOMIC DISEQUILIBRIUM

Restraints of Disequilibrium on Growth and Fluctuations

The late 1960s witnessed a great stride made in disequilibrium theory. In his two papers, "The Keynesian counter-revolution: a theoretical appraisal"[1] and "A reconsideration of the microfoundations of monetary theory,"[2] American economist Robert Wayne Clower came up with a notable argument on disequilibrium theory: Economic instability comes not from a specific market but from discordance between markets, a discordance that stems from the incompleteness of these markets and of the information transmission mechanism between them. If this argument on disequilibrium is applied to analysis of economic growth and fluctuations, the result will be obvious: Not only will the equilibrium equation of growth predicated on the complete conversion of savings into investment and the full utilization of the production capacities thus yielded become void, but the supposition about fluctuations that lists the restrictions of income and its changes on effective demand as a major destabilizing factor in an economic system will also be considered as having major limitations.

Shortly afterwards, Swedish economist Axel Leijonhufvud published *On Keynesian Economics and the Economics of Keynes*[3] among other books. Like

Clower, Leijonhufvud reinterpreted the Keynesian economic theory with a disequilibrium approach, and made his own analysis of the causes behind economic stability and instability. He maintains that between labor supply and commodity sales on the economic chain in real life, there are intermediary links, including employers hiring workers, workers producing commodities, employers paying workers, workers buying commodities with their wages, and employers selling commodities. Nevertheless, price rigidity, incomplete markets, and flawed information transmission may disconnect any one of these links, thereby severing the economic chain and inevitably destabilizing the economy. This is precisely a manifestation of economic disequilibrium. If this analytical method based on disequilibrium is applied to economic growth and fluctuations, it can likewise prove that it is neither possible for the economy to follow the road of balanced growth as designed by those who subscribe to the equilibrium theory of growth, nor can economic fluctuations be overcome by negotiating the balance between aggregate demand and aggregate supply on the basis of the equilibrium equation for national income.

From the 1970s onward, French economist Jean-Pascal Benassy and Hungarian economist János Kornai probed deeply into the theory of disequilibrium from different points of view. They have made quite a few breakthroughs in disequilibrium studies, which is evident in Benassy's *The Economics of Market Disequilibrium*, *Macroeconomics and Imperfect Competition* and *Macroeconomics: An Introduction to the Non-Walrasian Approach*,[4] and Kornai's *Anti-Equilibrium*, *Economics of Shortage and Growth*, *Shortage and Efficiency*.[5] Their studies on macroeconomic operation contribute greatly to studies of economic growth and fluctuations.

Benassy's contribution to the theoretical study of disequilibrium lies mainly in his analyses of the restraining factors in economic disequilibrium and of the effects of quantitative quotas. According to him, when prices are rigid, traders ought to adjust demand and supply according to both market price and quantity signals. That is to say, traders are restrained by both prices and quantity.

The quantity constraint is embodied in quantitative quotas of various forms. That is to say, the market rations the limited supply among demanders when supply falls short of demand, and apportions the limited demand among suppliers when supply outstrips demand. The equilibrium achieved through quantitative quotas is called "rationed equilibrium," which is actually a kind of disequilibrium or, in a certain sense, temporary, ex post equilibrium. The position of this kind of equilibrium is determined by the shortest side in demand and supply. Benassy maintains that, when observing an economy in disequilibrium, not only should the presumption of price flexibility be abandoned, but price rigidity and asymmetric price elasticity should be taken into consideration as well. Although price rigidity is somewhat relevant to asymmetry in price elasticity, the two factors are different in their impact on actual economic activity. Asymmetry in price elasticity tends to complicate resource allocation in economic disequilibrium, and to further hold back the effectiveness of government policy. If the concept of expectation—that is, individual traders' expectations of uncertain behaviors in economic disequilibrium—is factored in, to stabilize the economy in disequilibrium will become a tougher proposition.

Kornai's analytical approach to the disequilibrium theory is distinctly his own. His study is focused on economic disequilibrium under repressed inflation, that is, disequilibrium characterized by supply shortfalls, where limited commodity supplies are rationed out to demanders by way of quantitative quotas. In that scenario, any increase in fiscal expenditure can further boost the demand on the commodity market, and further strain the distribution of the already limited supplies, thereby worsening the repressed inflation. If, on the contrary, the government attempts to curtail demand by tightening up expenditure, supply and demand will shrink simultaneously, thereby defeating the purpose of making up for supply shortages. Kornai's study of economic disequilibrium is valuable in that he focuses discussions on both hard and soft budget restraints, because the existence of firms' soft budget constraint can keep the economy in long-run disequilibrium and make it hard to eradicate supply shortfalls.

The studies by Western economists drive home clearly that both economic growth and fluctuation are inevitably restrained by economic disequilibrium.

The influence of the equilibrium theory runs deeply in the economic growth theories represented by the Harrod-Domar model, Neo-classical model and Neo-Cambridge model that came in vogue in the 1950s and 1960s. What sets the Neo-Cambridge model far apart from the other two models is that it incorporates two different kinds of income and the restraints of income distribution on economic growth. However, even with this legitimate contribution to growth theories, the Neo-Cambridge model still fails to eschew explicit or implicit assumptions of a complete market, flexible prices, and smooth information transmission. As a result, this model ascribes the difficulties encountered in the process of economic growth mainly to income distribution problems rather than to market imperfections and the incompatibilities between markets. In this way, the Neo-Cambridge model falls short of accounting for the restraining impact of persistent supply shortages on economic growth.

One thing that should be noted is that Joan Robinson and other major advocates of the Neo-Cambridge model were, theoretically speaking, against assumptions of economic equilibrium. Proceeding from Keynes's viewpoints on economic disequilibrium, they raised a series of arguments against mainstream post-Keynesian theorists. But why was it that they could not shake off the influence of the equilibrium theory in their analysis of economic growth? It was because their microeconomic theory was inadequate and weak, and because their neglect of analyses of market transaction behaviors, corporate operational mechanisms, and information transmission mechanisms determined the inherent drawbacks in their model of economic growth.

In economic fluctuation studies, the relevant theory represented by the IS-LM (investment · savings—liquidity preference · money supply) and Multiplier-Accelerator models that were popular in the 1950s and 1960s is preconditioned by equilibrium and equilibrium growth assumptions. According to these models, economic fluctuations are caused by overinvestment, oversaving, oversupply, or inefficient money supply, and by the inherent law of technology and equipment upgrading, and are not directly associated with market imperfections, price rigidity, and informational frictions. What is more, the IS-LM model also ignores the analysis of the microeconomic basis of the macroeconomy, while the Multiplier-Accelerator model does the same by leaning heavily on the economy's technical factors. Such oversight determines the serious flaw in the fluctuation theories that were current in the 1950s and 1960s.

The progress made in the late 1960s in researches on the disequilibrium theory provided no small inspiration for studies of economic growth and fluctuations. And the restraining effects of the imbalanced nature of the economy on growth and fluctuations were increasingly accepted in academic and economic circles thanks to constructive explorations made by researchers in the disequilibrium theory. These explorations were made without totally disallowing the significance and reference value of either the Harrod-Domar, Neo-classical and Neo-Cambridge models in the realm of theoretical research on economic growth, or the IS-LM and Multiplier-Accelerator models in their studies of the fluctuation theory. Such explorations were important in that they approached growth and fluctuations from a unique perspective, thereby putting their studies on a new and more realistic footing. That is why some of their conclusions are closer to reality than those derived from the theories popular in the 1950s and 1960s.

The studies of disequilibrium analyses of growth and fluctuations so far can be summarized in the following four major conclusions:

First, with incomplete markets, inflexible prices and inefficient information transmission, the conversion of savings into investment will be held back, and the imbalance between supply and demand, once it occurs, cannot be easily corrected. Shortages in supply and demand can be mitigated by the function of market to a certain extent, but will not disappear totally. The equilibrium thus achieved under a nonzero unemployment rate or a nonzero inflation rate can restrain economic growth or cause major fluctuations.

Second, disequilibrium makes it harder for markets (commodity market, capital market, labor market, etc.) to function in a coordinative way. Once supply or demand shortages occur in one market, they cannot possibly disappear and will go on to cause new shortages and exacerbate existing ones in other markets. This may become a restraint on growth or an important cause behind major fluctuations.

Third, disequilibrium is characterized by price rigidity. The major impact of price rigidity on growth and fluctuations is manifested in that economic agents have to make supply-demand decisions based on imprecise signals. However, price rigidity does not mean that a price will hold forever. On the contrary, it may entail sudden, large-scale, and asymmetric price changes. This is detrimental to economic growth, to be sure, and more importantly, it may cause or aggravate fluctuations.

Fourth, the presence of disequilibrium or equilibrium under nonzero rates of unemployment and inflation is bound to alter the expectations of market participants, which in turn gives rise to irregular and shortsighted economic behaviors. Such behaviors are likely to become not only a major cause behind intensified fluctuations, but also a stubborn retardant on steady and sustained economic growth.

Telling Two Kinds of Disequilibrium Apart, a Study of Growth and Fluctuations

Using disequilibrium analysis, and combining it with the country's actual economic situation, we will be able to get a better understanding of the guidelines for the ongoing economic reform and the way the economy develops.

Given that disequilibrium is caused by incomplete markets, inflexible prices and inefficient information transmission, either of the following arguments will make sense in theory:

Argument A: To avoid volatile fluctuations and stabilize the growth rate, it is necessary to remove price restraints and improve market conditions, and to put economic agents on equal competitive footings. Economic growth will be realized in a relatively complete market with flexible prices.

Argument B: With market mechanism flaws such as incomplete markets, inflexible prices and inefficient information transmission, it is necessary to tighten up macroeconomic management to make up for market deficiencies and rectify economic deviations with government regulation of quotas and prices. Steady and sustainable economic growth will be achieved mainly by allocating capital, labor, and production materials via quantitative quota. To put it another way, economic growth under disequilibrium can be achieved mainly through quantitative quota implementation.

Both arguments stem from analyses of economic disequilibrium. In fact, Argument A is a succinct interpretation of the theory on "price reform as the centerpiece of economic reform," while Argument B emphasizes "macroeconomic stabilization as the centerpiece of economic reform." Insofar as economic growth and fluctuations are concerned, Argument A attributes economic fluctuations in disequilibrium to incomplete markets and inflexible prices, so that flexible prices and better market conditions are the first steps to take to avoid fluctuations or maintain stable economic growth; while Argument B ascribes fluctuations to incomplete markets or limitations in the market mechanism itself, so the inevitable reform step is to strengthen macroeconomic management through government quota and price regulation.

However, a study of the actual performance of the Chinese economy proves that neither price reform nor macroeconomic stabilization, if chosen as the centerpiece of economic reform, can ward off wild fluctuations or maintain steady economic growth. This means that neither Argument A nor Argument B tallies with the current Chinese economic situation.

Given that both arguments are based on studies of disequilibrium assumptions and therefore inappropriate, one may wonder what really went wrong. Isn't it that the disequilibrium theory itself is wrong, or that analysis of this theory is not thorough enough to account for such complex issues as economic restructuring, growth, and fluctuations in this country? The disequilibrium theory is, without a doubt, an advance in economics.

Equilibrium assumptions are unwarranted in the absence of complete markets, flexible prices, and efficient information transmission. In reality, however, economies are always in disequilibrium; therefore, they can be observed only with disequilibrium analytical methods. For this reason, we cannot make light of the disequilibrium theory simply because the above two arguments do not fit. The problem does not lie in disequilibrium analysis itself.

What really went wrong? The problem dwells in the flaws of general disequilibrium analysis, so much so that it falls short of explaining such complicated issues as economic restructuring, growth, and fluctuations in China.

What merits attention is that general disequilibrium analysis does not take into account the dynamics of firms as microeconomic units. Instead, its assumption is that firms are dynamic enough. It thus follows that analysts attribute disequilibrium to incomplete markets, inflexible prices, and inefficient information transmission. This is how Arguments A and B are drawn, and why disequilibrium analysis is flawed.

In my book *Disequilibrium in the Chinese Economy*,[6] I propose to divide disequilibrium into two categories, one with incomplete markets, and the other with both incomplete markets and enfeebled firms. The current Chinese economy falls into the second category. This being the case, economic restructuring in this nation should proceed in two stages: Firstly, to transform firms more deeply until they become dynamic and profit-maximizing entities that enjoy decision-making autonomy and are liable for their profits and losses, so that the Chinese economy can complete its transition from the second category of disequilibrium to the first category of it; and secondly, to center economic restructuring on building a complete market and decentralizing prices, so that the economy can edge its way toward equilibrium. My book differs from the general studies of the disequilibrium theory in that I have differentiated between two categories of economic disequilibrium and observed the attributes of the second category of disequilibrium.

It makes sense to distinguish between these two kinds of disequilibrium, because it helps analyze Chinese economic growth and fluctuations. Economic growth is restricted to a larger extent and more vulnerable to fluctuations in the second category of disequilibrium. In the same vein, it is more difficult to maintain steady economic growth and avoid wild fluctuations under the second category of disequilibrium than under the first category of it. Without clarifying the difference between the two categories of disequilibrium, we may mistake incomplete markets, inflexible prices and inefficient information transmission for the main restraints on economic growth and the basic causes behind fluctuations. We will miss the point if we adopt economic policies in light of these judgments. It is like a doctor who, acting on a false diagnosis, writes out an inappropriate prescription and leaves an illness untreated.

If, instead of telling the two kinds of economic disequilibrium apart and seeing that China is in the second kind of it, we set improving market conditions and decentralizing prices or intensifying macroeconomic management as our major policy decisions to stabilize economic growth and avert fluctuations, we are ignoring the most forceful restraints on economic growth and fluctuations imposed by weak firms that, as investors and consumption fund issuers, are not responsible for their management decisions, profits and losses. Under the second category of disequilibrium, firms are yet to become independent commodity producers liable for their management decisions, profits and losses, so their status as investors and consumption fund issuers is nominal and unrestrained. In that scenario, the following problems will occur:

1. Owing to their lack of autonomy, firms may not be able to make investment even when it is profitable to do so, thus making it hard to keep overall economic growth in pace with these firms' increasing economic returns.
2. Having no self-restraints on investment and bearing no investment, production and management risks, firms in the process of expanding investment will be susceptible to repetitive construction and fail to realize economies of scale. In that case, economic growth is likely to be a process of ballooning overstock and financial losses for such firms.
3. Myopic economic decisions such as allocating the consumption fund to serve immediate interests will impair firms' growth potentials and leave them with outdated equipment and technology. Economic growth will be held back as a result.
4. Firms with no self-restraints may issue more consumption fund than is allowed by their economic returns, and such economic returns are often adulterated even though they are pegged to wages and bonuses. Under these circumstances, the more tightly wages and bonuses are pegged to economic returns, the bigger the losses will become for firms and the state. Economic growth will invariably be held back as a result.
5. The negative macroeconomic impact of the lack of self-restraints on investment and consumption fund cannot be underestimated. Overinvestment and runaway growth in consumption fund are one of the manifestations of this negative impact. In that case, even if the

economic growth rate is increased, such an increase will be short lived and sow the seed for future economic disorder. Extended losses on firms and stressed fiscal balance are another manifestation of this negative impact, with stressed fiscal balance becoming a major cause behind economic instability and a huge obstacle to sustained economic growth.

6. The fact that firms take no responsibility for their own profits and losses and, in particular, cannot stop production or be closed down, merged or transferred because of government-business collusion, deprives the flow of corporate capital stock of proper channels and makes it impossible to optimize the reallocation of production factors. With bottlenecks like these, industrial restructuring can never go smoothly, and sustained economic growth is hamstrung as well.
7. When firms have no decision-making autonomy and bear no responsibility for their profits and losses, neither can their capital stock be made to flow, nor can the purpose of industrial restructuring through reinvestment be served. Increases in investment are limited, and limited increases in investment can hardly put an end to the disproportionate industrial structure. The problem, however, does not stop here. If we liken corporate capital stock to a pool of stagnant water, and reinvestment to flowing water, the real problem is that when year's increased amount of investment is reinvested in a firm, it becomes part of the firm's capital stock the next year. If this cycle is made to last, it is tantamount to constantly turning running water into stagnant water—no amount of running water can put an end to the situation. Consequently, bottlenecks persist and economic growth is greatly held back.
8. Under the second category of economic disequilibrium, because firms, as microeconomic units, remain as government appendages, whenever the government takes macroeconomic regulation steps, they either find it difficult to adapt their business activity to macroeconomic changes or cannot respond properly for lack of self-restraints. As a result, the government regulation steps fail to yield the desired results. The lack of elasticity—in the investment interest rate, the import-and-export exchange rate, and output prices—is exactly a telltale sign of the undesirable results of government regulation steps. In the absence of stability-oriented internal adjustment mechanisms, once economic fluctuations occur, the situation can only be tackled with government intervention. However, under the second category

of disequilibrium, government intervention from top on down to the grassroots level often comes seriously belatedly. The higher-up leadership (or decision-making authorities) will not take action until problems become serious enough. Furthermore, the negative impact of inappropriate government intervention on economy stability should never be overlooked.

These eight problems illustrate what is so unique about the growth and fluctuations in the Chinese economy in the second category of disequilibrium. Therefore, our studies of Chinese economic growth and fluctuations should proceed from the relevant factors, with the second category of disequilibrium as the precondition.

Understanding the Wooden Barrel Principle in Disequilibrium

An important principle in the disequilibrium theory is the "law of the shortest side," which is believed to be the key restraint on economic growth and the essential cause behind fluctuations. The "law of the shortest side" is tenable in this regard. This is because in a disequilibrium economy, the market cannot play a complete role in regulating the relationship between supply and demand, and therefore the existence of the shortest side becomes an inevitability, which forces production factors to be reallocated in compliance with the minimum demand. This is like a barrel composed of planks of different lengths. The capacity of the barrel is determined by the shortest plank rather than the longest one. If more water than the shortest plank allows is poured into the barrel, the water will spill out. This is what the "law of the shortest side" entails.

When applying the "law of the shortest side" to the study of growth and fluctuations in economic disequilibrium, the following problems are worth our further consideration:

1. Why can the shortest side persist for a long time? Despite years of economic growth, the shortest side of previous years remains to this day or becomes even shorter. That is, the shortest plank of the barrel becomes still shorter. What has gone wrong?
2. In theory, production factors are mutually replaceable and supplementary to a certain extent. This means that the shortest side could be

replaced or made up for by certain longer sides. In reality, however, the ability of longer-side production factors to replace or supplement shorter ones is very limited, a fact that has a considerable influence on economic growth and fluctuations. The issue here is: Why mutual replacement and complementation between production factors can be so difficult as to allow the "law of the shortest side" to become the key factor in inhibiting economic growth and causing fluctuations?

3. Reallocation of production factors can address economic problems caused by shortest-side factors, boost economic growth and curtail fluctuations. Take, again, the barrel for example. Since how much water a barrel can contain is determined by its shortest plank, the situation can be remedied in two ways. One is to saw a certain length off the longest plank and nail it onto the shortest one, so that the two new planks are level with each other. This can happen only when production factors are mutually supplementary. The other is to dismantle the barrel and put the old planks together to make a new one, hopefully a larger one. This is tantamount to the aforementioned reallocation of production factors. Nevertheless, in reality, such reallocation is an unrealistic proposition probably because the barrel is too solid to be torn apart for reassembling. Then we should ask why the barrel is so solid. Why can't we break it apart? Is it really difficult to reallocate production factors?

All these problems are relevant to the characteristics of growth and fluctuations under economic disequilibrium. Bearing in mind the differentiation between the two types of disequilibrium, and combing it with the fact that the Chinese economy is in the second category of disequilibrium, let us proceed from the "law of the shortest side" to observe these three problems, so as to better understand the "law of the shortest side."

Problem One: the Shortest-Side Syndrome in the Second Category of Disequilibrium

The shortest-side syndrome refers to the situation where shortest-side factors remain, or are growing even shorter in spite of years of economic growth and restructuring. Where is the problem? In economic equilibrium, shortest-side factors will disappear when the market mechanism promotes the free flow of production factors and resources are reallocated in response to price signals. In this way, even if new shortest-side factors emerge in the process of economic growth, the economy is immune to the shortest-side syndrome. Apparently, the shortest-side syndrome tends to occur when production-factor is stagnant and resources cannot be reallocated smoothly.

Supposing our economy is in the first category of disequilibrium, which is characterized by incomplete markets, inflexible prices and incomplete information, production factors can flow more freely by improving the markets and decentralizing the prices, and resource reallocation can take place in response to price signals. In this way, the shortest-side syndrome may disappear gradually. Though scarcity in some resources may make it difficult to reallocate resources and overcome the shortest sides, the syndrome can be avoided if this scarcity can be eased with replacements or imports.

However, the situation is more complicated in the second category of disequilibrium, which is peculiarly prone to the shortest-side syndrome. In this category of economic disequilibrium, clogged production-factor flow and troubles in industrial restructuring and resource reallocation can be imputed respectively to the "lack of information, incentive and channel."

"Lack of information" means that when faltering firms operate in an incomplete market, their access to price signals is bound to be inappropriate, untimely and incomplete. At the same time, because these firms, as microeconomic units, are under the strict control of their leadership authorities, the government cannot obtain timely and accurate information from both the market and these firms. Therefore, government quota adjustments are often at odds with market needs, and resources can only be reallocated in the absence of accurate information. As a result, shortest-side factors are mistaken for longest-side ones, and vice versa; and ineffective supply is regarded as being effective.

"Lack of incentive" means that the lopsided industrial structure is a solid fact, and firms have obtained adequate information about shortest- and longest-side factors and can respond accordingly, but they are not motivated enough to take action and run the risks. This is because, as government appendages that have not the final say in management and are not liable for profits, losses and production and management risks, these forms are neither motivated to restructure their products and nor willing to run such risks.

"Lack of channels" means that even if firms as microeconomic units and the government as macroeconomic authorities have both received adequate information about shortest- and longest-side factors and are willing to restructure the economy, there are no channels to facilitate the free flow of production factors. This is because firms are mere government appendages while the economy has been sectioned by a labyrinth of ownership boundaries, making it difficult to reallocate resources, let alone optimize them. All this bears out the unavoidability of the shortest-side syndrome.

Problem Two: Difficulties in Mutual Replacement Between Production Factors in the Second Category of Disequilibrium

As mentioned above, as long as production factors are able to replace each other, shortest-side factors can be eased with the help of longest side ones. This is not to say, however, that such replacement is absolute; rather, it is relative, and cannot work under all circumstances. Moreover, the replacement of one factor by another can either improve or reduce efficiency. Only when the margin of drop in efficiency caused by such replacement is narrower than that caused by the scarcity of the factors in question can such replacement be deemed feasible.

In an economy in equilibrium, whenever production factor replacement is possible, the price and cost-benefit ratio will motivate firms to alleviate the shortest-side syndrome by choosing effective methods for such replacement. In the first category of economic disequilibrium, replacement difficulties caused by inflexible prices and distorted price signals can be overcome by improving the market conditions and decontrolling the prices. However, the situation is worlds apart in the second category of economic disequilibrium, where the problem is not limited to the incomplete production-factor market. The fact that production factor suppliers and demanders are government appendages is more of a problem. For instance, when human resources are controlled by government quotas and sectioned to different departments, localities and firms, they are unable to make up for capital shortages even if replacement is possible. It is also necessary to make reinvestment and upgrade technology and equipment when there is a possibility of replacement between material production factors. On the one hand, because material production factors are supplied by some departments and localities, and demanded by others, it is hard to achieve supply-demand balance under intersected government administration. On the other, reinvestment involves problems concerning the investment system. If the old system continues, production factor replacement cannot take place. In a word, it is not easy for production factor replacement to be realized.

Problem Three: Hindrance to Production Factor Reallocation in the Second Category of Disequilibrium

We have noted that shortest-side factors can be compensated for through reallocating production factors. However, why is it so difficult to reallocate production factors in the second category of disequilibrium? Take the barrel again. Why is it so sturdy that it refuses to be torn apart and re-assembled? Herein lays the key to studies in the ongoing Chinese economic growth and fluctuations.

Production factor reallocation calls for at least three conditions: first, well-defined property rights; second, smooth flow of production factors; and third, competence of the organizer of such reallocation. The biggest reason why reallocation of production factors under the second category of disequilibrium is so difficult is that the first two conditions are not available. To be more specific, the second kind of disequilibrium is subject to ill-defined property rights under public ownership, business-government collusion, lack of responsibility for management, gains and losses, and lack of internal and external restraints on the part of firms. All these result in inefficient production factor flow, indeterminate beneficiaries of reallocation gains, and undefined risk bearers in such reallocation. These obstacles to reallocation arise when the first two conditions are not satisfied.

Judging from the third condition, the success of production factor reallocation lies in the organizer's proficiency for the task and ability to secure potential benefit from it. Who, then, is the eligible organizer in the second category of economic disequilibrium? As government appendages, firms have yet to become autonomous commodity producers, and are therefore not qualified.

If firms cannot organize the reallocation of production factors, how about the government? It is not that the government cannot do the job, but that it may not be able to fulfill the task in the absence of the first two conditions. Let me explain. If what is referred to here is the central government, it is powerful enough and in the possession of the means for such reallocation, but, as a macroeconomic regulatory institution, it cannot possibly be directly engaged in reallocating production factors. In fact, the government here refers to local authorities. Supposing a local government has difficulty in reallocating production factors due to institutional obstacles, to what extent can it break through those obstacles? Is it authoritative enough to overcome those obstacles? What's more, can a local government be highly efficient in directly organizing the reallocation of production factors? In any case, it is difficult for any local government to be fully competent in the second category of economic disequilibrium. Thus, the third condition is not available either. Furthermore, whether the organizer is a firm or a government, reallocation of production factors can succeed only when it is handled by someone who is highly innovative and capable of organizing modern production. In fact, innovators and organizers of this type are rare, a fact that also accounts for what a difficult task allocating production factors can be in this nation.

Production and Circulation in Economic Growth

The relationship between production and circulation merits due attention. In analyzing economic growth factors, some authors tend to emphasize elements in the production field, such as investment quantity and its proportion in national income, the input-output ratio, the contribution of production factors (technology, and human resources included) to economic growth, different combinations of production factors and their impact on corporate and macroeconomic returns. They tend to give a second seat to the circulation factor in economic growth in general and sustainable economic growth in particular. Three reasons may account for this analytical approach. First, they stress the decisive role of production in circulation to the neglect of the reaction of circulation to production. Second, they base their calculation of the economic growth rate on output value, as if increases in output value are equal to economic growth, regardless of the fact that the percentage of ineffective supply in output value cannot be counted as part of real economic growth. Third, insufficient attention to circulation and misunderstanding in the role of markets lead to inadequate understanding of circulation. Small wonder that circulation is held in a secondary seat in economic growth in these authors' analyses of economic fluctuations.

In the Chinese economy, however, the importance of circulation and consumption to production and distribution is becoming increasingly more pronounced in the traditional economic system's transition to a new one. It is because people's freedom and motivation in economic life are growing steadily. They are engaged in production to meet their needs. Those needs are satisfied on a daily basis through market transactions, and more and more commodities are reaching people through the market. Commerce promotes production, coordinates distribution, ensures circulation and guides consumption. As to all the consumer goods, most of the public goods, and a fair quantity of capital goods, the effectiveness of their supplies hinges on whether circulation can go smoothly. Poor circulation leads to ineffective supply, and goes further to hold back economic growth and give rise to major fluctuations.

The importance of circulation to economic growth is also evident in the flow and reallocation of production factors. Production factors fall into two categories: real ones and latent ones. The production factors that flow and reallocate through circulation are real ones, which is bound to activate latent ones. For instance, the full employment, free flow and reallocation of real labor resources will inevitably bring latent labor resources to the market to augment the real labor resources. The same is true with capital. If real capital is put to full use of and flows freely to effectively combine with other production factors, more latent capital will be brought forth. This is the way latent production factors are converted into real ones, to the benefit of economic growth. The role of circulation figures prominently in this regard in the current period of development in the Chinese economy. To maintain sustained economic growth in this country, which abounds in latent production factors but falls short in the supply of absolutely and relatively real ones, it is necessary to turn latent production factors into real ones through reform and hard work on circulation.

So much for the paramount importance of circulation to the Chinese economic life. In recent years, however, there has appeared an abnormal "debt chain" in circulation. Although this "debt chain" is directly related to economic austerity, overstocked inventory, shortage in capital investment, and the ensuing overdue obligations to suppliers, however, we can understand it more profoundly and in a new light if we turn our attention to economic disequilibrium, the second category of it in particular.

The "debt chain" is not to be perceived merely as a result of an inordinate industrial or product structure. It is understood that this inordinateness can lead to sluggish sales, overstocked inventory and overdue obligations to suppliers, but it is unfair to regard it as the fundamental cause behind the "debt chain." Inordinate industrial or product structure is nothing new, but why this "debt chain" has surfaced only in the last couple of years? What is more, why haven't we done anything about it? What has thrown the industrial or product structures off balance, or, in other words, what is the deep-seated cause behind the "debt chain"? Obviously, the answers cannot be found from structural inordinateness alone.

It is equally superficial to impute the "debt chain" to economic austerity. Austerity is nothing but a government policy, whereas the "debt chain" is deeply rooted in the economic system. It is thus unfair to blame the "debt chain" on a certain government policy, not to mention the fact that after this chain appeared, government policy has never stopped its move from austerity to relaxation, such as major increases in credit and loan grants. However, the loans issued to undo the "debt chain" never worked. It is all too obvious that austerity is not the culprit for the "debt chain."

In light of a study of the attributes of the second category of economic disequilibrium, the "debt chain" may be explained in this way: The development of a commodity economy is in direct conflict with government-business collusion, which is a hallmark of this category of disequilibrium. Therefore, the "debt chain" was born of the contradiction between government-business collusion and the burgeoning commodity economy. To be more exact, without the commodity economy, government-business collusion would not have resulted in overdue obligations to suppliers, let alone a "debt chain." If government were detached from business, the "debt chain" would not appear no matter how fast the commodity economy grows, not even when a temporary slump appeared. This is because when a creditor asks for repayment according to law, the debtor may liquidate his assets to honor the debt until he files for bankruptcy.

However, this is not the case with present-day China. On the one hand, a commodity economy is emerging; and on the other, the second category of disequilibrium persists. That is to say, the long-standing government-business collusion is yet to give way. When transactions between firms are taking place in increased frequency, if A is overdue in payment to B, and B to C, the debtor-creditor relationship can be very complicated. In government-business collusion, debtors are always backed by the government, so that creditors are not in a position to ask for due repayment, let alone demand for liquidating the assets. It is another story when a debtor is responsible for its own benefits and losses. This indicates that liability disputes between firms come down to disputes between government departments when the "debt chain" involves firms that are government appendages. Because such disputes cannot be settled by bankruptcies, the debts will be piled up, and the chain will grow in length with each passing day. Fundamentally speaking, the "debt chain" can never be eradicated if we fail to deepen corporate reform, detach government from business, and turn firms into commodity producers making their own business decisions and bearing their own profits and losses. In other words, the transition from the second category of disequilibrium to the first category of it must be accomplished at an early date to get rid of the "debt chain."

The nature of economic disequilibrium also sheds light on another major issue in the field of circulation, the issue of the outsourcing of circulation. Stable and sustained economic growth is determined not only by production, but also by circulation. Production bottlenecks, clogged circulation channels and ineffective supply all play a part in volatile economic fluctuations. Therefore, the outsourcing of circulation should become an indispensable part in our study of economic growth and fluctuations, the growth and fluctuations in the Chinese economy in particular.

At the first glance, clogged circulation channels bring about an overstock of some commodities and shortages of others, and strain supply. These problems merit attention, but they cannot be addressed by improving circulation alone. The outsourcing of circulation takes on a different meaning in economic disequilibrium from in economic equilibrium.

In economic equilibrium, where the market is complete, prices are flexible, information transmission is smooth and firms are liable for their management decisions, benefits and losses, the outsourcing of circulation is inevitably characterized by free circulation of commodities at flexible prices and by production and sales in the interest of firms.

In the first category of disequilibrium, firms are responsible for their own business management, benefits and losses. However, the market is incomplete, prices are inflexible, and information transmission is clogged. As a result, free circulation will run up against obstacles. Firms will find it hard to organize production and sell their products on their own. In addition, supply or demand shortfalls will make it hard for market prices to play a due role in economic adjustment, so much so that such shortfalls must be eased, to some extent, with quantitative adjustment either by the government or by the market.

The situation is much more complicated in the second category of disequilibrium. Apart from an incomplete market, inflexible prices, and clogged information transmission, firms are failing and yet to become autonomous. The disparity between supply and demand is more acute in capital goods than in consumption goods, and therefore, it is more pressing to develop capital goods than to procure more consumer goods. According to this interpretation, the outsourcing of circulation in the second category of disequilibrium should be interpreted in this way: We should develop all sorts of markets, capital goods markets in particular, while combining quantity regulation with price regulation in relevant markets, particularly in the markets for pivotal capital goods. Only thus can obstacles to circulation be lifted, and the effective combination of production factors optimized nationwide. The percentage of quantity quotas and that of price regulation should be decided in light of the degree of economic disequilibrium, because we can always make do with the second best choice where and when the first best choice is hard to come by.

It is in accord with the principle of the second best choice to understand the outsourcing of circulation in economic disequilibrium from the perspective of combining quantity and price regulation. What merits attention here is that the replacement of price regulation with quantity regulation in economic disequilibrium is not the same as replacing complete competition with incomplete competition. Rather, it is the replacement of one kind of incomplete competition with another. In economic disequilibrium, there will never be a complete market, and therefore the effort to improve the market is invariably in conflict with quantity regulation. It is unrealistic to deny the existence of such a conflict and its effect on economic growth and fluctuations. In the current stage of economic development, what we should and can do is to improve the management of circulation as much as possible, dredge up the circulation channels, further the commercial reform to minimize obstacles to the outsourcing of circulation. In the meantime, we should also mitigate economic disequilibrium in multiple ways to ease the conflict between market improvement and quantity regulation.

We have elaborated on the restraining impact of circulation on economic growth and fluctuations, probed into the deep-seated causes behind the "debt chain," and elucidated the need to outsource circulation in economic disequilibrium. Thus, we are able to better understand the economic growth and fluctuations in China in two ways.

Firstly, observed from the viewpoint of circulation alone, the profound impact of the second category of disequilibrium on the realm of circulation has clearly become a potent restraint on economic growth and an essential cause behind fluctuations. Only by taking into consideration the effect of the second category of disequilibrium on both production and circulation can the economic growth and fluctuations in this country be better interpreted.

Secondly, from our observations of circulation we can arrive at this conclusion: If, instead of proceeding from invigorating our companies to push economic restructuring, we allow government-business collusion to persist in the long run, sustained economic growth will be out of the question, and major fluctuations will become unavoidable. This fully bears out what economic restructuring is all about in the second category of disequilibrium.

Thoughts on Normal and Abnormal Fluctuations

The topic of this study being fluctuations in economic disequilibrium rather than in equilibrium, we are confronted with the issue of normal and abnormal fluctuations. Fluctuations are always deemed abnormal in economic equilibrium, where normal fluctuations are nonexistent. However, it is the other way round in disequilibrium, where gaps in either supply or demand are a common occurrence, and the market can bridge such gaps but cannot root them out. That is to say, disequilibrium is essentially balance with nonzero unemployment rate and nonzero inflation rate. To put it differently, disequilibrium is a kind of equilibrium that is accompanied by a certain unemployment rate or a certain inflation rate (or a balance with certain demand shortfalls and certain supply shortfalls).

Any economic gap can be interpreted as "shortage." For instance, a rise in prices, which means that excess money is chasing commodities that are in short supply, can be termed as "commodity shortage." Unemployment, which indicates that many workers are hunting for a few jobs, can be expressed as "job shortage." Similarly, undercapitalization denotes a "fund shortage," while overcapitalization points to "shortage in investment outlets." A bottleneck in resource supply indicates "shortage of a certain resource," while idle resources indicate "shortage of resource users." Since any gap can be regarded as a shortage, there must be two kinds of shortages in economic disequilibrium—normal shortages and abnormal shortages.

As stated above, normal shortages are common and inevitable in economic disequilibrium. However, it does not mean that a certain shortage cannot be eliminated by any means, but that one shortage can be eliminated probably at the cost of another shortage that causes even a greater loss in efficiency. For instance, a 2% unemployment rate is an indicator of a normal shortage of jobs, but someone insists to eliminate this normal unemployment rate. We are not saying that he has no way of accomplishing it, but that in doing so, some firms may be overstaffed and suffer major efficiency losses. In other words, the normal job shortage is eradicated in return for a higher disguised unemployment rate and a greater loss in efficiency. We may follow a similar line of thinking to prove how a visible inflation rate that is within a normal range of shortage in economic disequilibrium is made to disappear in return for an increased disguised inflation rate and a major efficiency loss.

From this analysis, we can see that the alert line for macroeconomic operation in disequilibrium cannot be marked with zero shortages (zero unemployment rate, zero inflation rate, etc.). The alert line in question is designed to guide government regulation. When the economy runs below this line, there is no need to take action. Only when the economy surges above the line should the government take appropriate steps to regulate it. Under disequilibrium, the position of the alert line is directly relevant to the extent of normal shortages. Assuming there is a zero shortage level in the economy (zero unemployment rate, zero inflation rate, etc.), the alert line must be somewhere above this level. The space between the two lines represents normal shortage; the space above the alert line is abnormal shortage, as is shown in Figure 12.1:

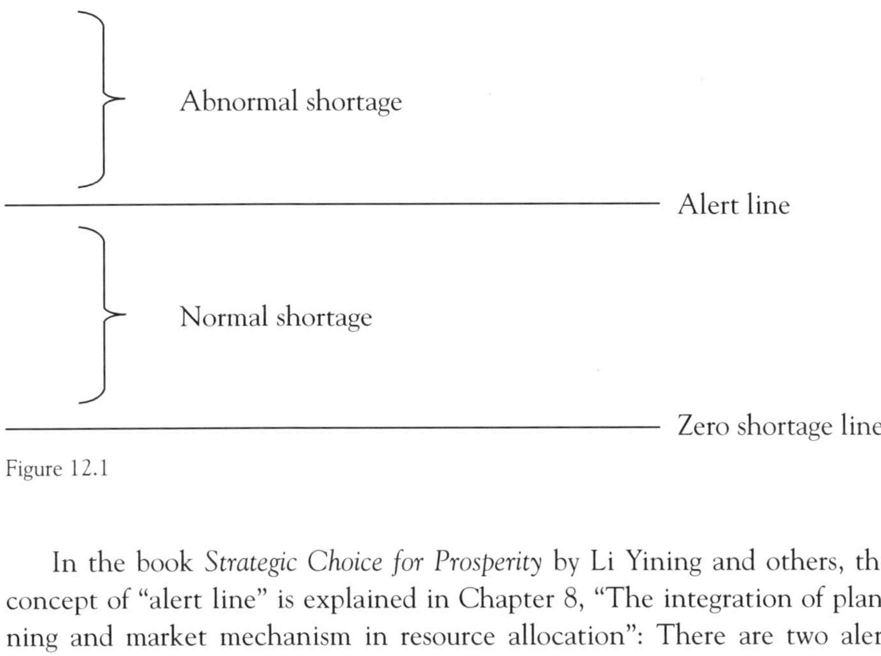

Figure 12.1

In the book *Strategic Choice for Prosperity* by Li Yining and others, the concept of "alert line" is explained in Chapter 8, "The integration of planning and market mechanism in resource allocation": There are two alert lines—the first alert line and the second alert line. The first line sets the boundary between market regulation and government-planned regulation. The second line runs above the first one. Whether the government should give priority to direct regulation or indirect regulation depends on the space above the first alert line. When the economy operates between the two lines, it comes mainly under indirect government regulation. When it runs above the second alert line, it is evidence that indirect regulation has not achieved desired results and, therefore, it is time to shift the emphasis to direct regulation in place.[7]

With a second alert line added to Figure 12.1, Figure 12.2 is drawn. The alert line featured in Figure 12.1 is presented as the "first alert line" in Figure 12.2:

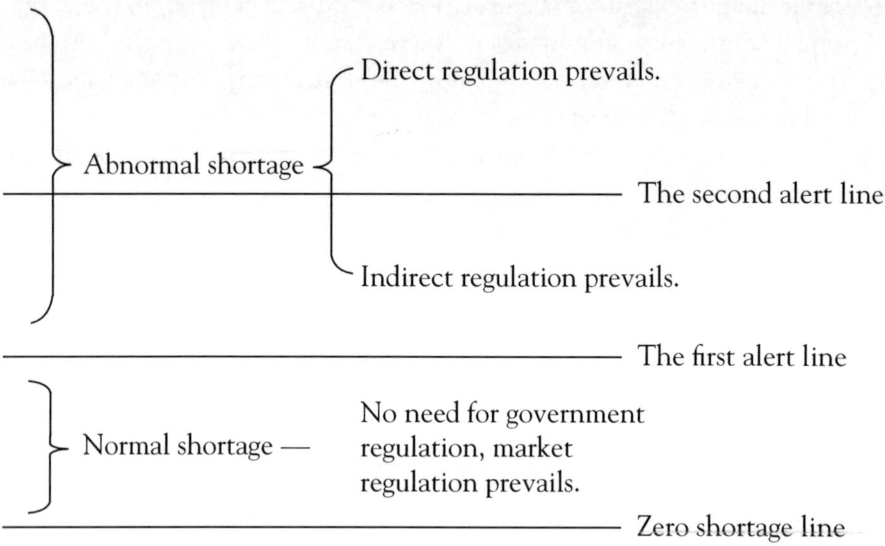

Figure 12.2

In *Strategic Choice for Prosperity*, an additional explanation is made: "Whether it is indirect regulation or direct regulation that prevails, the adoption of planned quotas should not be excluded when restraints on resource become strong and shortages run high, and changes in market prices and supply and demand must be followed."[8]

As shown in Figure 12.2, the second alert line divides abnormal shortages into two sections. Let us call the section between the second and the first alert lines "abnormal shortage I," where the government gives priority to indirect regulation. The section above the second alert line is dubbed "abnormal shortage II," where the government gives priority to direct regulation. If abnormal shortage in the economy is serious enough to necessitate forceful intervention, the government can turn to the "last resort," unconventional intervention in the economy. The reservation of this "last resort" testifies to the government's resolve and strength to regulate the economy—it will never look on with folded arms as the economy goes from bad to worse.[9] This can be shown in Figure 12.3:

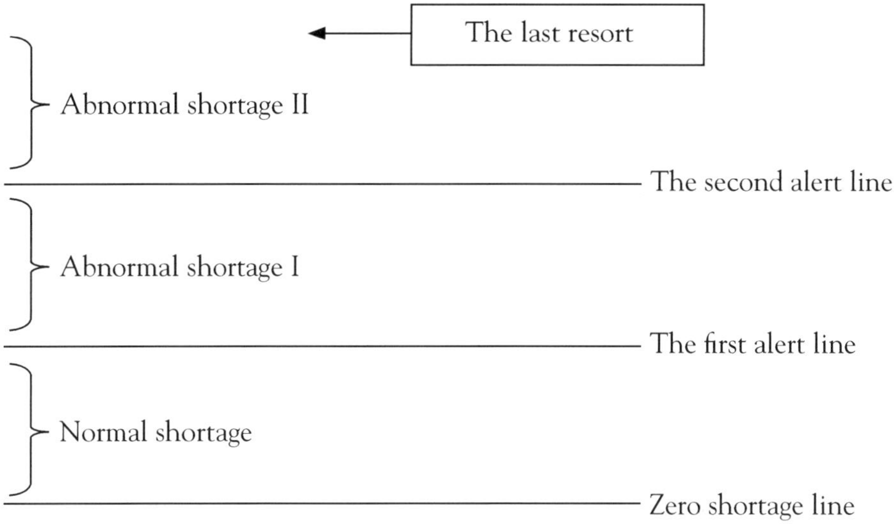

Figure 12.3

With these concepts in mind—zero shortage line, normal shortage, abnormal shortage I, abnormal shortage II, the first alert line and the second alert line—we gain a better understanding of what normal fluctuations and abnormal fluctuations are all about.

What are normal fluctuations in economic disequilibrium? We can reach this preliminary conclusion: When the economy operates above the zero shortage line and below the first alert line—that is, within the scope of normal shortage—fluctuations are normal.

What about abnormal fluctuations in economic disequilibrium? We can also arrive at the following preliminary conclusion: When the economy operates above the second alert line but is still within the scope of abnormal shortage II, fluctuations are abnormal.

Figure 12.3 indicates that the section between the zero shortage line and the first alert line represents normal shortage. When the economy runs within this range, normal fluctuations in economic disequilibrium occur; what happens in the section above the second alert line is abnormal shortage II, in which abnormal fluctuations in disequilibrium take place. This poses the question: Are fluctuations normal or abnormal when the economy operates between the first and second alert lines? Further analysis is needed to give a reasonable answer.

Fluctuations are usually indicated with changes in the economic growth rate. However, the economic growth rate cannot accurately reflect shortages. A high growth rate can be achieved under both normal and abnormal shortages, and so can a low growth rate. Therefore, when studying the economy's performance in a specific year or a period of years, we find it hard to discover the close ties between economic growth rate and the degree of shortages. In addition, changes in the degree of shortages are concealed when fluctuations are measured by economic growth rate. Therefore, if we judge whether fluctuations are normal or not merely by changes in economic growth rate, we are courting two mistakes.

First, fluctuations seem to have nothing to do with economic disequilibrium. The difference between normal and abnormal fluctuations under disequilibrium conditions is concealed in the changes of economic growth rate. Thus we cannot see through fluctuations and predict their future course of development.

Second, a high economic growth rate can be achieved in the presence of abnormal shortages, whereas a low growth rate may happen amidst normal shortages. This being the case, if we judge fluctuations on the basis of growth rate changes, we will probably go astray in attempting to maintain a high economic growth rate by expanding abnormal shortages instead of maintaining a low growth rate by curtailing such shortages.

Obviously, we cannot jump to a conclusion on normal or abnormal fluctuations in economic disequilibrium simply according to changes in economic growth rate. Rather, we should base our observation on changes in the degree of shortages. We will get a clearer picture of this if we observe the economy for a longer period of time. This is because, supposing the economy operates within the range of abnormal shortages under disequilibrium conditions, problems caused by such shortages will definitely affect economic growth rate and betray themselves in the form of marked fluctuations.

Now let us return to the previous question: Is it normal or abnormal fluctuation under disequilibrium when the economy operates between the first and second alert lines? The answer should be based on changes in shortages during an extended period of economic growth. There are two scenarios:

The first scenario: The economy has been operating within a normal shortage range, and economic growth has been achieved on this basis. If the economy runs above the first alert line and fluctuates between the two alert lines, such fluctuations are deemed abnormal.

The second scenario: The economy has been operating within abnormal shortage II, that is, above the second alert line, and economic growth has been achieved on that basis. If the economy operates between the two alert lines and fluctuates within abnormal shortage I, it is considered a normal fluctuation, because compared to the previous period, the economic fluctuations are moving towards normalcy.

(*Translated by Zhong Zhilan*)
— A speech at a meeting to summarize the "Growth Theories and Mathematical Models of the Chinese Economy," a research project of the National Natural Science Foundation of China
March 21, 1993

Notes

1. Hahn F. H. and F. P. R. Brechling (eds.) (1965), *The Theory of Interest Rates*, London: Macmillan.
2. *Western Economic Journal*, issue No. 6, 1967.
3. Leijonhufvud Axel (1968), *On Keynesian Economics and the Economics of Keynes: A Study in Monetary Theory*, New York: Oxford University Press.
4. Benassy Jean-Pascal (1982), *The Economics of Market Disequilibrium*, New York: Academic Press; Benassy Jean-Pascal (1986), *The Macroeconomics and Imperfect Competition*, Paris; Benassy Jean-Pascal (1986), *Macroeconomics: An Introduction to the Non-Walrasian Approach*, New York: Academic Press.
5. Kornai János (1971), *Anti-Equilibrium: On Economic Systems Theory and the Tasks of Research*, Amsterdam: North-Holland; Kornai János (1980), *Economics of Shortage*, Amsterdam: North-Holland; Kornai János (1982), *Growth, Shortage and Efficiency*, Oxford: Basil Blackwell.
6. Li Yining (1990), *Disequilibrium in the Chinese Economy*, Beijing: Economic Daily Press.
7. Li Yining et al (1991), *Strategic Choice for Prosperity*, Beijing: Economic Daily Press, p. 204.
8. Ibid, pp. 204–205.
9. Li Yining (1990), *Disequilibrium in Chinese Economy*, Beijing: Economic Daily Press, pp. 70–71.

· 13 ·

PROPERTY RIGHTS REFORM OF RURAL ENTERPRISES

I

More and more people are coming to terms with the importance of rural enterprises to the Chinese economy, an importance that has been borne out by reality. The reform of large and medium-sized state enterprises and the development of rural enterprises are part and parcel of the effort to reshape the microeconomic foundation of the socialist market economy being developed in this nation. Academic discussions are elaborate and thorough concerning the property rights reform of large and medium-sized state enterprises, but somewhat lacking on the significance of similar reform of rural enterprises and the approaches to it. Indeed, discussions about the latter have merely touched upon the development of the "joint-stock cooperative system." In truth, the property rights reform of rural enterprises is no less important and difficult than that of state enterprises. Moreover, the term "joint-stock cooperative system" is yet to be clarified. All this necessitates some in-depth study.

To begin with, we should not take the burgeoning development of rural enterprises over the recent years for granted. Rather, we should contemplate the role of the market in the survival and development of these enterprises, and look at the question of what is to be done to adapt them further to the market.

Rural enterprises have no lack of competitors. On the home market, they compete with each other, but their competition comes mainly from state enterprises, large urban collectives,[1] private businesses, equity joint ventures with Chinese and foreign investment, and imported commodities. After a rural enterprise is built or expanded, its managers must think about where its market is, how to carve out a niche in the market for its products, and how to expand its market shares.

Rural enterprises cannot count on local governments for incentives or fringe benefits. They are mistaken if they believe that local governments can help them secure local markets, bar the entry of outsiders, monopolize local supply of raw materials, and prevent local raw materials from being shipped to other areas. This is because local protectionism runs counter to market economy principles, and, judging from the requirements of either the planned economy or the market economy, is bound to be ditched. From the perspective of the planned economy, the practice of monopolizing the supply of raw materials and carving up local markets among local businesses flies in the face of the principle of centralization and of quota-based distribution. From the perspective of the market economy, local protectionism violates the principle of fair and square market competition and market unification. In the short run, this protectionist practice may benefit rural enterprises, but in the long run, it is wrong in that it protects backwardness, strangles businesses, and can backfire on rural enterprises themselves. Enterprises must grow in strength through market competition, because their survival hinges on product quality, profitability, and creativity.

If flexible business mechanisms can stand rural enterprises in good stead when competing with state enterprises and big urban collectives under the planned economy, that competitive edge can do them little good when they are pitted against equity joint ventures and private enterprises. Competition between rural enterprises themselves can be tough, too, as their competitiveness is neutralized by the common business mechanisms they employ and the common incentives they receive from local governments. Market competition is merciless; its result is always the same: in the course of it, some rural enterprises collapse, some grow in strength, and new ones keep appearing.

Therefore, it is reasonable to conclude that market conditions are the test of rural enterprises. Today, such enterprises are burgeoning everywhere in the country. Will this robust development grow to disastrous proportions? Under central planning, fast proliferation of rural businesses would have been the undoing of the national economy. However, that was then, this is now. The rural enterprises we have today are worlds apart from their predecessors in that they must face the market and be tested by it. The underdogs in market competition are doomed. Their predecessors might have still been muddling along under central planning and gone on consuming all sorts of resources no matter how inefficient they were and how deeply they sank into debt. The test of the market was always there, but under central planning, businesses could ignore such a test or stay impervious to it. Not so for the rural enterprises of today. They are sensitive to the test of the market because their survival is on the line. They must strive to raise economic efficiency and produce nothing but what the market needs. In other words, under central planning, the existence of too many losing companies was a disaster to the national economy because they could be established but were not allowed to die, they were allowed to hang around but not allowed to disappear. By contrast, rural enterprises today are allowed to rise or fall of their own accord; those doing poorly are phased out without mercy; the national economy is immune to fluctuations caused by drastic increases in the number of rural enterprises; and society is in no danger of turmoil when large numbers of such enterprises collapse. This being the case, if people are saying there are too many enterprises, that is because too many ill-managed enterprises are still dragging along under old-fashioned central planning and because too few enterprises can measure up to market economic requirements and stand the test of the market. If people are saying enterprises are growing too fast, we know they are complaining about the unbridled development of enterprises that are insensitive to market changes and never bother to cater their production to market demand, while enterprises that produce only for the market and whose products sell briskly on the market are not growing fast enough. Rural enterprises of today belong in the latter category.

II

I deem it necessary to say something about repetitious construction. Should repetitious construction be discontinued? Generally speaking, it should be disallowed. This is because with a given supply of resources, repetitious production is synonymous with waste, or unwarranted use of resources that serves nothing but to aggravate the already strained supply. With a given level of market purchase power, repetitious construction or production often means that, for lack of demand, some products become a drag on the market or are stockpiled, which again is tantamount to wasting or abusing resources. This double waste or abuse of resources is a cost or a menace that repetitious construction poses for the economy.

When censuring repetitious production, people tend to lump rural enterprises in with it, as if there were an indissoluble bond between the rise and expansion of these enterprises and repetitious production. Yet they have forgotten what really matters with such production is not whether an enterprise is rural or state-owned, but whether it has changed its operational mechanisms and whether its investment system is new or old. Rural enterprises are flexible in management, and they make their own business decisions while bearing their own gains and losses. Common sense tells us that repetitious production is a losing cause because it inevitably strains resource supply, inflates production costs, and inhibits sales because of the market's limited purchasing power. Rural enterprises do not meddle in repetitious production in the same way that a man never bangs his head against a wall, knowing perfectly well that such an action spells nothing but headache. By contrast, enterprises that do not have to bear the consequence of investment risks under central planning may willingly go after large production scales and as many production projects as possible at all costs, even if such investment brings no returns at all. The crux of the issue is precisely whether an investing enterprise is accountable for the investment risks it chooses to run. Rural enterprises do not embrace redundant production because they can, of their own accord, shun investment and redundant production projects that bring no economic returns.

From a macroeconomic point of view, we should go a little further in our observation of what people really want out of repetitious production. The term generally refers to building a new factory to make a product that someone else is already making. It is a typical behavior of waste. But the question here is: Does banning repetitious production protect monopoly and backwardness? Is repetitious construction detrimental to the national economy on all occasions? Should competition be allowed between manufacturers of the same product? Take, for instance, a certain product being manufactured by a factory, which is in short supply and leaves a considerable market share to be filled. The dilemma here is whether to allow the factory to expand production or to build a new one to make up for the shortage. In this case, construction of a new factory should obviously not be regarded as repetitious. Again, if the factory already in existence can meet market demand for the product in question but its price is too high and its quality leaves something to be desired, whereas the same product to be made by the factory to be built will be better in quality and lower in price, is it wise to allow the existing factory to monopolize the product and bar the participation of the new factory? It simply does not make sense to tolerate one factory making an inferior product and reject another factory that can offer the same product with a lower price and better quality. In all, repetitious construction should not be used as an excuse to justify protecting monopoly and backwardness.

Now, a look at the waste of resources associated with repetitious construction. It should be pointed out in the first place that it is a waste or abuse of resources to allow a factory to go on making a product at high price and with poor quality while banning the construction of a new factory to produce the same product more competitively. If, under the pretext of sanctioning repetitious construction, we choose to ban the construction of the new factory that can use the same amount of resources to produce a superior product, and tolerate the existing factory's poor performance, isn't that an abuse of resources? Moreover, it should be reiterated that the market is the test of all enterprises, rural enterprises included. As long as the principle of "survival of the fittest" is followed in economic affairs, those making expensive and shabby products will be eliminated and those making cheaper and better products will survive even if both the amount of capital goods and the market purchasing power are limited. The limited supply of capital goods and market share should be awarded to the latter and denied to the former. Through a period of competition, the fittest survive, and the least fit are phased out. The waste of resources is naturally taken care of through market competition. Isn't there any reason for us to insist that repetitious production is bad? Overlapping production of expensive and shabby commodities should be banned, and so should the overlapping construction of factories producing such commodities, whether the factories involved are owned by the state or farmers.

A profound lesson to be drawn from practice is that rural enterprises can never measure up to the requirements of the market economy if they fail to speed up property rights reform, organize production according to market needs, give precedence to profitability, and establish a managerial system that fuses incentives with restraints. We dare say that the good days are numbered for those rural enterprises that are doing well despite their ill-defined property rights. The market economy is pressing them to overhaul and transform themselves before it is too late.

III

This justifies the need to elaborate on the importance of rural enterprise property rights reform. This reform is designed to standardize the organization and behavior of market participants. At the present stage of development in this nation, its mission is to revamp those enterprises in which government administration is entangled with business management and property rights are ill defined, and which cannot make their own management decisions and bear responsibility for their gains and losses. Only when management is free from government intervention and property rights well defined can enterprises have the final say in economic activity, and account for their own profits and losses. The property rights reform entails transforming old enterprises and establishing new ones. According to the reform guideline, new enterprises should, from day one, have their management detached from government patronage and their property rights clarified, make their own decisions and be liable for their own gains and losses.

As is mentioned above, the market is the test for enterprises, and "survival of the fittest" the rule of market competition. To root out repetitious production, enterprises must be overhauled and new ones set up according to the guidelines for property rights reform. Only thus can they restructure their products in light of market changes, phase out unneeded products and turn out products that are needed and can elbow out competitors' high-priced shabby products. More importantly, property rights reform puts all enterprises on the same scratch line and detaches their management from government administration. Abiding by law and paying taxes according to rules, they are not directly under government administration and their production and business activity are immune from direct government intervention. Through property rights reform, every company bears investment risks and is liable for their gains and losses, instead of living off the government's egalitarian system of distribution and preferential treatments. The significance of property rights reform as a fundamental step towards a modern market economy is self-evident.

People are still wondering if property rights reform is as much needed by rural enterprises as by state enterprises or large urban collectives. The answer is in the positive: Rural enterprises need property rights reform. Such enterprises' survival and further growth are predicated on changing their operational mechanisms, making independent business decisions, bearing responsibility for their gains and losses, and ceasing to be government appendages. If they do not have the final say on business decisions and cannot take responsibility for their own profits and losses, how can it be said they have stood the test of the market and followed the "survival of the fittest" rule to compete for all their worth? If they are still subject to stringent government restrictions and intervention the way state enterprises and large urban collectives used to be, how can it be said they are a force powerful enough to breach the dyke of central planning? The saying that rural enterprises are following a different property right system than the state enterprises and urban collectives is a vague statement. It does not tally with reality in two ways.

On the one hand, only a fraction of rural enterprises have radically changed their business mechanisms to qualify as independent commodity producers. Many others are not qualified as such because they are still following the beaten track of central planning—they are rural enterprises in name but "rural-owned" or "town-owned" enterprises in reality. In other words, they are still appendages of local governments at the grass roots level. For them, property rights reform is yet to begin, and local rural or town governments are yet to come to terms with the necessity and importance of such reform. That is why it is absolutely wrong to believe property rights reform is not a requisite for rural enterprises.

On the other hand, even those rural enterprises said to have changed their operational mechanisms have, in fact, only begun to do so. Their property rights structure is yet to be standardized, and their relationship with rural governments is yet to be readjusted before they can qualify as one hundred percent independent commodity producers.

Therefore, the pressing task for rural enterprises today is to push property rights reform, standardize their property rights configurations, and put their property rights structure on a sound footing. To believe their immediate task is expanding production and increasing investment is to overlook the key to their development. It matters, of course, for rural enterprises to expand production and increase investment. But that should come as an inevitable result of property rights reform rather than a substitute for such reform.

The impact of rural enterprise property rights reform does not stop just there. There are other aspects where its impact is apparent. Firstly, it enhances farmers' awareness of their status as owners of their enterprises and thereby fortifies their resolve to boost production and transform their homeland; secondly, it improves farmers' cultural endowment and business acumen and puts rural socioeconomic development on a fast track; thirdly, it promotes rural government reform and shores up the nation's political power at the grass roots level; and fourthly, it improves farmer income and livelihood and furnishes beneficial conditions for the achievement of common prosperity in rural areas. The following is a further elaboration of the impact of rural enterprise property rights reform in these four aspects.

Enhancing Farmers' Awareness of Their Status as Owners of Rural Enterprises

It should be noted that without genuine property rights reform, the property rights of rural enterprises can remain vague and ill defined, and farmers' self-respect as owners—even if they are just partial owners—of rural enterprises will be hurt, and this will further shake their commitment to production and investment. If, on the contrary, property rights reform has been carried out in all seriousness so that every farmer-investor in such an enterprise becomes clear about his or her share of property rights, their awareness of themselves as owners of their enterprise will be vastly enhanced. They will become more attentive to the incremental value of the assets in their enterprise, and be personally concerned with their business performance and more enthusiastic for production and investment. When rural enterprises are energized by property rights reform to increase their profits and output, they can open the eyes of their farmer-owners and investors to the prospects of rural development and the impact of their economic growth on rural development. Their resolve to turn their villages into brand-new ones will be greatly fortified as a result. It is often reported that, bored or disheartened by village life, able-bodied farmers are quitting farming and leaving their country homes, causing a drain on the rural workforce. True, this is what happens in some rural areas. However, it is equally true that in areas where rural enterprises have grown to a sizeable scale, and particularly where such enterprises are using part of their profits to improve rural cultural and living conditions, farmers are in a peaceful frame of mind and live a contented life. Not only are local able-bodied farmers staying put, but farmers are coming from elsewhere to join them as well. Therefore, there is every reason to believe that once property rights reform has boosted farmers' awareness as owners of rural enterprises and vastly energized their enterprises, tremendous changes are bound to take place in the rural economic and cultural landscape, and local farmers will become more committed to building up their homeland than ever before.

Improving Farmers' Cultural and Technical Proficiency and Management Acumen

Farmers' cultural and technical proficiency and business acumen can be improved in many ways. An important way is property rights reform of rural enterprises, which is meant to turn farmers into true owners and investors of such enterprises, give them the opportunity to attend enterprise meetings, and open up new avenues for them to improve their cultural endowment, skills, and business acumen. This is because without such a reform, farmers are just nominal owners of their enterprises, and have no opportunities to attend these enterprises' meetings and make their voice heard, to say nothing of improving themselves through the activities of these enterprises. Under these circumstances, farmers' relationship with their rural enterprise is reduced to the point where they are mere workers or people who have spent some money on them—no enterprise would regard them as its masters. That situation can change dramatically through property rights reform, which serves to clarify farmers' status as owners and investors as well as their share of property rights to rural enterprises. As owners and investors, they can take part in the decision-making process or send representatives to meetings. In this way they gain a gradual understanding of their enterprise's business and financial situation, and get to know the causes for their successes or failures behind the rise and fall of the value of their assets. If a farmer happens to be working in the enterprise he owns or invests in, he is entitled to participate, directly or indirectly, in the making of production and business decisions. If several rural enterprises are presented to him as investment options, he may compare them, and upgrade his technological and economic know-how through such comparisons. The market economy is often said to be a great school in which people can learn a lot of things that cannot be learned from books. However, farmers can learn a lot more from the market economy as rural business owners and investors than if they are mere workers. The more they come to know the market economy, the more smoothly the market economy can grow. To help farmers understand the market economy deeply, it is necessary for them to participate not just as consumers, workers, or bank-savings depositors but as investors and managers as well.

Bolstering Up Rural Governments at the Grass Roots Level

The building of governments at the township level involves a number of issues, such as promotion of democracy in rural government elections, the building of Party organizations at the grass roots level, and the character building of rural government officials. It also involves readjusting the relationship between grass roots governments and rural enterprises. Rural government reform is intimately related to the property rights reform of rural enterprises, and the key to the success of both reforms lies in unfettering businesses from government intervention and turning rural enterprises into independent commodity producers with well-defined property rights and decision-making autonomy and bearing their own gains and losses. When rural enterprises cease to be government appendages, rural governments can no longer regard them as their own businesses, let alone turn them into their slush funds. This is something that can never be achieved without genuine property rights reform. As a matter of fact, there is no lack of local governments which, by capitalizing on rural enterprises' ill-defined property rights, put these enterprises under their control and turn them into their slush funds even if they are not making a profit. This inevitably saps the energy of these enterprises and dampens their farmer-owners' ardor for production and investment. As a hotbed for corruption among rural government officials, these illegal "off-book coffers" also spoil the image of grass roots political power, rob local governments of popular support, and destabilize local political and economic life.

The dire consequences of the wanton behaviors of rural government officials in this regard have been borne out by a series of legal cases that have been cracked in recent years. As *de facto* bosses of some rural enterprises with political and economic power in their control, these people have wantonly violated the norms of the market economy by willfully withdrawing money, extorting reimbursement for personal expenses, and practicing nepotism in enrolling workers. Shouldn't these behaviors be sternly sanctioned in the course of reforming the property rights of rural enterprises?

Obviously, it is not just a paramount economic issue, but also a political issue with a close bearing on whether rural political power can be consolidated and whether rural social stability can be maintained. We have got to follow the principle of defining property rights and separating administration from management when we readjust the relationship of rural enterprises with grass roots governments and turn them into independent commodity producers that enjoy well defined property rights and decision-making autonomy, and bear their own gains and losses. On no account should this task be taken lightly.

Raising Farmer Income and Striving for Common Prosperity in Rural Areas

Improved rural livelihood is a fruit of increased farmer income. The issue here is how farmers can increase their income quickly. Simply put, there are two ways to achieve this. First, developing farm production (animal husbandry, fishery, forestry, sideline occupations included), and boosting labor productivity by a large margin. Second, striving for fast growth in rural enterprises in the primary, secondary, and tertiary industries and for major growth in labor productivity, so that farmers can make more money immediately as laborers and investors. In addition, rural enterprises may also use part of their profits to support agriculture, improve rural cultural and living facilities and ameliorate farmers' livelihood.

Some farmers have left their home villages for somewhere else, but many of them end up working in rural enterprises away from home. It is thus clear that the property rights reform of rural enterprises and the effort to revive rural enterprises for further development are conducive to increasing farmer income and improving rural material and cultural lives.

What is to be done to help the rural poor to beat poverty? What is the relationship between the development of rural enterprises and the drive to help the rural poor? First of all, helping the rural poor is a social issue that can be addressed only by the concerted efforts of the entire society. This calls for special policies addressed to impoverished areas and households, aid from urban businesses and institutions for economic, technological, and educational and medicare development of underdeveloped areas, as well as help from families that have become affluent earlier than others to poor families. Another method that works is to enlist help from rural enterprises for poverty-stricken areas and underprivileged households. For instance, enrolling workers from poor areas and investing in these areas for developmental purposes helps tap local resources and boost local income. Rural enterprises in relatively more developed regions may pair up with counterparts in less developed regions. In all, the enthusiastic participation of rural enterprises can vastly accelerate increases in the income level of households and regions in financial difficulties. Such actions are an embodiment of the fruits of property rights reform.

IV

Now look at the goals target model for rural enterprise property rights reform. That the contract responsibility system cannot become a target model for enterprises under the market economy is a foregone conclusion among many accomplished economists, and therefore does not need further elaboration. Instead, what target model should be set for this field of property rights reform merits further study.

The cooperative system can be a target model for rural enterprise property rights reform, as it defines the economic nature and organizational form of enterprise properties. What this goal can achieve can be summarized in four points.

First, when adopted to establish or transform rural enterprises, the cooperative system helps separate government administration from business management, clarify property rights and enable enterprises to enjoy business autonomy and hand gains and losses on their own.

Second, when employed to establish or transform rural enterprises, the cooperative system helps combine farmer-investors and farmer-workers into one, thereby motivating farmers as both investors and workers.

Third, when used to establish or transform rural enterprises, the cooperative system can foster a congenial internal environment, thereby enhancing internal cohesion, and promoting labor productivity.

Fourth, when applied to establish or transform rural enterprises, the cooperative system enables them to tighten up their management system under a standard corporate constitution, restrain their leaders and protect the lawful rights of workers and investors, thereby paving the way for their smooth development.

With the aforementioned strengths, the cooperative system for rural enterprises should not be overlooked as an organizational form for corporate properties. The notion that cooperative enterprises are outdated does not tally with reality. It need be stressed that the rural enterprises established or transformed according to a standard principle are different from their counterparts that existed under central planning or still exist nowadays. Ill-defined property rights make it hard for those rural enterprises that are known as collectives in name only to identify who their investors are. Some of these firms are established with money raised by individuals, but they do not treat their investors as owners, and the investors themselves do not regard themselves as owners, either. By contrast, the rural enterprises that have adopted the cooperative system take on a new look that distinguishes themselves categorically from firms under collective ownership. The cooperative system may also be a form of collective ownership, but it is a new form of collective ownership adapted to the socialist market economic system.

The cooperative system, nevertheless, is just one of the target models for rural enterprise property rights reform. Compared with joint-stock rural enterprises, cooperative rural enterprises have five limits.

First, the cooperative system works smoothly when rural enterprises are small, but it falls somewhat short when they grow larger. When it is adopted to set up or transform a small rural enterprise, its investors are also its workers, thereby creating a congenial corporate atmosphere in which the "one man, one vote" decision-making system—the slogan of the cooperative system—works perfectly. But if the enterprise is big and has a lot of people on its payroll, the same decision-making system is likely to dwindle into a mere formality if it is put in place, for it cannot work as effectively in coordinating the enterprise's internal relationships as it does in a small enterprise.

Second, from a financing and fund-raising point of view, a cooperative rural enterprise compares unfavorably with a joint-stock one. A joint-stock rural enterprise can raise funds from a wide spectrum of public avenues, whereas a cooperative rural enterprise may have trouble raising more money than its internal fund-raising mechanism allows, especially under its "one man, one vote" decision-making system. This limit of the cooperative rural enterprise becomes more pronounced when it grows in size or when it lets a major profit-making opportunity slip through its fingers because of lack of money.

Third, when a rural enterprise sets about redefining its property rights, it is often harassed by the issue of converting its capital stock into stock shares. The same problem can be easily addressed under the joint-stock system. Yet under the cooperative system, it can be solved only by selling the capital stock evenly among members, something that is easy for a small enterprise but becomes unwieldy for a large enterprise.

Fourth, an enterprise in the course of development sometimes needs to acquire another enterprise's stock, or take control of it through such acquisition. Sometimes it needs to sell its stock shares to other enterprises. It may also grow into an enterprise group through mergers. These normal economic behaviors can go smoothly if rural enterprises are regrouped or transformed under the joint-stock system, but may hit some snags under the cooperative system.

Fifth, the cooperative system differs from the joint-stock system in that the stock shares of such a rural firm can be withdrawn freely, which can be a destabilizing factor for its production and business scale, whereas in a joint-stock rural enterprise, shares can change hands only among colleagues, which helps maintain its production and business scale. Moreover, under the joint-stock system, stock shares are transferred at the current price instead of the original price, which puts investors at a relative advantage. Under the cooperative system, it is hard to price the withdrawn shares—if the original price is applied, the man withdrawing his stock will find himself at the losing end of the deal, but if a higher price is set on the basis of reevaluating the assets, it may trigger off an exodus of stockholders. If that happens, how can the enterprise go on with its production? However, if a cooperative rural enterprise bans such withdrawal altogether, doesn't this violate the cooperative principle? Herein are some operational snags for such an enterprise in dealing with voluntary withdrawal of stock shares.

Cooperative rural enterprises are also confronted with the quandary of whether or not to admit new participants. If they do not accept new members while allowing those on the payroll to withdraw freely, won't they shrink in size constantly? At least their membership will keep diminishing. If new participants are welcome, what price should they pay for admittance? If the original price is used, it will do a great favor to newcomers and attract more new arrivals, leaving old members to feel cheated. Thus the conflict between old and new members will go from bad to worse. If newcomers are asked to pay at a price based on a reevaluation of the assets, the going will be tough for the enterprise. For joint-stock rural enterprises, where stock can only be transferred internally, the problem becomes a lot simpler.

V

Despite all that has been said, the beauty of the cooperative system for rural enterprises can hardly be gainsaid. It works as effectively as the joint-stock system in helping rural enterprises meet their goals by reforming their business mechanisms, keeping government administration from interfering in business management, defining their property rights, making their own business decisions and bearing responsibility for their gains and losses. The problem, however, is that the cooperative system works perfectly in small rural enterprises, but not as effectively as the joint-stock system in large rural enterprises, particularly where large and medium-sized enterprises are established or transformed. In other words, the cooperative system is appropriate for the property rights reform of small rural enterprises, while the joint-stock system should be pursued where the property rights of large and medium-sized enterprises are reformed.

This brings forth another topic for our discussion: the joint-stock cooperative system. What is the "joint-stock cooperative system" all about? Most of the rural enterprises that claim to be under this system are small companies under joint partnership. The others are irregular joint-stock enterprises. Rural enterprises that follow the textbook-perfect cooperative or joint-stock system are few and far between. For this reason, not just those rural enterprises that have not reformed their property rights should carry out such reform—those already passing themselves off as "joint-stock cooperative" enterprises should also undertake this reform in earnest, so as to standardize their operational system. They may either be transformed into cooperatives or joint-stock firms, or, in the light of their property rights situations, become private firms under either single ownership or partnership.

The term "joint-stock cooperative system" is somewhat off the mark. The cooperative system and the joint-stock system entail different organizational forms of corporate assets. An enterprise may or may not choose either system. It is impossible for a firm to adopt both at the same time, or combine them in one. Nevertheless, the "joint-stock cooperative system" catches the fancy of many a rural enterprise out of three probable considerations.

First, concern over being dubbed "capitalist," a term that may cause some raised eyebrows in socialist China. Out of the belief that the cooperative system is socialist and the joint-stock system capitalist, some enterprises choose to call themselves a "joint-stock cooperative enterprise" when regrouping or transforming themselves to measure up to the requirements of the joint-stock system. They do this to avoid unnecessary controversy and enhance their sense of security even though the name bears little meaning for a joint-stock company. Such concern is uncalled for today. The joint-stock system is, if anything, an organizational form of corporate assets. It is therefore contentious to call it either socialist or capitalist. The joint-stock system can stand on its own. There is no need to pass it off under the ill-fitting title of "joint-stock cooperative system."

Second, the belief that the adjective "cooperative" can help attract government policy incentives. This again is unnecessary. Government policy incentives may be granted in two ways. Firstly, an enterprise that meets national or local policy requirements for industrial restructuring naturally qualifies for such incentives whether or not its name contains the word "cooperative." It is the industrial nature of the enterprise's investment and production that counts. Secondly, cooperative enterprises deserve certain policy incentives in compliance with relevant national and local legislation. An enterprise must be regrouped or transformed under the cooperative system to qualify for such incentives. It won't do to add "cooperative" to the name of an enterprise that is not really a cooperative one. If a "joint-stock cooperative" is truly cooperative, why don't they simply call themselves "cooperative"? It is useless to gild the lily.

Third, mistaking the "joint-stock cooperative" system for a corporate property organizational form with Chinese characteristics, which is different from both the cooperative system and the joint-stock system. It so happens that some enterprises have divided their stock into "collective shares" and "corporate shares." Believing that this division does not accord with the standard joint-stock system, and that "collective shares" and "corporate shares" smack of the cooperative system, they have renamed themselves "joint-stock cooperative enterprises." It also happened that some people—on the ground that the cooperative system allows investors to withdraw their shares but the joint-stock system does not, and that in a cooperative enterprise under the "one man, one vote" decision-making system, votes are decided by the number of stock shares—have coined the term "joint-stock cooperative" system in the hope of incorporating the strengths of both systems, so that old investors can withdraw their shares while new investors, individuals and legal entities included, can be attracted. They assert this "joint-stock cooperative system" is distinctively Chinese. This way of thinking, however, is misleading. For their tremendous role in Chinese economic development, rural enterprises are "distinctively Chinese" enough. There is absolutely no need to concoct an ill-fitting joint-stock or cooperative system. Such irregular systems, if allowed to exist, can only hold back the growth of rural enterprises.

VI

Property rights reform is under way among rural enterprises. The rise of the "joint-stock cooperative" rural enterprises is a nascent phenomenon no matter how you look at it. They deserve help and guidance to meet established business norms. They should not be discriminated against, still less rebuked or disbanded. Their rise is spontaneous to a large extent. Rural government officials and local farmers have embraced them with great gusto. Some of these enterprises, though looking somewhat outlandish, are the brainchild of local people. If the rise and development of rural enterprises had played a positive role in the development of China in the 1980s, part of that contribution came from the "joint-stock cooperatives." If, with their presence and growth, rural enterprises are a powerful onslaught on central planning, the contributions of "joint-stock cooperative" rural enterprises cannot be denied. Practice proves that in comparison with the "orthodox" enterprises which are collective in name but centralized indeed, the "joint-stock cooperative" rural enterprises may well qualify as "heterodoxy." However, to unshackle the national economy from central planning, we would do better to have more of such "heterodoxy." Property rights reform should be carried out variously in light of specific circumstances, and different measures are called for to institutionalize the property rights configuration of rural enterprises. Such reform should also be allowed to go at different speeds. The general trend is that the cooperative system will be the target model for property rights reform in small rural enterprises, and the joint-stock system for this reform in large and medium-sized rural enterprises. Having made this point previously, I will not labor it further.

Joint-stock rural enterprises need not be listed on the stock market. Under the joint-stock system, only a few companies eventually become listed. Someday, however, some rural enterprises may qualify for it, a likelihood that should never be excluded. Most joint-stock rural enterprises, however, may be converted into limited liability companies, which I believe is a property organizational form universally applicable for rural enterprises. A certain number of them may be transformed into limited liability companies with internal stock shares. It should be noted that the joint-stock system cannot be divided into "urban enterprise joint-stock system" and "rural enterprise joint-stock system," nor can it be split into "joint-stock system for regrouped state enterprises" or "joint-stock system for regrouped rural enterprises." The joint-stock system applies to all manner of shareholding companies.

Some enterprises, out of one consideration or another, choose to stay with the name "joint-stock cooperative enterprise." What is to be done about this? In this case, impetuosity gets us nowhere. The goal of property rights reform is to prevent the government from interfering in business management, to define property rights, and delegate enterprises with autonomy to make business decisions and handle their own gains and losses. A rural enterprise may still be known as a "joint-stock cooperative enterprise" provided it has reached the goals of property rights reform, adopted effective business operational mechanisms, and has already been organized and operated under a standard joint-stock or cooperative system. Someday, it may awaken to the need to change its name to "joint-stock enterprise" or "cooperative enterprise."

The "joint-stock cooperative system" is a transitional corporate property organization form. The "rural enterprise" is transitional, too, and many firms have stuck to this name since its debut for two reasons: first, to differentiate them from enterprises under the dominant central planning, such as state enterprises and large urban collectives; and second, to take into consideration the fact that they are located in villages and towns, with their workforce coming mainly from among local villagers. What will become of these "rural enterprises" in the future? Will there be any more "urban enterprises" in contrast with "rural enterprises"? Can "rural enterprises" be established only in villages or towns, and can their workforce come only from local villages? If, in these early days, it is necessary to use the term "rural enterprise" to highlight their differences in business operational mechanisms from those under central planning and their identity as "above-norm" commodity producers, is there any need to differentiate "above-norm" commodity producers from "planned" commodity producers in a future market economic environment? As mentioned in the foregoing, enterprises are enterprises, joint-stock enterprises are joint-stock enterprises. There is absolutely no need to divide them into "urban" and "rural" enterprises, still less "urban" and "rural" joint-stock enterprises. "Rural enterprise," as a transitional name, will disappear at last, and so will "rural joint-stock enterprise."

This, however, will not happen anytime soon. Returning to reality, we should pursue joint-stock reform among rural enterprises and devise proper ways and means to establish and operate them. Moreover, to repeat once again, even though the notion of "joint-stock cooperative system" is inaccurate, and the establishment and operation of such enterprises can be very difficult, we may as well let such a title stay, considering the fact that it has been widely accepted by rural officials and farmers. The use of the name "joint-stock cooperative" system, or simply the "joint-stock system," represents a departure from the status quo. In property rights reform, instead of haggling over names endlessly, we should set our eye on the essence of things. If an enterprise is traveling down the road of property rights reform, it will not reach its goal in just a single leap. A more realistic approach is to go step by step toward the final destination.

— *Study & Exploration* bimonthly, issue No. 3, 1994

Note

1. Large urban collective, a term dating back to the Big Leap Forward of 1958, referring to firms in which capital is owned collectively while workers are accorded the same wages and welfare benefits as state enterprise employees. (*Translator*)

· 14 ·

RATIONALITY AND PROPORTIONALITY IN INCOME DISTRIBUTION

What does an equitable income distribution entail? Is rationality a better benchmark than equity for income distribution? These are major questions pertinent to the theory of income distribution. My answer is that the term "equitable income distribution" is vague and smacks of a rehash of the old idea of egalitarianism, so the word "equitable" does not make as much sense as the word "rational" in this regard. This being the case, it is probably appropriate to replace "equitable income distribution" with "rational income distribution."

What kind of income distribution can be considered as being rational? Let us start this topic from the double meanings of rational income distribution.

Double Meanings of Rational Income Distribution

The term "rational income distribution" means two things: the rationality of income *per se*, and the rationality of income disparity among people. These two meanings, though closely related, are different. For instance, both Mr. A and Mr. B have taken part in market activity as production-factor suppliers with A earning *n* yuan and B making *m* yuan in return. The first meaning of rational income distribution poses the following questions: Is the distribution rational for A to make *n* yuan and for B to make *m* yuan? Should they be paid higher than *n* yuan and *m* yuan, or lower? If they should be paid higher than *n* yuan and *m* yuan, how higher should it be for their income to be called rational? If they should be paid lower, how lower for it to be called rational? Such questions pertain to the first meaning of the term "income distribution rationality." The second meaning of the term poses the following questions: Supposing A earns *n* yuan and B earns *m* yuan, how little should the disparity between *n* and *m* be for it to be called rational? How wide should the disparity between *n* and *m* be for it to be called irrational? A and B are of course not the only production-factor suppliers and market participants, and there are income gaps among them. We may divide all production-factor suppliers and market participants into groups according to their incomes, to make it convenient to study the meanings of income distribution rationality by looking into the income disparities among these groups in the light of the second meaning of rational income distribution, or "income distribution rationality."

There are both differences and correlations between the two meanings of income distribution rationality. Studies of the first meaning should serve as the basis for studies of the second meaning. If Mr. A's earning of *n* yuan is rational and Mr. B's earning of *m* yuan is also rational, then the income disparity between *n* and *m* may also be deemed as rational. However, if A's earning of *n* yuan is irrational, it is hard to believe that the income disparity between *n* and *m* is rational no matter how rational B's earning of *m* yuan may be; and vice versa. People may argue that income distribution in China's recent past under central planning could still be regarded as being well-coordinated because despite the meagerness of people's income, the income disparity among them was not so glaring.

Does that argument hold water? The question can only be answered after we have understood the double meanings of income distribution rationality. We have to acknowledge that in those years under central planning, when income distribution was dominated by egalitarianism, everyone was underpaid as production-factor suppliers. Given that the earnings of all people were irrational, their income disparity was irrational as well. When income distribution is irrational in either meaning of income rationality, well-coordinated income distribution is out of the question in principle.

What Is Meant by Income Distribution Proportionality

Having clarified the double meanings of the rationality of income distribution in the previous section, let me explain what income distribution proportionality means.

Income distribution proportionality is based on both the first and second meanings of income distribution rationality. As was pointed out in the previous section, without the first meaning of income distribution rationality, there can be no income distribution rationality in its second meaning. Well-proportioned income distribution is impossible without matching income distribution rationality's double meanings. This being the case, we cannot talk about income distribution proportionality in the absence of income distribution rationality.

It was also mentioned in the previous section that if income distribution is well-proportioned at a low income level for every market participant, it is proportionality in a false, disguised form. This point can be understood only from the perspective of egalitarian income distribution. Egalitarianism is associated with low efficiency, low productivity, and low income level. A seemingly moderate income disparity under egalitarianism should never be interpreted as evidence of near-perfect income distribution proportionality. Well-coordinated income distribution can only be realized when income is distributed according to people's production efficiency so that every production-factor supplier can receive a rational income. Only then can we say that income disparity among people is rational as well. When everybody's income is low regardless of productivity level, income distribution proportionality is an improbable proposition no matter how income is distributed.

Talking about whether income distribution is well-coordinated or not, people usually refer to the proportionality not only of income distribution among individuals, but also of income distribution among regions. Regional income distribution is another topic of income distribution. We should see that although the effort to guarantee proportionality in income distribution among individuals may run up against some difficulties, it can still be handled with relative ease in comparison with the effort to achieve balanced regional income distribution. This is because whether income distribution among individuals is balanced or not is directly related to whether income distribution is rational or not. The evaluation of the rationality of income distribution among individuals can be relatively easy once the degree of income distribution rationality is measured (even though such measurement is somewhat difficult, a point that I will elaborate on later). By comparison, it is far more difficult to determine whether regional income distribution is well-coordinated or not for the following two reasons.

First, although individual income distribution rationality can be benchmarked by the amount of income individuals earn according to their production efficiency, such a benchmark does not apply to the rationality of regional income distribution. Individual income rationality means individuals earn on the basis of their productivity as production-factor suppliers. However, regional income distribution rationality is not well defined. Regional income may refer to a region's GNP and national income. If that is what regional income is all about, then it is hard to judge the rationality of regional GNP or regional income. If regional income equals the average income that individuals make as production-factor suppliers, it is still hard to decide whether it is rational or not, because the average income conceals the differences in efficiency between production-factor suppliers. Given the difficulties in evaluating regional income rationality in its first meaning, it is likewise impossible to judge whether regional income distribution is well-coordinated or not.

Second, rationality of income distribution in its second meaning (i.e., rationality of income disparity) is based on income distribution rationality in its first meaning. This should be the case with both individual and regional income distribution rationality. Since income distribution rationality in its first meaning does not apply to regional income distribution as described previously, there is no way to judge the rationality of regional income distribution. The most we can say is that the income disparity between coastal and inland regions is so glaring that something has to be done to reduce it. However, we cannot decide, due to the lack of empirical evidence, how little the disparity should be to put income distribution between the two regions on a rational footing.

Thus it can be said that even though the rationality of regional income distribution and of income disparity calls for in-depth theoretical study, it is better to focus on individual income distribution proportionality. We may as well leave regional income distribution proportionality for the future as a theoretical research topic. Of course, this does not mean we cannot use in general the term "promoting proportionality in regional income distribution," which is meant mainly to keep regional income disparity from growing out of control.

Efficiency or equality, which should come first? The answer will become clearer by treating individuals, rather than regions, as production-factor suppliers. This is because changes in efficiency—which is about effective use and allocation of resources—are relevant to the changes in the effectiveness of the production factors provided by suppliers. Equality—which refers to well-coordinated income distribution in the principle of equal opportunities—applies to individual income distribution and the income disparity arising from it, but not to regional income distribution and the income disparity resulting from that, because, as to income distribution rationality of a certain region or income disparity rationality among regions, there are no well-defined criteria from which to make such a judgment.

Differences in Economic and Social Senses of Income Disparity Rationality

Although we cannot but set individual income distribution as the focus for our study of income distribution rationality and proportionality, we must still answer the questions: What is on earth rational disparity in individual income distribution? And why does the economic sense of income disparity rationality not tally completely with its social sense?

From an economic perspective, let us imagine that production-factor suppliers are given the same opportunity to participate in market activity but end up with non-equal income. This inequality in income distribution is an outcome of distribution on the basis of production efficiency in compliance with the principle of equal opportunities. Therefore income disparity rationality in an economic sense can exist under two conditions: First, all production-factor suppliers are given equal opportunities so that they can join market activity from the same starting point; and second, these suppliers earn their income according to their production efficiency. Needless to say, irrational income disparity in an economic sense stems either from unequal opportunities (meaning they are not at the same starting point) or from failing to follow the principle of distribution according to efficiency, or from both. In a purely economic sense, income disparity stemming from either or both of the two factors is irrational, and is a manifestation of poorly coordinated income distribution, whether such a disparity is glaring or not. Such irrational income distribution should be remedied through redistribution by government. In other words, in an economic sense, as long as income distribution is the result of all production-factor suppliers having equal opportunities in market activity, with each supplier getting his pay in the principle of distributing according to efficiency, the income disparity, big or small, should be regarded as a sign of rational income distribution, or proportionate income distribution.

To define whether income disparity is rational or irrational in a social sense is more difficult than in an economic sense. Why? This can be answered in two ways.

On the one hand, to judge whether income disparity is economically rational or not, the conclusion should be strictly based on whether market activity opportunities are equal and whether income is distributed among production-factor suppliers according to their production efficiency. Yet in judging the rationality of income disparity in a social sense, it is impossible to find a criterion as strict as that for income disparity rationality in an economic sense. If the criteria used to measure the rationality of income disparity in an economic sense are the same as those for the rationality of income disparity in a social sense, then income disparity rationality would be the same in both senses. If so, isn't it unnecessary to separate the economic sense of income disparity rationality from its social sense? It seems the criterion for judging income disparity rationality in a social sense should not be limited to whether participants have equal opportunities in market activity and whether the principle of distribution according to efficiency is followed when income is distributed among production-factor suppliers. A new criterion should be set, but it is not easy to find out exactly what it should be.

On the other hand, the results of rational income disparity in an economic sense will be eventually reflected economically in efficiency improvement, productivity growth, and per capita income rise no matter how great the disparity is. Thus it is safe to say that the presence of a rational income disparity in an economic sense can yield positive results in the immediate future. However, if income disparity is too big in a social sense, it will cause social unrest whether it is economically rational or not. Moreover, social unrest caused by a large income disparity in a social sense cannot be felt immediately—it takes time for problems to crop up and conflicts to brew to the point where social turmoil breaks out. So it is not easy either to judge income disparity rationality from its aftermath in a social sense.

Given the differences between the economic and social senses of income disparity rationality, and the difficulty to define income distribution rationality in its social sense, we cannot but ask: Is it necessary to define such rationality in a social sense apart from defining it in an economic sense? We ought to say the necessity is warranted. If income disparity is rational economically, it would be ideal if it is rational socially as well. However, things may turn out like this in reality: An income disparity deemed rational economically is irrational socially; whereas an income disparity deemed irrational economically may turn out to be rational socially. For this reason, it is necessary to explore income disparity rationality in its social sense despite the difficulties involved.

Income Disparity Rationality in a Social Sense

As mentioned above, whether opportunities are equal or not for all production-factor suppliers in the market is one of the criteria for assessing income disparity rationality in both economic and social senses. The other criterion is whether income is distributed according to efficiency. The two criteria are necessary conditions for income disparity to be economically or socially rational. However, they are not sufficient conditions for judging an income disparity in the social sense. It is not easy to find the missing pieces, but we are not helpless either.

Irrational income distribution disparity, manifested in a social sense by income disparity among people, can lead to social instability. Social instability holds back economic development, and causes improvements in production efficiency to slow down, stagnate, or decline, thereby reducing the per capita income level, or inhibiting its growth. Therefore, we can say income distribution disparity is rational in its social sense if social stability is not affected by income disparity among people, if the economy continues to grow in a sustained way, if production efficiency grows as usual, and if per capita income keeps rising steadily. Thus whether or not income distribution disparity leads to social instability can be adopted as a third criterion for judging whether income disparity is rational or not. At least it is a sensible criterion at the current stage of Chinese economic development.

To scrutinize the issue further, at least three questions come to surface.

First, what is the signal for social stability or instability? The economic growth, efficiency, and per capita income resulting from rational income disparity in an economic sense can be reflected in statistical indicators that are at once computable and comparable. What statistical indicators should be adopted to signal social stability based on rational income distribution disparity in its social sense? How can those statistics be calculated and compared?

Second, as I have said previously, whether income gap rationality or irrationality has contributed to social stability or caused social instability cannot be determined overnight. It takes a brewing period before social instability becomes keenly felt, but that period can last for a long time, which makes it harder to judge if an income gap is socially rational or not.

The catch is to find out how the degree of latent social instability can be measured. When judging if an income gap is rational or not, how can latent social instability not be mistaken for social stability?

Third, social instability can stem from many factors, and irrational income gap is just one of them. This gives rise to the question: How should the role of irrational income gap in causing social instability be determined in a social sense, and to what degree? In particular, when the income gap is found to be rational socially, can social instability not be caused by other factors? Both questions can make it more difficult to see if the income gap is socially rational or irrational. The secret lies, firstly, in determining how to measure, in a social sense, the role of rational income gap in promoting social stability and to separate this role from the other factors that are also contributing to social stability, and secondly, in discovering how to benchmark, socially, the role of irrational income gap in causing social instability and to separate it from other factors that are also precipitating social unrest.

I do not list these three major questions to say that we need not to probe any further because of the aforementioned snags. It is precisely because of these problems that I believe we should not and cannot lean heavily on quantitative analysis in this field of study. Rather, we had better adopt a rough-sketch type of approach. To be specific, we may use, as a benchmark, people's satisfaction with their own income and with a comparison of income with other members of society. As people's satisfaction differs in degree in both regards, the findings should be studied separately.

The degree of people's satisfaction with their income may be termed "an individual's absolute degree of income satisfaction." This term refers to the degree of correspondence between the income someone receives from the production factors he has supplied on the one hand, and the value of his expected income on the other. A production-factor supplier will be satisfied with his absolute income if what he earns meets his expectation. He will stay satisfied if his earning exceeds his expectation even if the two are not symmetrical. If he earns less than what he expected, he will be dissatisfied with the gap between reality and expectation. The more his actual earning falls below his expectation, the more dissatisfied he becomes, and the lower the degree of his absolute satisfaction is with his individual income.

The degree of a member of society's satisfaction with a comparison between his income and those of others can be abbreviated as the "degree of individual relative income satisfaction." This term denotes the degree of correspondence between the actual ratio of income gap between an individual and the others and his expected ratio. He is satisfied with his relative income if the two ratios correspond with each other. He is even more satisfied if the actual ratio exceeds his expectations, even though the two factors do not correspond with each other. He is dissatisfied if the actual ratio falls below his expected ratio, that is, the two factors are ill-matched. The more the actual ratio falls short of his expected one, the more dissatisfied he becomes with his relative income, or the smaller the degree of his satisfaction is with his relative income.

Society consists of numerous members who differ in absolute or relative income satisfaction. No matter what the mode of income distribution is, there is always a gap between the degrees of a person's absolute and relative income satisfaction. However, an individual's low satisfaction with his absolute or relative income is unlikely to cause social instability. Social instability takes place only when most members of society have registered a low degree of satisfaction over individual absolute or relative income. Theoretically speaking, society's average degree of satisfaction with absolute or relative income at a given moment in time can be pinpointed. Social instability happens only when this average degree of satisfaction with absolute income falls below a threshold point. The deeper it sinks below the threshold point, the greater the degree of social instability becomes. Social instability occurs when this average degree of satisfaction with relative income drops below a certain point. The more it dips below the threshold point the greater the degree of social instability becomes.

It is worth noting that there is a difference between the degree of individual absolute income satisfaction and that of individual relative income satisfaction, with the former serving as the basis of the latter. If the degree of an individual's absolute income satisfaction is relatively high, his impact as a production-factor provider on social instability will be negligible even if his relative income satisfaction is low. If the degree of his absolute income satisfaction is low, his impact on social instability will grow even if the degree of his satisfaction with his relative income is high. The degrees of the impact of individual income satisfaction on social instability may be aligned in the following sequence:

1. A high degree of individual absolute income satisfaction alongside a high degree of individual relative income satisfaction, will have a minimum impact on social instability.
2. A high degree of individual absolute income satisfaction accompanied by a low degree of individual relative income satisfaction, will have a relatively small impact on social instability.
3. A low degree of individual absolute income satisfaction coupled with a high degree of individual relative income satisfaction, will have a relatively big impact on social instability.

4. A low degree of individual absolute income satisfaction together with a low degree of individual relative income satisfaction, will have a maximum impact on social instability.

As I have said previously, both the degree of individual absolute income satisfaction and that of individual relative income satisfaction should be indicated according to society's average degrees of absolute and relative income satisfaction. The above sequence of order in the degrees of impact of individual income satisfaction on social instability should also be expressed in the same way. Considering that the impact of individual absolute income satisfaction on social stability is greater than individual relative income satisfaction, when combining society's degrees of average absolute and relative income satisfaction to derive society's average degree of income satisfaction, the former should take a larger portion than the latter. Thus a threshold value can be set for society's average degree of comprehensive income satisfaction. Society's average degree of comprehensive income satisfaction and its threshold value may be applied to back up judgment of income gap rationality in a social sense of the term.

Finally, a rundown of the above discussion:

A: individual income;
B: individual's expected income;
C: the degree of correspondence between A and B, known as the degree of individual absolute income satisfaction;
D: the actual ratio between one's income and someone else's income;
E: the expected ratio between one's income and someone else's income;
F: the degree of correspondence between D and E, known as the degree of individual relative income satisfaction.
G: the average degree of social satisfaction with absolute income as derived from C;
H: the threshold value of the average degree of social satisfaction with absolute income;
I: the average degree of social satisfaction with relative income as derived from F;
J: the threshold value of the average degree of social satisfaction with relative income;
K: based on the impact of the degree of individual absolute and relative income satisfaction on social stability, to determine the portions of both factors in their combined impact on social stability;

L: to derive from G, I, and K the average degree of social comprehensive income satisfaction;

M: the threshold value of the average degree of society's comprehensive income satisfaction;

N: based on L and M, to determine, in a social sense, the degree of income gap rationality or irrationality.

A Further Look at the Relationship Between Income Disparity and Social Instability

In my previous analysis, social instability is a criterion for income disparity rationality or irrationality. I have said that social instability requires a period of time to gather its momentum. Only when problems come to a head can social instability be keenly felt. Income disparity is only one of several factors that cause social instability. This being the case, we have to look deeper into the relationship between income disparity and social instability based on the previous study of the average degree of society's comprehensive income satisfaction and its threshold value.

First, consider the cumulative nature of social instability. As the old Chinese saying goes, "It takes more than one cold day for rivers to freeze three feet deep." It takes a relatively long cumulative period for social instability to amount to social upheaval. When people's absolute or relative income satisfaction begins to decline, and once it progressively reaches its threshold value, the situation can turn grim in no time. Just as the old refrain puts it, "Things can take a sudden turn for the worse, and, if mishandled, can run out of control." A possible way to prevent this situation from happening is to break the threshold value of the average degree of society's comprehensive income satisfaction into Threshold Values I and II.

When the average degree of society's comprehensive income satisfaction dives below Threshold Value I, social instability will begin to be felt—meaning such instability is relatively mild or partial.

Social instability deteriorates when the average degree of society's comprehensive income satisfaction falls further below Threshold Value II—meaning that it will soon turn into an overall social upheaval.

Thus the grey zone between Threshold Values I and II merits close government attention. Threshold Value I provides a warning sign. When the average degree of society's comprehensive income satisfaction approaches

Threshold Value I, the government should be alerted and take action to avoid social upheaval by alleviating income disparity and relevant problems. If the decline in the average degree of society's comprehensive income satisfaction continues beyond Threshold Value I, the government should be further alarmed, because problems are boiling over and conflict is intensifying. Social upheaval becomes unavoidable once the average degree of society's comprehensive income satisfaction plunges below Threshold Value II. So Threshold Value II is another warning sign. It seems to me that the establishment of Threshold Values I and II can help further clarify the relationship between income disparity and social instability.

The role of income disparity in precipitating social instability, coupled its relationship with other causes of social instability, is a difficult research topic. It is oversimplifying to attribute social instability solely to income disparity. Social instability can be caused by a mixture of many factors that are affecting each other. This makes it hard to quantify the role of income disparity in causing social instability, not to mention the complex relationship between income disparity and its role in causing social instability. For instance, a small income disparity leads to low efficiency, which may result in a low average degree of society's comprehensive income satisfaction (such as in those low-income years when most members of society were disgruntled about the egalitarian practice of "everybody eating from the same big pot"), but it will have little impact on social stability. If income disparity is huge but the average degree of society's comprehensive income satisfaction is tolerable (meaning that most members of society find such an income disparity acceptable), it will not have a major impact on social stability. If income disparity is huge while the average degree of comprehensive social income satisfaction is low, its adverse impact on social instability can be felt; if the disparity grows to a certain degree and the average degree of society's comprehensive income satisfaction has also dropped below a certain threshold, the income disparity may lead to social unrest.

With the complex relationship between income disparity and social stability or instability in mind, we may handle the issue this way:

Let us take income disparity and the average degree of society's comprehensive income satisfaction as two indicators, and let income disparity be represented by the Gini Coefficient. The lower the Gini Coefficient, the smaller the disparity in income distribution. The higher the Gini Coefficient goes, the bigger the income disparity becomes, that is, the further it drifts away from equal income distribution. Thus the relationship between income disparity and the average degree of society's comprehensive income satisfaction can be replaced with the relationship between the Gini Coefficient and the average degree of society's comprehensive income satisfaction.

Whether the average degree of society's comprehensive income satisfaction is high or low, social stability will not be considerably affected by income disparity when the Gini Coefficient is low. Let us therefore forget about this scenario for the time being.

When the average degree of society's comprehensive income satisfaction is high, income disparity will not grow to a point where it can adversely impact social stability whether the Gini Coefficient is high or low. Therefore this scenario can also be ignored as far as this study is concerned.

Thus our study is narrowed down to the scenario where the Gini Coefficient is high and society's average comprehensive income satisfaction is low. Let us set the Gini Coefficient at Levels 1, 2 and 3. The higher the Gini Coefficient, the lower its level. We may also divide society's average comprehensive income satisfaction into three tiers: Tiers 1, 2 and 3. The lower society's average comprehensive income satisfaction, the higher its tier. The three levels of the Gini Coefficient and the three tiers of society's average comprehensive income satisfaction can be paired to serve as benchmarks for judging the relationship between income disparity and social instability. Generally speaking, when the Gini Coefficient stands at Level 1, and society's average comprehensive income satisfaction at Tier 1, the adverse impact of income disparity on social stability is the highest, thereby pinpointing income disparity as the primary reason behind social instability or upheaval. When the Gini Coefficient stands at Level 3 with society's average comprehensive income satisfaction at Tier 3, social instability may be caused mainly by other factors, or a combination of factors that may or may not include income disparity, even though income disparity is also affecting social stability. Under these circumstances, it is difficult to quantify the impact of income disparity on social stability, but at least we can get a rough idea about it by studying individual cases.

Conclusions

1. "Equitable income distribution" is a vague notion that smacks of egalitarianism. "Rational income distribution" is a better term. In fact, rational income disparity denotes a reasonable gap in individual income

distribution. However, it is necessary to distinguish the economic sense of income disparity rationality from its social sense. A rational income disparity in an economic sense is not necessarily the same as it is in a social sense. In the context of social stability, the government is obliged to take the social sense of income disparity rationality into consideration when intervening in income distribution.

2. To judge if income disparity is rational or irrational in a social sense, and to decide on the degree of such rationality or irrationality, two indicators can be employed—society's average comprehensive income satisfaction and its threshold value. To maximize the effect of government regulation of income distribution, we may benchmark society's average comprehensive income satisfaction with Threshold Values I and II. In that way the government may use them as warning signs in regulating the economy.

—*Social Sciences Front* monthly, issue No. 6, 1994

· 1 5 ·

MESHING FISCAL POLICY WITH MONETARY POLICY

Limitations of Fiscal Policy in an Incomplete Market

Policy Effectiveness in Relation to Economic Growth

The interaction between fiscal and monetary policies was a much-debated issue between Keynesians and Monetarists. According to post-Keynesian mainstream economics, in macroeconomic regulation the government should, except in times of crisis, avoid adopting fiscal and monetary policies that are tight or loose at the same time. A better choice is to pair tight fiscal policy with loose monetary policy, or loose fiscal policy with tight monetary policy. Monetarists, in principle, are not opposed to the interaction between fiscal and monetary policies, but they maintain that fiscal policy has great limitations. For example, a loose fiscal policy may not achieve the expected goals because fiscal expansion tends to partially "crowd out" private consumption and private investment, but if fiscal policy is tight, it cuts into the economic growth rate, resulting in fiscal expenditure cutbacks that invariably bring down fiscal revenue, thereby diverting the fiscal policy from its prescribed goals. Consequently, they believe that monetary policy is more effective than fiscal policy. Such is the basic policy preference of Monetarists.

In a policy debate with Monetarists, Keynesians further argue that the coordination between fiscal and monetary policies should be discussed in combination with economic policy goals. To be specific, they argue that it is necessary to observe the effects of the coordination between these two policies from the perspective of whether it is conducive to economic stability and sustainable growth.

A loose fiscal policy is supportive of economic growth and plays a positive part in GNP growth. But can it "crowd out" private consumption and private investment? Sweeping generalizations should be avoided in answering that question. The key to the answer lies in whether the market is restrained or not, that is, whether the market can expand in time with GNP growth. If the market expands constantly, a loose fiscal policy in interaction with an equally loose monetary policy in the course of economic growth will squeeze out neither private consumption nor private investment. To put it another way, the "crowding out" effect can happen only when a loose fiscal policy interacts with a tight monetary policy. Only in that scenario can the Monetarist hypothesis make sense.

Nevertheless, to pair a loose fiscal policy with a loose monetary policy is bound to aggravate inflation. But this consequence can be forestalled if, on the one hand, the monetary policy is loosened only to a certain extent, and on the other, inflation is kept within bounds by boosting economic growth and aggregate supply. If this condition prevails, it broaches the topic of to what extent should monetary policy be loosened to avoid inflation resulting from increased money supply without allowing increased fiscal expenditure to suppress private consumption and private investment. Research on this topic has yet to be fully completed.

Whether the pairing is between a loose fiscal policy and a tight monetary policy or between a tight fiscal policy and a loose monetary policy, it calls for a comparison of effectiveness between the two parings, as well as that between a tight policy and a loose one. Without such a comparison it is hard to decide how the two should be paired.

Impact of Market Completeness on Policy Effectiveness

The above summary of Keynesian and Monetarist viewpoints about coordinating fiscal and monetary policies makes a valuable reference. It is hard to judge which school is correct, because it involves the margin of economic growth and the margin of growth in aggregate supply. If the economic growth rate is too low while aggregate supply grows too slowly, neither fiscal policy nor monetary policy can work whether they are tight or loose, because fiscal expenditure will crowd out private expenditure or decline along with financial revenue. In that way, coordination between fiscal and monetary policies is out of the question. The analysis of monetarists may be warranted in this case. Otherwise, the Keynesian position may sound even more reasonable.

However, the experience of China and that of some other developing nations indicate that the effectiveness of fiscal and monetary policies is associated with the degree of market completeness. To be specific, both fiscal and monetary policies work most effectively if the market is fairly complete. By comparison, a tight fiscal policy tends to meet more impediments than a tight monetary policy in the course of enforcement, and, as a result, its effectiveness will be more or less curtailed.

The situation will be different if the markets—capital market, securities market, foreign exchange market, property rights market, and so on—are less than complete. In this scenario, monetary policy may come across more obstacles in the course of implementation than fiscal policy, and its effectiveness may be limited to a larger extent. By the same token, a tight monetary policy may face more hindrance than a tight fiscal policy. This is because monetary policy works through the capital market, securities market, foreign exchange market, property rights market and so on, whose incompleteness can deprive the monetary policy of its transmission mechanism or make its transmission mechanism less effective.

Fiscal policy differs from monetary policy in that it impacts the commodity market directly. If the general market is incomplete, the commodity market is usually less incomplete than the other markets, while the capital, securities, foreign exchange and property rights markets tend to be most incomplete. This is exactly true of the Chinese experience, where fiscal policy works relatively more effectively even though a tight fiscal policy may still encounter a lot of obstructions.

This point may be illustrated with the effect of fiscal policy on economic growth. Because fiscal policy has a direct bearing on the commodity market and can change GNP through the extension and contraction, or ebb and flow of that market, it can either restrain or stimulate the rate of economic growth. Even if the commodity market is incomplete, fiscal policy can still act on GNP through corresponding changes in that market, which is ultimately indicated in changes of economic growth rate. This is something monetary policy cannot do, as its impact on the economic growth rate can be considerably lessened—and therefore cannot be as pronounced and direct as the impact of fiscal policy—as long as the capital, securities, foreign exchange and property rights markets remain incomplete. In China, a loosened-up fiscal policy works better than a loosened-up monetary policy in stimulating economic growth, but conversely, it is also more likely to play a larger part in aggravating inflation.

The effects of a loose policy and a tight policy are asymmetrical in an incomplete market. Given the same money market tightness benchmark, a relaxed policy is more effective than a tight policy. This is particularly true of monetary policy in an incomplete market. This is because—under the assumption that the capital, securities, foreign exchange and property rights markets are incomplete while the monetary policy lacks a transmission mechanism—the impact of a tight money market is different than that of a loose one even though the effect of monetary policy is restricted to a certain extent. When the money market is loosened up, investors can always obtain credit from different channels, and the economy will be animated correspondingly even if the market remains incomplete. When the loose money market is tightened up, however, some investors will still act on prescribed plans, because market incompleteness has made them oblivious to the pressure of a rising interest rate or a rising reserve requirement ratio. This is because the more incomplete the market is and the bigger the informational restraints are, the more unfair competition becomes. As a result, some privileged investors can still obtain credit and make investment. They may gradually feel the pressure, but generally speaking, the effect of a tightened-up monetary policy on them always comes belatedly.

Pairings of Loose and Tight Policies in an Incomplete Market

This gives rise to the issue of how to pair a loose policy with a tight one in macroeconomic regulation of an incomplete market. Such pairings are different from those in a complete market in two ways.

Firstly, in a complete market, the effects of both fiscal and monetary policies are keenly felt. Even though a tight fiscal policy tends to hit more snags than a tight monetary policy, it works reasonably well, when and where necessary, to coordinate a loose fiscal policy with a tight monetary policy, or to pair a tight fiscal policy with a loose monetary policy. Yet, for reasons mentioned above, things are different in an incomplete market: Fiscal policy is more effective than monetary policy. To meet the goal of macroeconomic regulation, fiscal policy is preferred over monetary policy, whose role can be very limited unless robustly enforced. Therefore, it is impractical to count on monetary policy in this regard. Such is one of the salient features of macroeconomic regulation under conditions of an incomplete market.

Secondly, a tight fiscal or monetary policy will strain money supply, bring down the economic growth rate, and curtail the inflation rate, whereas a relaxed fiscal or monetary policy will loosen up money supply, boost economic growth, and reduce unemployment. However, all this can happen only in a complete market. In an incomplete market, macroeconomic regulation will be slow to take effect, and worse, the results might be unexpectedly distorted. This is because the securities, foreign exchange and property rights markets are more incomplete than other markets, and therefore the transmission mechanism of monetary policy becomes even more flawed. If curtailing inflation is the goal of government policy regulation, the adoption of a tight fiscal policy can quickly cool down the economy and reduce inflation because this policy works especially well in this field when it is tightened up. However, the tight fiscal policy needs to be paired with a loose monetary policy if we are to prevent the economy from being cooled to such an extent as to thwart economic growth. Furthermore, because of the incompleteness of the market, and the flaws in monetary policy's transmission mechanism, a loosened monetary policy cannot work properly in the course of enforcing a tight fiscal policy, thereby defeating the purpose of maintaining the economy's momentum. As a result, with the tight fiscal policy having a strong effect and the loose monetary policy having a weak effect under incomplete market conditions, the economy is likely to be over cooled or even bogged down in stagnation. That echoes the saying, "It is easier to stop a car than rev it up."

Similarly, when raising economic growth is the goal of government policy regulation, a relaxed fiscal policy can be adopted in interaction with a tight monetary policy because this is where the relaxed fiscal policy works particularly well. Stimulated by expanded fiscal expenditure or tax reduction or exemption, the economy achieves rapid growth, but it is necessary for the relaxed fiscal policy to be accompanied by a tight monetary policy to curb inflation in this process of accelerated economic growth. However, the incompleteness of the market and the flaws in its own transmission mechanism prevent the tight monetary policy from working properly in the course of enforcing the relaxed fiscal policy, thereby failing to achieve the goal of keeping economic growth and inflation from running too high. Thus, under incomplete market conditions, the strong effects of the relaxed fiscal policy, coupled with the weak effects of the tight monetary policy, can result in excessive economic expansion, and make it hard to contain hyperinflation.

Therefore, the troubles met in the coordinated application of fiscal and monetary policies in an incomplete market are attributed to the "limping status" of both policies. In other words, the pairing of an effective policy with a less effective one makes it hard to achieve the goals.

This, however, does not preclude the combined use of fiscal policy and monetary policy in an incomplete market. Rather, it means that the forcefulness of both policies should be taken into account when pairing them up. For instance, given the strong effect of fiscal policy and the weak effect of monetary policy, we can implement the latter with more impetus than the former, so as to maximize the outcome of the combination.

Conclusion: It Is Easier to Stop a Car Than to Rev It Up Again

In the previous chapters I have made a tentative study of the coordinated adoption of fiscal and monetary policies. What does this mean for the Chinese economy in the present stage of development? As I have stated in the foregoing, the effectiveness of monetary policy is considerably restrained in an incomplete market, which makes it even harder to be coordinated with fiscal policy. For this reason, I would like to draw attention to the following two points:

First, in the current stage of economic development in this nation, it is inappropriate to adopt a relaxed fiscal policy alongside a relaxed monetary policy, or a tight fiscal policy together with a tight monetary policy, because the former tends to lead to runaway inflation and the latter a stifled economy. The only option is to couple a tight fiscal policy with a relaxed monetary policy, or vice versa. Given the different attributes of the effects of the fiscal and monetary policies under incomplete market conditions, I would suggest a relatively tight fiscal policy alongside a relaxed monetary policy.

Second, under incomplete market conditions, the Chinese economy is typical of the saying, "It is easier to stop a car than to rev it up again." It is also where the asymmetrical nature of the effects of macroeconomic regulation is most pronounced. That is to say, when macroeconomic regulation tightens up, its effect is quickly felt and the economy retrenches as a result. By contrast, if macroeconomic regulation slackens only slightly, it can hardly serve the purpose, because the economy can only revive slowly or stay stagnant for a considerable time before it comes back to its own. Why? Because the economy can be dynamic, the purchasing power stays strong and the market thrives only when businesses and investors are optimistic about the prospects of good profits and consumers are confident in anticipation of higher income. Nevertheless, it takes time to boost optimism and confidence. Expansionary policies cannot make people sanguine about market prospects right away, while the "limping state" in which fiscal policy outplays monetary policy can land macroeconomic regulation in an impasse. It will be even harder to rev up the economy with a tight fiscal policy in the absence of a relaxed monetary policy.

Hence the foregone conclusion: At the present stage of development, China can only slightly tighten up its fiscal policy while loosening up its monetary policy a little. Otherwise, the economy can never be delivered from the dilemma in which "it is easier to stop the car than to start it up again."

Be Prudent With Unconventional Monetary Policy Tools

Three Basic Monetary Policy Tools Predicated on Market Completeness

Monetary policy impacts GNP through its effects on the capital, securities, foreign exchange and property rights markets. If changing GNP is the policy's ultimate goal, a series of intermediary goals are needed. If changing inflation and GNP are the dual ultimate goals, they cannot be fulfilled before the intermediary goals are attained. Therefore, in our research on the impact of monetary policy on the economy, we should study this policy's transmission mechanism, and observe, through its different tools, the policy's impact on the intermediary goals, for the purpose of finding the ways and means with which to attain the ultimate goals through these intermediary goals.

Interest rate is one of the intermediary goals of monetary policy. Under complete market conditions, the central bank applies a rediscount policy to influence the interest rate. When the rediscount rate is readjusted, it will change commercial banks' cost of borrowed funds, thereby precipitating readjustments in the interest rate on the market, and compelling investors to raise or reduce their monetary demand. Money supply thus becomes the most important of all intermediate goals that, alongside the interest rate, influences society's monetary demand, aggregate demand, and GNP. If the monetary policy's transmission mechanism is effective, it can exert its impact, through the central bank's rediscount policy, to attain both the intermediate goals and the ultimate goals. This, however, also has something to do with the economic environment as a whole. If the market is incomplete, rediscount policy cannot work as a monetary policy step on money demand the way it does in a complete market, nor can it work effectively for the attainment of another intermediate goal, the volume of money flow. Unless the rediscount policy is executed with government intervention, changing the rediscount rate cannot work on the increases or reductions in money flow.

We may take a further look at the impact of the rediscount rate. For the changing rate to exert a desired influence on interest rate, there need be full competition among commercial banks that are supposed to grant loans to clients strictly in line with the norms of market competition and selection, while the clients are likewise expected to compete on an equal footing. Otherwise, the impact of rediscount rate readjustments on interest rate will be much confined.

Adjusting reserve requirement ratio is another monetary policy tool to influence commercial banks' derived deposit, restrain their lending behavior, and ultimately affect money supply. Here, another intermediate goal—the volume of money supply—can be attained through adjusting the central bank's reserve requirement ratio. This, however, can materialize only when this ratio stays at a high level. Otherwise, even though the reserve requirement ratio can work as a monetary policy tool, it cannot serve the purpose of forestalling any financial crisis. Furthermore, the reserve requirement ratio cannot function as a policy tool without two preconditions. For one thing, commercial banks should set maximum profits as their goal, for without such a goal, the effectiveness of readjustments in the reserve requirement ratio and of the reserve requirement system itself will be greatly blunted. This precondition is hinged on the soundness of the commercial banking system. For another, central bank's adjustment of the reserve requirement ratio should be compulsory rather than elastic; otherwise it could defeat the purpose of this monetary policy tool to intervene in money supply. Although the adjustment of reserve requirement ratio is not a frequent monetary policy tool, the effectiveness of its transmission mechanism still rests on the degree of market completion.

The central bank's open market operation is yet another monetary policy tool that should also be observed from an economic environment perspective. In comparison with other monetary policy tools, open market operation calls for more stringent market conditions—a complete and mature securities market over and above a rational market interest rate and sensible investors. Pitfalls in the transmission mechanism of open market operation cannot only make it hard to achieve the intermediate goal of adjusting money supply but also frustrate open market operation as a monetary policy tool.

The rediscount rate, the reserve requirement ratio, and open market operation discussed here are three essential monetary policy tools. Their transmission mechanisms are, without exception, associated with the soundness of the market and the commercial banking system. They invariably become crippled or totally ineffective under incomplete market conditions or a flawed commercial banking system.

Unconventional Policy Tools Also Depend on Market Completeness

Now a look at two unconventional policy tools besides the three aforementioned monetary policy tools: (1) credit scale control or credit rationing; and (2) rediscount quotas and relending quotas. The central bank uses the former to control the lending scale of commercial banks, and the latter as a supplement to rediscount rate readjustments. Both are adopted under incomplete market conditions or under a flawed commercial banking system, but each uses a different transmission mechanism.

The central bank decides credit scale on the basis of its judgments of the economic situation. Differences in the grounds and perspectives for such judgment, and errors in evaluating credit scale effectiveness invariably lead to considerable arbitrariness in the central bank's credit scale control. The will of the government plays a big role therein as well. Controlled credit scale can change the money supply volume directly and rapidly, and in that sense, the transmission mechanism of the credit scale control policy is effective. However, prompt response and an effective transmission mechanism are not necessarily conducive to the attainment of the monetary policy's ultimate goal. This is mainly because resource allocation must be optimized constantly if economic growth is to be sustained and inflation is to remain low. Optimized resource allocation indicates improved efficiency. However, the effectiveness of credit scale control is a different story. The problem with credit scale control is that money supply may change the way policymakers want in the short run, but in the long run, with policymakers' will imposed on it, this monetary policy tool is detrimental to optimizing resource allocation, and will inevitably derail the monetary policy's ultimate goal.

Rediscount and relending quotas are adopted as another unconventional policy tool to make up for the limitations of rediscount rate readjustments. Rediscount quotas may enable the central bank to manipulate commercial banks' money-lending capacities by increasing or decreasing such quotas, and starting from there to further control overall money supply. The same purpose can be achieved by increasing or decreasing the relending quotas. However, the central bank's rediscount quotas and relending quotas, being arbitrarily decided by the government, are so subjective that they do not necessarily fit the reality of money supply. Therefore, whether such quotas are beneficial or detrimental to the realization of the monetary policy's ultimate goal is open to question. On the other hand, these unconventional tools may impair the optimization of resource allocation, and, in the long run, will hold back the attainment of the ultimate goal of the monetary policy.

Using Credit Scale Control and Other Unconventional Measures With Prudence

From our study of monetary policy's transmission mechanisms we may conclude that if the market is complete and the commercial banking system sound, these transmission mechanisms may work effectively. If the market is incomplete and the commercial banking system flawed, it is impossible for conventional monetary policy tools to achieve expected results. As to such unconventional monetary policy tools as credit scale control, rediscount quotas and relending quotas, although their transmission mechanisms may remain effective in such a scenario, they are, in the long run, detrimental to the optimization of resource allocation and the attainment of the monetary policy's ultimate goal.

The question at hand to be answered is: What is to be done to reactivate the economy after a period of economic retrenchment? As is noted in the previous section, the adoption of a relatively tight fiscal policy in coordination with a loosened monetary policy under these circumstances is better than the pairing of a loosened fiscal policy with a tightened monetary policy, and even better than coupling fiscal and monetary policies that are both rigid or both relaxed. Our analysis of monetary policy's transmission mechanisms is further proof that this conclusion tallies with the reality of our nation.

Unconventional monetary policy tools—credit scale control, rediscount quotas, and relending quotas included—are often resorted to under incomplete market conditions. Worse, the trend is to regard these unconventional measures as conventional ones, as if the ultimate goal of the monetary policy can never be attained without doing so. In fact, this is sheer misunderstanding. Just as is discussed in the foregoing, despite being somewhat effective, these unconventional measures are harmful to optimizing resource allocation, and, corrupted by government will, cannot satisfactorily fit the money supply situation in economic operation.

To rejuvenate the economy after a period of retrenchment, it is imperative to loosen up the monetary policy more forcefully along with a relatively tight fiscal policy. Thus prudence must be applied when employing such unconventional policy measures as credit scale control, and for three reasons:

First, the transition from economic entrenchment to economic revival hinges on restoring and enhancing public confidence in market prospects, but confidence can be built up only through a cumulative process. The adoption of unconventional monetary policy tools can engender nothing but uncertainty whether they are relaxed or rigid. If the government can employ relaxed measures, it can also choose rigid ones. In either case there are no norms to go by, because things are at the mercy of those who adopt such measures. The result can be the same: People feel their confidence draining away. That being the case, little or no use should be made of unconventional measures. We would rather adopt conventional monetary policy tools that are sure to help boost people's confidence. Although incomplete market conditions may somewhat tarnish such measures' effectiveness, that can be remedied with redoubled enforcement efforts.

Second, because unconventional monetary policy tools are often misleading to investors, and thus of great disservice to optimizing resource allocation even if a relaxed monetary policy has been adopted to activate the economy, the ultimate goal still cannot be attained due to the failure of these tools to optimize resource allocation. To rejuvenate the economy and keep it primed after a period of retrenchment, it is really important to focus on optimizing resource allocation so that production factors can be grouped and resource use efficiency increased according to market demand. In this regard, unconventional monetary policy measures compare unfavorably with conventional ones. It must be pointed out that, the restraints imposed on conventional measures by an incomplete market can always be overcome through redoubled implementation efforts.

Third, monetary policy can be loosened up a little more than usual, but this should be done on condition that commercial banks issue loans only according to the redeemability of such loans and the borrowers' fund use efficiency. Otherwise bad debts will pile up, and economic vitality will suffer. What, then, is to be done to avoid the accumulation of debts under a relaxed monetary policy? What kind of monetary policy measures—conventional or unconventional—should be employed in this regard? Obviously, unconventional monetary policy measures are susceptible to arbitrariness and government intervention, making it hard to curtail bad debts, let alone achieve the anticipated results of the relaxed monetary policy.

The Eclipse of Monetary Policy's Effectiveness

What Makes Monetary Policy Increasingly Less Effective

The eclipse of monetary policy's effectiveness becomes an issue when our study comes to the position and impact on objective economic regulation of such policy. This refers to the fact that after a monetary policy has been executed for some time, its positive impact on attaining the ultimate goals of economic growth and monetary stability will ebb steadily while its negative impact on the economy will increase.

The waning of a monetary policy's effectiveness may be a universal occurrence. It happens whether the market and commercial banking system are flawless or not. Naturally, the decline in policy effectiveness becomes more serious when the market is incomplete and the commercial banking system faulty.

The decreasing effectiveness of monetary policy is attributed mainly to the fact that market participants—commercial banks, other monetary institutions, and non-governmental investors—are sensible economic agents that react rationally to the monetary policy adopted by the central bank. Even if the market is complete and the commercial banking system healthy, these agents will take countermeasures against the changing economic landscape and policy if their overriding thought is to maximize their own interests. Such countermeasures may cause the effectiveness of a certain monetary policy measure to decrease correspondingly, or force the central bank to reconsider its policy's effectiveness and readjust it. This phenomenon is undoubtedly more pronounced under incomplete market conditions and a flawed commercial banking system.

Monetary policy's waning effectiveness has also something to do with the limitations of its transmission mechanisms. The policy attains the ultimate goal through intermediate goals. However, the economy is in a state of constant restructuring that constantly updates money demand. That is to say, the relationship between money supply and demand always changes in pace with economic restructuring. The monetary policy tools taken are, without exception, focused on changing money supply, to the neglect of the new money demand of economic restructuring. As a matter of fact, this means the central bank's monetary policy should be designed to adapt such demand to money supply, not the other way around. Changing the money supply is an intermediate goal of monetary policy; changing the demand for money is not. To put it another way, the monetary policy impacts directly on money supply, and indirectly on money demand by changing money supply. Thus it can be said the monetary policy does not have a transmission mechanism that directly impacts money demand. Precisely because of this missing point in the transmission mechanism, investors in the chain of money demand inevitably seek to meet their demand for money or influence the aggregate demand for money through other channels, which are beyond the reach of policymakers. Thus the steady decline in the monetary policy's effectiveness becomes inevitable even if the market is complete and the commercial banking system perfect. The achievement of this policy's ultimate goal, observed from a monetary point of view, is predicated on changes not only in money supply but also in money demand. Only by coordinating such supply and demand can a monetary policy be effective in the attainment of the ultimate goal.

The Eclipse of Monetary Policy's Effectiveness Under Incomplete Market Conditions

The unstoppable ebb of a monetary policy's effectiveness under incomplete market conditions and an imperfect commercial banking system is also ascribed to the following causes that are perhaps more important than the aforementioned ones.

First, in an incomplete market and under a flawed commercial banking system, the central bank habitually resorts to unconventional monetary policy tools like credit scale control, rediscount quotas, and relending quotas. However, because the design and use of such tools smack of government intervention, the central bank is actually not in a position to make adjustments relevant to the changing economy. As a result, these tools become rigid policy measures that can only defeat the purposes. Moreover, because these policy measures are usually introduced and backed by the administration, their effectiveness is invariably whittled down because they are rejected, openly or covertly, by commercial banks and other monetary institutions.

Second, under incomplete market conditions and an unhealthy commercial banking system, the central bank's quantitative monetary control over the entire economy is limited. The more incomplete the market and the commercial banking system are, the more likely that firms and investors choose to obtain money beyond the central bank's control. Similarly, under the same conditions, the more the central bank tightens up its quantitative money control, the more firms and investors will try to dodge such control and seek money in areas beyond the reach of the central bank, resulting in a reduction in the effectiveness of the monetary policy.

Third, under incomplete market conditions and a flawed commercial banking system, the activity of the central bank and commercial banks may be interfered with by government at all levels that demand, including the demand for more loans and—in extreme cases—bank overdrafts. This manner of government intervention inevitably cuts deeply into the monetary policy's effectiveness and makes it difficult to reach its prescribed goals. To unshackle them from such intervention, not only should the commercial banking system and the market be straightened out, but the central banking system itself should be rectified as well. This calls for normalizing the relationship between the Ministry of Finance and the Central Bank, and between local governments and the Central Bank's local branches.

Monetary Policy Needs to Be More Loosened and Forceful—Judging From Its Eclipsed Effectiveness

Now let us return to the issue of coordinating fiscal and monetary policies in the post-retrenchment years. Now that we have seen that the eclipse of a monetary policy's effectiveness is unavoidable and even more so under incomplete market conditions, we have every reason to believe that, to reactivate the economy in the wake of the retrenchment, it is necessary to adopt a slightly tightened up fiscal policy in coordination with a monetary policy that is loosened up more forcefully. Such a necessity is justified from three aspects:

First, the countermeasures taken by those under the impact of a monetary policy—commercial banks, other monetary institutions and nongovernmental investors—against the changing situation brought about by that policy can keep eroding its effectiveness. As a result, the monetary policy may not work as it should on a relaxed money market if it is not loosened up with appropriate forcefulness. Sensible investors always take countermeasures according to experience and government behavior, and are especially cautious in action after going through the retrenchment years.

They will tend to hold back and bide their time, lest an ill-advised investment move put them at a disadvantage. This being the case, the monetary policy has to be relaxed a little more vigorously if its effectiveness is to stop its decline, and if its prescribed goals are to be achieved.

Second, as illustrated above, to rebuild and enhance public confidence in market and investment prospects is vital to post-retrenchment economic revival. Because this calls for a cumulative process, to loosen up the monetary policy more forcefully in coordination with a relatively tight fiscal policy is a sensible recourse for the government to prevent the monetary policy's effectiveness from diminishing endlessly and to boost people's confidence in market and investment prospects. Whether or not a consumer chooses to buy something he can do without is a conventional benchmark of his confidence or the lack of it. The consumer may make that decision on the spur of the moment, but its impact on the market cannot be underestimated. If the monetary policy is tight, people tend not to buy things they can dispense with, and thus the hope for a revived market is dashed. That tendency will remain unchanged if the monetary policy is not loosened up enough. People will not be confident enough to buy commodities in the gray zone between necessity and non-necessity, and the economy and market will not come back to their own unless the monetary policy is loosened up adequately.

Third, it should be noted that a booming stock market alone is not enough to put the economy back on track right after a period of retrenchment. On the contrary, if the stock market is the only thing that is thriving, it may be evidence that the economy is still in a quandary, as dim investment prospects in many other fields are channeling large sums of money into the stock market. Furthermore, a bustling stock market may most likely be built on a flimsy foundation when investment prospects are grim in other fields. Under these circumstances, we should go out of our way to boost the other investment fields, at least those industries that can bolster up the economy. In conjunction with this, the monetary policy must be loosened up more emphatically to give precedence to the indispensability of its structural nature. That is to say, the policy must not be loosened up in a disorderly fashion and regardless of the industrial and investment structures. Rather, it should be designed, in the first place, to revive selected industries that can bring the economy to life and cause a chain reaction in other industries. To loosen up the monetary policy a little more liberally for these industries helps increase effective supply to the extent where inflation will not be aggravated. Growth in effective supply means true economic growth. In addition, we have got to realize that economic growth at the present stage is not without bubbles. Of all the bubbles foaming in the economy, those in economic growth are the most obvious. To get rid of such bubbles, ineffective supply must be eradicated. This can be done by liberalizing the structural monetary policy a little more.

All in all, to shift the economy back on boom conditions in these post-retrenchment years, we should not only coordinate a relatively tightened fiscal policy with a relaxed monetary policy, but also step up our effort to loosen up the latter. In the meantime, we should apply unconventional monetary policy measures with prudence, and make more use of conventional monetary policy measures. Such is the keynote of this thesis, entitled "Meshing fiscal policy with monetary policy."

— Carried in excerpts in *Asia Pacific Economic Times*
May 29, June 5 and June 12, 1997

· 16 ·

THE DUAL FOUNDATIONS OF EFFICIENCY

The Human Factor in Efficiency Studies

In a market economy efficiency is regulated by market, as economic activity is driven by interests. To gain interest, every resource investor must group his production factors in light of supply and demand and prices, and raise his efficiency. Therefore, the mechanism behind efficiency in the market economy is none other than the interest mechanism, or market mechanism, and the investor's goal is to maximize his interest. Thus motivation for interest and the lure of goals are unified insofar as efficiency is concerned.

Where there is government regulation besides market regulation, there will be the impact of government regulation on efficiency. The lure of goals is by and large a manifestation of such impact. Government goals are multiple rather than single. To meet its goals, the government needs to influence resource investors by way of regulatory means, and compel them to choose investment fields and forms of investment in line with government goals. Efficiency is affected as a result.

Because market regulation works hand in hand with government regulation, efficiency, whether high or low, is under their combined influence. Our study of this issue, however, does not stop just here. We need to probe deeper into it, because those engaged in market activity are individual traders, each being a resource investor. Market participants are subject to government regulation. As resource investors, they are concerned with both their own interests and the impact of government regulatory steps on their interests. This raises the questions: What is on the minds of resource investors? What factors are affecting their behaviors? Apart from market and government regulation, are there any other factors?

Take, for example, any normal firm. The relations in such a firm fall into two categories: relationships between people and materials, and interpersonal relationships. The relationship between people and materials finds expression mainly in the relationship between the means of production and those who use them. The condition and average quantity of the means of production per worker are basic indicators of a firm's technological level, which in turn determines its efficiency level. The interpersonal relationship is a lot more complicated. It can be broken up into a number of relations such as the relation between the firm's leadership and workers, between members of the leadership, between the leadership and the managerial body, between members of the managerial body and between workers. Some of these interpersonal relations are congenial, others are not. Some interpersonal relations are agreeable under one condition, but disagreeable under another. The agreeability of these interpersonal relations impacts efficiency in ways different from the impact of technology. If the technological level is low, it may be upgraded as a sine qua non for efficiency growth by increasing investment, adding new equipment, constructing new factory buildings, putting workers through training, or encouraging them to hone their skills. If interpersonal relations are disagreeable, can reinvestment be effective? How can it send efficiency skyrocketing?

Supposing the technological level of a company is fixed, the human factor—managers and workers included—will become so prominent as to determine the efficiency level. In this human factor, every employee's work hours, cultural attainment and skill adeptness, and how well-defined is work-post responsibility are observable factors, but there are also unobservable factors. For one thing, people's diligence level is elusive, for it is hard to tell exactly how hardworking everyone is. For another, employees are under the effect of a certain level of inertia. Those who are less affected by it are more motivated and aggressive in work; those affected more by it are lethargic. To what extent they can overcome inertia is another unknown factor. Moreover, efficiency grows when employees' goals match their firm's goals, and drops when their goals are at odds with each other, but whether or not these two kinds of goals can match each other is anyone's guess. The impact of these unobservable factors on firm efficiency merits careful study, for it is a hard nut to crack for both market and government regulation.

Therefore the study of efficiency needs to go beyond the scope of market and government regulation. This is not to say that market regulation and government regulation mean little to the rise and fall of efficiency. It only shows the limits of their impact, limits that, in particular, can affect our analysis of the sources of efficiency. For instance, in our research on a firm's interpersonal relationships, the impact of unobservable factors such as diligence and inertia on employees should be probed. Work ethics affect human behavior and go on to affect efficiency in many ways. What is the true source of efficiency? It is the human factor. Efficiency hinges on people's motivation and innovativeness, so work ethics should never be overlooked. Efficiency improves greatly when full scope is given to people's potentials, and when they are highly motivated and innovative under the influence of work ethics.

It should be noted that the above analysis is predicated on a given technological level. Technological level, judged from the perspective of the relationship between people and the means of production, is relevant to efficiency level. If the technological level of a country, region, or firm is a lot higher than that of another country, region, or firm, it makes comparing the impact of work ethics very difficult. Only by accurately reading the impact of work ethics on efficiency at a given technological level can such comparison make sense.

Efficiency Stems From Organizational and Social Cohesion

As illustrated in the previous chapter, the source of efficiency at a given technological level lies in people's motivation and innovativeness. To make the most of such motivation and innovativeness, it is essential to develop rational economic operational mechanisms and agreeable interpersonal relationships.

The cohesion parameter of the agreeability of interpersonal relationship falls into two categories: cohesion of an organization, and cohesion of society. The cohesion of an organization or society hinges on the agreeability of its interpersonal relationships. Cohesion generates efficiency. Organizational cohesion delivers efficiency inside an organization, and social cohesion endows efficiency on society.

The organization in this context refers in general to businesses, institutions, communities, villages, households and others. Organizations may vary in size, but each has its own cohesion. Organizations may be structurally loose or tight. Tight structure is not synonymous with high cohesion, while loose structure does not always mean a lack of cohesion. The structural looseness or tightness of an organization is irrelevant to cohesion or the lack of it, but is directly relevant to the agreeability of the relationship between the organization and its members and between its members. If the members of an organization are given to scheming against each other or are in discord with their leaders, this organization will be devoid of cohesion no matter how close-knit its organizational structure is. By contrast, if members of a community are in an amicable relationship with one another and with their leaders and work with one mind to make progress, such a community will enjoy cohesion, and a strong cohesion at that, even if it is loosely organized.

A firm consists of workers and managers. Its cohesion is one of many kinds of organizational cohesion. To foster corporate culture helps cultivate corporate cohesion. A highly cohesive firm can not only improve its efficiency steadily but also overcome difficulties and tide over adversities.

Some questions come to mind at this point of this study: How does society's cohesion come about? What is the relationship between organizational cohesion and social cohesion? How should such a relationship be handled to achieve both organizational and social cohesion?

Social cohesion is the force that rallies members of society together as one to achieve common goals. There is no lack of outstanding examples in this regard, such as the concerted effort, hard work, and self-sacrifices of people rallying against foreign invaders or natural disasters. Under such unusual circumstances, this kind of cohesion can generate high social efficiency and work wonders. Under normal circumstances, a society with harmonious interpersonal relationship and strong cohesion invariably enjoys an agreeable social environment that is a boon to the growth of efficiency.

As to the relationship between organizational cohesion and social cohesion, they may either promote or circumscribe each other, depending on what the organization's nature and goals are. There are all sorts of organizations in society that differ in nature and pursue different goals. If separatism is a political organization's overriding call, then the more cohesive it is, the more destructive it becomes to society. Of course this is an extreme example that can be excluded from my discussion. Generally speaking, an organization and society can get along if they have compatible goals, and consequently the cohesion of the organization and that of society are complementary. Below let me take firms for example again.

In a market economy, maximization of interest is the primary goal of firms that function as commodity producers making their own business decisions and being accountable for their profits and losses. To meet that goal, they must beat competition by constantly adjusting their production and business directions, improving their management and enhancing their internal cohesion.

Competition on a level playing field is essential to the proper handling of the relationship between firms, in which their shared interest lies in the belief that the more stable society is and the more the economy thrives, the better off the firms become. The rise of one firm does not necessarily mean the downfall of another. In an environment of social stability and economic prosperity, every firm has the opportunity to grow and convert their good intentions into reality. However, even in such a friendly environment there are still firms that have to downscale production, go bankrupt, or be annexed due to decision-making errors or failure to keep pace with technological development. These occurrences are a normal reflection of the regrouping of resources. As long as such regrouping proves salubrious to efficiency of the economy as a whole and brings new opportunities to investors, the common interest of the business world will not be hurt by the aforementioned production cuts, bankruptcies, or mergers.

Organizational cohesion and social cohesion, however, are not the same thing. Whether the former can be unified with the latter, or whether enhanced organizational cohesion can strengthen social cohesion, is determined by the substance and efficacy of advancement in culture—corporate culture, community culture, campus culture, etc.—as a major element in the promotion of organizational cohesion. If a firm's corporate culture emphasizes not only its own goals but also the goals of society, and aims not only at cultivating its own corporate spirit but also at fostering fine social mores, the achievement of such a corporate culture will be reflected in the improved cohesion of both the firm and society. The unification of corporate and social cohesion precisely embodies the social function and value of a sound corporate culture. Conversely, if a firm is bent on pursuing its own corporate and workforce interests at the expense of its corporate culture's social function and value, it will have no way of coordinating its cohesion with that of society, nor can its improved corporate cohesion result in improved social cohesion. This point should not be overlooked when analyzing the sources of efficiency.

A more nuanced understanding of the issue enables us to see that growth in national wealth is connected with society's economic prosperity and development in culture and education. A prosperous society with advanced culture and education is better endowed to promote cultural development and coordinate its own cohesion with organizational cohesion. Moral values also play an outstanding role in enhancing social and organizational cohesion, a role that cannot be superseded by market or government regulation. This is because only moral values can demonstrate to members of organizations that their own organizations' goals are in line with those of society and that the interests of individuals and organizations are, fundamentally speaking, compatible with the interests of society. That realization enables them to identify themselves completely with society's goals, thereby bolstering both organizational and social cohesion. Both organizational and social cohesion can be steadily enhanced under the impact of moral force.

Hence my conclusion: In the past, researchers of the source of efficiency have often stressed economic and technological factors to the neglect of non-economic and non-technological factors, emphasized the impact of interests at the expense of public goals and a sense of social responsibility, and reiterated material values regardless of human values. Under the sway of such outdated ideological and methodological approaches, researchers could neither probe into the deep-seated issue concerning changes in efficiency, nor explain that the human factor and interpersonal relations—rather than the material factor and the relationship between people and materials—are the true fountainhead for efficiency. Organizational cohesion generates organizational efficiency, and social cohesion brings forth social efficiency. This being the case, the source of efficiency and its enhancement lies not in market mechanisms or government interventional behavior, but in the force of morality and its impact on people.

Where Super Efficiency Comes From

It is generally acknowledged that efficiency rests on a material foundation. Such a foundation encompasses production equipment, raw materials, technological conditions, workers with a certain level of technical proficiency, and social infrastructure (including means of communications and transportation, telecommunications facilities, water and heat and energy utilities). The importance of the material foundation is common knowledge. Efficiency suffers when the material foundation stops improving itself.

Does efficiency have only one foundation, the material foundation? Is it true that where there is a material foundation, there will be growing efficiency? As noted previously, a material foundation alone is not enough to account for the ebb and flow in efficiency. Due consideration must be given to the other foundation—the moral foundation. Manufacturing equipment and raw materials are used by people. The efficacy of technology cannot operate without man's proficiency, motivation and creativity. In other words, workers with a certain level of proficiency are an integral part of the material foundation of efficiency. However, workers are not robots. They are human beings who think, feel, and pursue ideals and goals. They may take one attitude or another towards life, and be either devoted to or uncaring about work. In addition, they are not isolated, but interact with one another to form all sorts of interpersonal relations with varying degrees of coordination. All this constitutes the other foundation for efficiency, the moral foundation.

The material and moral foundations of efficiency exist alongside each other. Neither of them can stand alone to account for a rise or fall in efficiency. Let us imagine that two firms have the same material and technological conditions and make the same product needed by consumers: How is it that one firm is more efficient than the other? The answer can be found by comparing the differences in the moral foundation of their efficiency.

Thus it makes sense to say that efficiency has dual foundations, material and moral.

Organizations—as small as families, companies or villages or as large as communities or nations—cannot survive without spiritual cohesion, norms of conduct, and moral values in the same way as they cannot dispense with science and technology. In handling interpersonal relations, morality comes to assist when and where science and technology are helpless. Once interpersonal relations are finely tuned, once full scope is given to people's initiative and creativity, efficiency grows as a matter of course. This shows that efficiency does indeed have a moral foundation.

Efficiency's material foundation changes constantly with economic growth, technological advancement, and the renewal of knowledge on the part of those who use the means of production. Moreover, its changes are unstoppable. Does efficiency's moral foundation ever stop changing itself? Is there any unalterable moral principle that forms this foundation? Given that the material foundation is ever-changing, can the moral foundation stay intact alongside it? If the answer is in the positive, does the moral foundation ever change on its own or only in unison with circumstances? If it changes on its own, this refers to changes in moral values, rules of conduct, and evaluation criteria. If it changes in unison with circumstances, this means that it can adapt itself to the material foundation. However, it is difficult to distinguish between these two kinds of changes, which, in fact, are often intertwined with each other.

Now consider this question: Where does super efficiency come from? While the material foundation usually offers conventional efficiency, the moral foundation not only ensures conventional efficiency but also provides super efficiency.

The super efficiency of the immigrant societies of yore has been a topic of perennial academic interest. During the millennium-long war and turmoil following the demise of the Han dynasty (206 BC–220 AD), immigrants from central China hacked their way through brambles and throngs and settled in what are today's Guangdong and Fujian provinces, where they dredged rivers and converted barren land into fertile farmland. Beginning from the 12th century, immigrants into the western European region now known as the Netherlands reclaimed the land, built water conservancy projects and developed farming and animal husbandry. What these immigrants embodied was precisely a kind of super efficiency. How did they achieve such efficiency with medieval tools, limited manpower, and harsh environment? There was neither market force nor government intervention during the process of immigration and the rise of the immigrant society, so what had motivated these people to toil with such high efficiency? This can only be attributed to the magical forces of morality, cohesion, and creativity. We may as well say that given the historical circumstances, these immigrants performed pioneering feats with extraordinary strength under extraordinary conditions. Even their social organizations were extraordinary. These factors combined to work miracles in human history. In the absence of a commensurate moral foundation, there could not have been such extraordinary immigrant social organizations, the immigrants could not have mustered such extraordinary strength as individuals, and such super efficiency would have been out of the question.

The achievement of super efficiency fully testifies to what potential efficiency growth can do. Such potentials can be tapped by relying on the moral foundation of efficiency. Examples in this regard are aplenty, besides the aforementioned immigrant societies. The role of morality, confidence and faith in stimulating human willpower and abilities can be seen in people's death-defying behaviors in resistance against foreign invaders, in combating natural disasters, and even in the effort of members of an organization—as small as a family or clan and as large as a nation or region—in attaining their goals or in safeguarding dignity and honor. Super efficiency arises precisely from among these people. Can the material foundation also contribute to the rise of super efficiency? Efficiency can certainly not do without its material condition. For instance, our forefathers would not have accomplished their pioneering cause without certain means of production in their possession no matter how motivated they were. We cannot combat natural adversities empty-handed. However, without the tremendous impact of morality and faith under these circumstances, material conditions can only yield mediocre efficiency. We must admit to ourselves that in the absence of a moral foundation, our efficiency may still be inadequate, low or even negative despite the provision of an efficient material foundation.

The longstanding controversy about the conflict between the efficiency standard and the moral standard is settled through our analysis of super efficiency. The conflict between these two standards is about judging economic behavior with two criteria. One is a standard of efficiency, meaning that an economic behavior is good when it boosts efficiency, and bad when it reduces efficiency. The other is a standard of morality: Efficiency is good if it accords with the moral principle and evil if it violates it. These two standards are often in discord because rising efficiency may run counter to the moral principle, whereas efficiency that accords with the moral principle may fall. This longstanding issue cannot be settled mainly because of uncertainty about which standard to use in judging the moral good or evil of efficiency.

The efficiency standard is an issue in economics, and so is efficiency judgment. However, neither the moral standard nor moral judgment is a subject or research task for any economists. Both belong in the realm of economics where and when an economic issue touches upon the relationship between moral standard and efficiency standard, and the need arises to determine whether or not a moral judgment corresponds with an efficiency judgment. In my *Socialist Political Economics* I put it this way, "The moral judgment of economic behavior should be tested in practice, otherwise the moral principle for the economy could become elusive. … We may as well regard 'maximum workforce interests' as the moral standard for economic behavior. That is to say, an economic behavior is sound when it complies with 'maximum workforce interests,' and is evil when it does not."[1] This approach to coordinating efficiency and moral standards may serve to support my judgment of certain economic behaviors.

After all, the conflict between efficiency and moral standards may still occur in evaluating some other economic behaviors, to the bewilderment of the economists of today. However, the emergence of super efficiency testifies to the accord between both standards. Extraordinary efficiency itself is evidence of an impressive boost in efficiency, and therefore, the efficiency standard is entirely applicable here. How, then, does super efficiency come about? It is directly related to the role of morality, as I have stated before. Without morality, super efficiency would have been out of the question in an immigrant society or in combating foreign invaders or major natural catastrophes. Thus super efficiency that measures up to the efficiency standard is also up to the moral standard.

Tapping Potentials in Efficiency Growth

The mention of the moral foundation for efficiency brings the following question to mind: Under which condition is the potential greater for efficiency growth—the more the initiative is taken into the hands of individuals, or the less the initiative is taken into the hands of individuals while the more closely individuals are attached to their organization or society?

Why should I raise such a question? It has something to do with the moral foundation of efficiency. Given the technical nature of the means of production, given objective production conditions, and provided the cultural and technical proficiency of individuals as producers is fixed, individuals with more freedom of choice may become highly motivated and innovative, and thus have greater potential for efficiency improvement. That is to say, the larger the number is producers and workers with freedom of choice in economic activity, the more dynamic the economy becomes, the better the economy's capacity for growth is, and the easier the potentials of efficiency growth are to be tapped. Therefore, it is wrong to believe that the more autonomy is allowed for producers and workers, the more detrimental it is to the economy. On the other hand, however, given that the source of efficiency also lies in harmonious interpersonal relations and in people's compatibility with their organizations or society, it is more likely to coordinate these relations and enable individuals to adapt themselves to their organizations and society if they are subordinate to those organizations or society as a whole. Does this also point to greater potential for efficiency growth?

As a matter of fact, this question is not unanswerable. Individual autonomy and subordination to a particular organization or society can be mutually compatible instead of mutually exclusive. The moral foundation for efficiency entails not just making the most of people's enthusiasm and creativity; it also involves coordinating and harmonizing interpersonal relations. It is senseless to emphasize the former to the neglect of the latter, or vice versa. Nor can we believe that efficiency can grow continuously rather than temporarily when individuals are deprived of autonomy and lack enthusiasm and creativity as members of a particular organization or society, or when individuals enjoy a lot of autonomy while interpersonal relations are growing increasingly more inordinate and incompatible. Thus it is ideal to have both individual autonomy and coordinated and compatible interpersonal relations, with neither aspect neglected. This being the case, there should be individuals subordinate to organizations and society on the one side, and organizations and society holding individuals in due respect on the other—the coexistence of both conditions can keep efficiency growing steadily. In other words, individuals' subordination to organizations and society should be genuine and voluntary. Instead of being imposed upon them, their subordination should be conditioned by coordinated interpersonal relations and mutual respect, but at the same time, individuals should also conduct themselves with dignity and self-respect.

That should be the way it is in reality. People living in society are inevitably its members. A member of society invariably participates in certain organizations or institutions. The family is the smallest cell of society, and everyone belongs to a particular family. If a man is a worker, he works in a factory, where he may also be a trade union member. If he is a farmer, he may become a member of a villagers' self-governing organization, if such an organization ever exists. If he is an urban dweller, he belongs to the local community or neighborhood. If he is a private or self-employed business owner, he must belong to a certain association in which he handles interpersonal relations the best he can in order to live and work in harmony with fellow members. Meanwhile, as an individual, he should have his own wishes and demands, follow his own principles in dealing with people and daily life, and take the initiative into his own hands to stay motivated and innovative. In all, he should be a dynamic human being. Self-dependence is the prerequisite for someone to be in good interpersonal relations and get along with his organization and society. Good personal and interpersonal relations can mean nothing, and there will be no coordination and compatibility to speak of, if people are deprived of self-dependence and personal initiative. Doesn't this mean that personal initiative should be put in the first place in comparison with harmonious interpersonal relationships?

Society consists of numerous individuals, and an organization or institution comprises a certain number of individuals. If these individuals enjoy self-dependence, are motivated, energetic, and innovative, and have the latitude to pursue their own goals while adapting themselves to organizational and social goals, interpersonal relations can be better handled, and efficiency can grow faster and by bigger margins. Isn't this exactly what society and organizations hope for?

Based on the above study, we know that the moral foundation of efficiency is an objective reality, but efficiency growth may either be real or potential, and the potential in efficiency growth is not necessarily tapped to capacity. To give full scope to such potential, we have to do two things: first, to respect people's self-dependence and give full scope to their motivation and innovativeness; and second, to coordinate interpersonal relations and adapt individuals to their organizations and society.

—*Journal of Peking University* (*Humanities and Social Sciences*), issue No. 6, 1998

Note

1. Li Yining (1986), *Socialist Political Economics*, Beijing: Commercial Press, pp. 438–439.

· 17 ·

WHAT ARE THE IMPLICATIONS OF CHINA'S DUAL TRANSITION FOR THE DEVELOPMENT OF ECONOMICS?

A Speech on the Hot Issues of China's Economy in Commemoration of the 60th Anniversary of His Teaching Career

Today, on this occasion, I would like to discuss the implications of China's Dual Transition for the development of economics.

First, the opportunities for breakthroughs exist in the weakest link of the chain. China's Dual Transition refers to the transition of economic system and the way of development, that is, from planned economic system to market economic system and from an agricultural society to an industrial, modern society. The two of them must go hand in hand.

How could we break the chain of planned economy that was so stiff and rigid? To answer that, we should work on the weakest link and agriculture was indeed the weakest in planned economy. Why? Because the peasants did not enjoy the same benefits as city residents did. You would always get ration stamps for food and other living necessities as long as you were born a city resident. One kilogram of meat was guaranteed every month to even the poorest families in the cities. Unemployed citizens could still make a living by planting trees or building roads as long as they were willing to do such kind of jobs. But things were different for the peasants because they were excluded from the ration stamps. Some of them were even starved to death during famines. Therefore, agriculture was no doubt the weakest link. The peasants did exactly as the government planned, sweating on their small pieces of farmland with no guarantee for a basic living. How to deal with this problem? These peasants would have the strongest desire to reform and change the status quo should there be signs of policy shifts. Opportunities for breakthroughs were destined to emerge in the rural areas because in 1979, after the Third Plenary Session of the 11th Central Committee of the CPC, the policies for the countryside started to change and the "all-round contract" system was gradually popularized, from Anhui province, Sichuan province, to many other places, raising the curtain on the unstoppable reform across China.

The second, and the most urgent issue was to ensure people's initiative and motivation in the process of China's reform and development. How? Ever since the adoption of the "all-round contract" system, the grain output shot up and the peasants became more motivated since they didn't have to starve any more. A lot of them began to flock to cities, crowded in the construction sites, looking for employment. This marked a great change in China. Another significant difference worth mentioning was the change in labor force. Before the popularization of the "all-round contract" system, China was experiencing a serious labor shortage. But this specific problem was solved by the entrance of rural labor force, which also pointed out a new direction of development—setting up township and village enterprises. The villagers built workshops on their own, purchasing scraps as raw materials from state-owned factories. Thus born the first batch of township and village enterprises. But then another question came: who was going to sell these products? They had to figure out the answer and find customers by themselves. So back in the 80s, though many of you weren't even born, people could often see peasants traveling by train or coach and wearing ill fitting suits, sometimes even a tie, with loads of heavy bags. What for? They were traveling around the country, vigorously marketing for their own products produced by the township enterprises because they had no other way.

This told us a very important point: the commodity market of township enterprises had begun to form, which was in parallel with the market under planned economy. The stubborn and uniformed planned economy was later broken. Who did it? The peasants. The reform in the rural areas started exactly after the implementation of "all-round contract" when peasants became motivated to go to other places for better opportunities.

The third change was in human resources. The peasants were no longer stranded in the field and came to the cities for employment. Although the problem of registering for city residents remained unsolved, they only cared about the money. These cases were unseen in any other developing countries when we look back at the development of economics in China. But here's an important question: all the other developing countries in Asia and Africa aimed at the establishment of market economy, that is, capitalist economy. In order to achieve this, they had to get rid of the pre-capitalist society and keep moving toward capitalism because such a process was non-reversible.

China, however, was different from those countries due to its dual transition. Not only from an agricultural society to an industrial society, but also from planned economic system to market economic system. So we had to be very careful in this process to guarantee a steady and successful reform. It was very important to improve people's livelihood and we should not let them down because they had experienced planned economy before and, in the past, city residents were endowed with the privilege of the stamp rations. They might miss the "good old days" for secured jobs and the "big-pot" distribution system. Social stability would be put in hazard if the new system failed to improve people's livelihood. Therefore, the dual transition in our country was new to the development of economics and the possibility of reverse would only exist in a country that is experiencing such kind of transition. This is a problem that all the participants of China's reform should pay attention to in the future.

Why do I emphasize on improving people's livelihood? Where did the "big-pot" distribution system come from? In fact, there was more than one "pot", sometimes two, or even three. So let's have a look at *Outlaws of the Marsh*. In Chapter 19 and 20, Chao Gai drew up the allocation principle of Mount Liang. Having robbed things from the outside, the part for distribution would be placed in the hall. The leaders would take half of the loot and their followers would share the other half. The allocation principle of Mount Liang was an example of equalitarianism.

So was planned economic system. The "pot" you belonged to, or the city you lived in, determined your share of the allocation. So there were different scales from big, medium, small to special. But in the past, people didn't know the differences and they wouldn't interpret the novel in that way. At least the people I knew all belonged to the same "pot". They couldn't imagine there were other "pots", let alone what those "pots" could offer. It was not until the downfall of the Gang of Four did we find out that Jiang Qing and her kind lived in Diaoyutai, the State Guesthouse, and their "pot" was certainly better than ours. But we didn't know this in the past. It was not easy to restore to the old distribution system, but, after all, it's not impossible. The beginning of China's reform was indeed unprecedented and enriched the content of economics.

At the beginning of the reform and opening up in the early 80s, the government was about to introduce the price leverage to the market. At that critical moment, I made a report in this very auditorium, so crowded with curious people that some of them had to sit down on the ground. The first statement I made was that the failure of price reform might eventually bring defeat upon the overall reform across the country and the key to its success lied in the reform of ownership because price reform would be infructuous if state-owned enterprises didn't change and take risks. Then how should we conduct the ownership reform and clarify the property rights? The answer was to introduce shareholding system. This marked the beginning of the great debate in the office building. But, finally, Deng Xiaoping's speeches during the inspection tour in south China and the 14th and 15th National Congresses of the CPC made clear that introducing shareholding system was the right direction for the reform of state-owned enterprises. Attendants and witnesses of this debate included not only the students and teachers in School of Economics and Management but also those in science departments or even from other universities. This suggested that ownership reform must be put in a crucial place in the process of transitioning from planned economy to market economy.

The most challenging part during this process was probably the employment problem in China. Why do I always emphasize on the problem of employment? Because China's rural population was, and still is, too large. At that time, I suggested giving priority to employment and paying attention to price stability to prevent inflation. But employment always comes first. Why? We must keep in mind the real situations in this country. With so many peasants continuously coming to the cities, employment would always be an important issue. So is the prevention of inflation. Therefore, we have a lot of new problems to deal with in the next stage of economic reform.

I recently visited a factory with an observation team. It was a construction site. The head of the enterprise invested hundreds of million Yuan. I asked him how many jobs would such a modernized factory increase. Surprisingly, he answered: none, on the contrary, I planned to cut down the current staff. Robots would be used in the factory in order to improve productivity and compete with our foreign rivals. I would hire a few managers but they got to be well qualified. As you can see, investment brings back the workforce.

There was another problem facing many factories. When I asked an entrepreneur about the current situations in his factories, he complained that it was just too hard to find enough workers. Due to the shortage of skilled workers, two of his friends moved their factories to Southeast Asia and now are regretting it. Why? They were attracted by the lower labor cost there since the salary for local workers was only half of that paid in China, which, apparently, was supposed to be an advantage. However, it didn't work out and there was no way back because the factories were already set up. First, Southeast Asian workers didn't observe disciplines as Chinese workers did and the attendance rate was simply terrible. Second, they were not willing to work hard on improving their skills and all they really wanted were holidays and having fun, which was completely different from the hardworking tradition of mentorship among Chinese workers. This suggested a significant challenge in the next phase of China's development, that is, improving the skills and quality of its labor force. The shortage of skilled workers would only become severer in the future if this problem weren't properly solved.

I used to be the head of the expert advisory group, and now the chief consultant, for Bijie experimental zone in Guizhou province. I came there for a field visit recently and found out a new problem: first, Bijie, as a pivotal experimental zone in the national poverty relief program, should take risks doing what others dare not to do. And that's the point of establishing experimental zones. If you would only follow others' steps and play it safe, how could you call it experimental? Back in 2003, shortly after I was transferred from Standing Committee of NPC to Standing Committee of CPPCC, I was appointed leader of an expert team by the United Front Work Department and went to Bijie with delegates from Peking University and CPPCC. During the symposium, they reported to us their achievements since the establishment of the experimental zone in 1988. From selecting and planting trees to soil reclamation, they managed to overcome a series of challenges and their hard work was fully recognized. But I asked them a few questions about how much the state-owned enterprises had changed and how many peasants had left the mountains. The answer was none. How could you call it an experimental zone with these two problems remained untouched? I suggested that they come to other provinces and learn the experience of bringing in private enterprises for the reform of the state-owned enterprises. Without prompt and telling reform, the burden would only become heavier as the government was getting no tax from the state-owned enterprises and, what's worse, spending a large amount of money trying to cover their losses, eventually leading to social instability. So Bijie took my advice and sent a team to advanced regions, bringing back experience and private enterprises into the reform of the state-owned enterprises. Now, burden relieved.

Second, the peasants living in the barren mountain areas must leave for other places to get better opportunities. It wouldn't pay to build a road and wire a small village for electricity if only a few households lived there. If they could just find a job nearby, adding to the local labor force, and get trained with skills in order to be sent to other provinces, they would be lifted out of poverty and backwardness. They felt that this was a great approach and skill training was indeed important but there was a difficulty to be solved. The separation. There are more than two hundred million migrant workers in China, among which tens of millions of husbands and wives are now in long-term separation. No one paid attention to this problem during the observation tours in the countryside but there were horrifying cases where the husbands went outside but the wives stayed at home and were later allured by bad guys. After the husbands got home and found this, tragedy happened as all of the family members were murdered. So the separation of tens of millions of families is definitely an urgent issue to deal with. During this process, we need to provide accommodation for migrant workers and try to figure out how to bring families working in different places to reunion. That is the current problem facing the countryside and, as the status quo of the countryside is changing, new challenges will appear constantly.

This time in Bijie, I saw a new phenomenon: people's life is getting much better now but some of them didn't come back home for the Spring Festival anymore because the tradition of giving "Hongbao," a red packet containing money as a gift, was getting increasingly expensive. Giving "Hongbao" is a prevailing custom for weddings, funerals, and other special occasions in China. It used to contain only 3 to 5 Yuan and wasn't a big matter. But nowadays, the "Hongbao" should contain at least one hundred or, more commonly, two hundred Yuan. For those who did come back for the Festival, "Hongbao" would devour almost all of their hard earned savings if their own families didn't have any special occasion to celebrate. To avoid such kind of losses, they choose to come back secretly when the Festival season was over. In the process of poverty relief, there are and will be many new problems.

I brought a research team from CPPCC to Hanzhong, Shaanxi province earlier this year. What for? It was all about the Han River that runs across the Hanzhong region and then into the Danjiangkou Reservoir, which is in the route of South-to-North Water Diversion Project. Therefore, all the existing factories have now been commanded to leave this area and polluting factories have been strictly forbidden. What about the peasants then? Fertilizers and pesticides were also prohibited to prevent water pollution. Otherwise, it would affect the quality of the water that eventually goes to Beijing. How could the peasants get rid of poverty under such circumstances? That was the major challenge facing us. We went to a county called Xixiang first. The fields that once grew crops are now growing tea trees because selenium enriched tea is a specialty here and has a ready market. The tea trees have changed everything because, different from crops planting, the chemical fertilizer-free and se-enriched tea requires processing and marketing. Migrant workers in Hubei, Sichuan and other provinces are now coming back because Xixiang has become a promising tea-exporting region.

And then we went to Yang County, the habitat for the endangered Crested Ibis. A sanctuary has been set up for its protection and breeding. After artificial reproduction, the birds will be set free batch by batch. There's a special trait about Crested Ibis. They are monogamous and once their lifetime partners are dead, they will never find another. So today, with beautiful scenic spots scattering around the Crested Ibis Lake, Yang County has become an ideal place for wedding ceremony. Brides wearing wedding gowns chose this place, including not only the newly weds but also those who got married in the past without the ceremony. Some of them are even throwing Golden or Silver Wedding ceremonies here because Crested Ibis is a symbol of eternal love. In this way, tourism has largely boosted local economy.

The third county we went to was called Liuba County, where Zhang Liang was conferred a noble man and titled the Marquis of Liu. What's special about this place? Well, Liu Bang, the founding emperor of the Han dynasty, used a trick to cheat his rival, Xiang Yu, pretending to advance along one path while secretly making a detour. Then Han Xin, Liu Bang's general, immediately brought his troop to Xi'an for the north expeditions. And now Liuba County has become a tourist attraction. The villagers are selling portraits of Zhang Liang and other local souvenirs and tourism has also become a booming industry here.

The forth place we went to was called Mian County. Dingjun Hill, where Huang Zhong slaughtered Xia Houyuan, is located there. On his deathbed, Zhuge Liang asked to be buried in Dingjun Hill. The tomb and ancestral hall of Zhuge Liang, as well as the famous Chinese novel *Romance of the Three Kingdoms*, have made tourism a supporting industry here. Therefore, when it comes to economic development, the most effective way is to give full play to local advantages.

The next step for Bijie is to make great efforts to develop vocational education, sending skilled workers to the southwest provinces and central region of China. Have they got any major achievement due to our support? Absolutely. During the early years of Guanghua School of Management, we sent people to Bijie College as supporting faculty to help improve the skills of the local teachers and give lessons to the students as well. But after all these years, Bijie College has changed so much that we couldn't even recognize it in our recent visit. Once a Normal College, it is now called Guizhou University of Engineering Science, training general college students who have no advantage over those from top universities. In my opinion, the college should focus on training high-end professional technicians instead.

So here the important point is that most of the difficulties we have encountered in the process of China's reform were unprecedented in the development of economics. Today, China has a new situation. The government bulletin of the third quarter of 2015 issued by National Bureau of Statistics of China just came out and one of the indicators caused great attention: the output value of China's tertiary industry has reached 51%. It is a sign of modern industrial development because there are three stages in the ongoing process of human society: the earliest one is agricultural society where the first industry makes the major part of economy; then enters the period of industrialization as the second industry grows rapidly and becomes the backbone of economy; and the post-industrial era comes when the output value of the tertiary industry accounts for more than half of GDP. China has already begun to gradually enter the post-industrial era. Therefore, it's important for us to figure out what we should do next.

As we all know, once a developed country has entered the post-industrial era, 60% to 70% of its GDP will be generated from the tertiary industry and its economic growth will be slowing down. In the stage of industrialization where the second industry leads the way, the economic growth can be very fast. A 3% annual growth would be regarded as economically prosperous in developed countries. How about China? Our economy is still growing by 6% to 7% per year in a rather speedy manner. China should pay attention to the following three points in the next stage.

First, China should make great effort to develop the tertiary industry. Now that the consumption rate has improved, we need to push it even further. This year, I paid an observation tour to Hebei province. The local entrepreneurs asked me to give them a brief speech and I said a few words: uniqueness is the key to becoming a best-selling product. Many department stores are having troubles in selling the garments because the styles are out of date and customers always want fashionable clothes. That's quite a simple rule. And don't be intimidated by online shopping. It will never replace department stores. This is exactly the case in foreign countries. Department stores are still full of stylish garments and female customers because the experience of window-shopping is an irreplaceable enjoyment. So the first point is to bring uniqueness to the products and then to the whole industry. Second, the service sector should be more people-oriented, proactively providing quality service to the customers. The third point is to bring about world-famous brands. China Brand Marketing Society told me that the best-known Chinese brand among foreign businessmen, judging from the questionnaires they have frequently conducted, was Maotai. Maotai is no doubt a Chinese brand, but it cannot represent all the good products China has produced. The influence of Chinese brands is weak. Forth, keep the customers. Customers are now flocking abroad for better and cheaper products since there's no tariff and no need to worry about the fakes. Therefore, developing the tertiary industry is the center of our work.

Second, never forget that China has not accomplished its process of industrialization yet, although the tertiary industry has accounted for 51% of GDP. Why's that? Because we are still far away from the goal of a high-end, sophisticated manufacturing industry, capable of producing complete sets of equipment. The factories have to buy equipment from Germany, Japan, Italy, France, the US, or other foreign countries if they wish to update the facilities. They would not think of purchasing equipment from Shanghai, Beijing, Tianjin, or Harbin. We can't convince them to buy domestic products if the quality fails to meet the standard. It's OK to buy things from foreign countries but to some degree it's a great loss for China. One trillion Yuan was spent on cosmetics, bags, and other products abroad each year, increasing the employment and tax in foreign countries. However, the fact is that now we are able to buy the same things in China. I visited several shops in the Free Trade Area of Xiamen and found that the German milk powder there was even cheaper than that in Germany due to the duty-free policy. As a result, the second point we should keep in mind is that China's process of industrialization has not yet finished and it's not a good time for us to lower the guard and slack off.

Third, the future of China's agriculture is very promising. If you are willing to pay a visit to the countryside, you'll realize the difference immediately. In the Hangjiahu region of Zhejiang province, I went to a county-level city called Pinghu with a delegation team from CPPCC. Having arrived there, we couldn't even recognize the roads because thick, red scraps of firecrackers covered the ground. The local people were celebrating the completion of confirmation of land right. It was a spectacular event even greater than the Land Reform. What benefits does confirmation of land right bring to the local peasants? Now that they have got management license for the contracted land, usage license for the homestead, and property certificates for the house, the atmosphere in the rural area is much more alive. First, their concerns and worries are relived. Second, they finally have something to mortgage on and use the money to open a shop, do small business, or invest in agriculture.

Family farms have been largely promoted in Zhejiang province. Originated from the United States, family farms is now common in Canada and the Europe. China has also started to implement this system. Parents are encouraging their children to learn about agriculture and technology because otherwise they won't be able to take over the farms in the future. That's the new situation in China. Many people have torn down their old houses and built new ones with at least four floors. The first and second floors would be rented to people from other places for small business and accommodation. The owners would live on the third and forth floors. In this way, their incomes have been boosted largely and, according to the report from the government of Jiaxing, the income ratio of urban citizens to peasants was 3.1:1 before the confirmation of land right. But now, it's 1.9:1. As you can see, the income difference has been greatly reduced.

Another difference we have noticed in agriculture is that the local peasants have gone to other places and left the farmland to people from other places. For example, peasants from Anhui province, according to our observation, have been cultivating the farmland in Zhejiang province while the local people are seeking greater opportunities elsewhere. So this time in Bijie, I found the farmland there was being ploughed by the peasants from the mountain areas or Yunnan province. The truth is that, no matter who, someone will manage the farmland. In my hometown, Yizheng, Jiangsu province, the peasants from northern Jiangsu are cultivating the farmland. We should know about these new situations in China.

After the confirmation of land right, the farmland has increased by 20%. How could that be? We did some research and found out the following reasons: first, at the beginning of the land contraction system, the farmland was separated into small pieces and contracted to the peasants. There were fertile land and less fertile land. Two *mu* of less fertile land was equal with one *mu* of fertile land. After 30 years' intensive and careful cultivation since the contraction, the quality of the less fertile farmland has improved and now that all the pieces of farmland are basically the same, the total amount is sure to increase. Second, in the past, the farmland was ploughed by cattle and separated into small pieces by ridge. But that's not the case anymore due to the introduction and popularization of tractors, rice transplanters and other agricultural machines. The ridges have been flattened and used as farmland as well, adding to the total amount of arable land greatly. The 20% increase means China's 1.8 billion *mu* farmland will soon become 2.13 billion *mu*. Third, nearly all the peasants used to underreport the amount of their farmland because they had to pay agricultural tax before. But there's no point in doing so since the government has already lifted agricultural tax. Only fools would underreport nowadays, said the peasants. If you underreport, the land to be rent in the future would be less and therefore you would get less share in the future. At the same time, they can't over report as well because the amount of the arable land of each household has already been registered. So we will be dealing with this new situation soon.

The current trend of cooperative management of cultivated land reveals that the peasants are now becoming more confident and wiser in the approach they have chosen to improve their life. After the confirmation of land, the peasants are willing to join the shareholding system and real cooperation would only start at this point. Judging from the new situations I have mentioned, China's reform is still moving forward fast and has added a lot of new stuff to the development of economics. We hope that all of you, teachers and students from Guanghua School of Management and other departments, would pay close attention to China's reform and development.

INDEX

N

O

P

Q

R

S

T

U

W

Made in the USA
Columbia, SC
30 March 2026

474bbfee-db3d-45f8-a2c9-27d0f2fce76fR01